Hollar

Holland Flowering

*How the Dutch Flower Industry Conquered
the World*

Andrew Gebhardt

AUP

Cover illustration: *Still Life with Flowers*, Ambrosius Bosschaert the Elder, Hallwyl Museum, Stockholm

Cover design: Sander Pinkse Boekproducties
Lay-out: Crius Group, Hulshout

Amsterdam University Press English-language titles are distributed in the US and Canada by the University of Chicago Press.

ISBN	978 90 8964 617 0
e-ISBN	978 90 4852 259 0 (pdf)
e-ISBN	978 90 4852 260 6 (ePub)
NUR	761

© A. Gebhardt / Amsterdam University Press B.V., Amsterdam 2014

Tutelary

Solace from anemones,
sepals of instinct pushing the air.
Why do they matter so much, there
in the room at noon while nothing moves
around them: scarlet, creams, and burgundies,
magenta, bone-white, and bruise-like blues;
the wind's daughter, or bride, for some,
for others a temple to the wounds of Tammuz –
or living itself, wordless, longing.
Where is that luminous lusciousness from?

Peter Cole

Table of Contents

Holland Flowering

The bud
stands for all things,
even for those things that don't flower
Galway Kinnell

As different as the world would be, it could run without contemporary financial institutions, people could thrive without nation states, and our current political and economic systems could be jettisoned or radically reimagined. But without the botanical and biological contributions of flowers, entire ecosystems would collapse and most non sea life would quickly perish. Also, the history of civilization shows that our cultivation of plants (as opposed to hunting and gathering) marked a profound switch, affecting every area of human development and social organization, from gender and sexuality to health, religion, eating habits, and more. Due to the rise of agriculture, in a short time span humans went from small, scattered, nomadic groups to settlements of larger and larger communities where land, tools, and property became significant. Today's commercial horticulture does not involve such dramatic transformations, but flowering plants remain central to contemporary society, especially our food system. Industrial agriculture and horticulture share many characteristics, use the same infrastructure, and in the Netherlands, the two often overlap in policy and social networks. All of these considerations suggest the relevance and background in which to understand our relationship to horticulture.

Today, reliance on fossil fuels spans the chain of flower production, from breeding, irrigation, and planting, through watering and spraying, to harvesting, processing, packaging, refrigerating, and distributing. Almost every aspect requires oil and gas, including the roads, vehicles, ships, and planes criss-crossing the globe with goods, as well as the construction and repair of equipment, including tractors, greenhouses (both heating and cold storage), and processing facilities. And most pesticides are petroleum-based, while commercial fertilizers are ammonia-based, ammonia being produced from natural gas. In the twentieth century, governments and private industry have entrenched this oil and gas intensive system. As Michael Pollan has pointed out, after the Second World War, the U.S. government converted much of the munitions industry into agricultural fertilizers – since ammonium nitrate is the main ingredient of both bombs and chemical fertilizer – and shifted nerve-gas research toward inventing new pesticides. It was a rather sadistic twist on the spirit of the expression 'swords into plowshares,' since this destructive mode of agricultural production may ultimately prove even more insidious and harmful than war. During the same period in the Netherlands, agriculture and horticulture also became increasingly industrialized, especially accelerating in the 1960s and 1970s after the 1959 discovery of gas fields off Groningen in the North Sea made cheap gas available for greenhouse heating and for fertilizer production.[1] Though green technology is beginning to have an impact, Dutch horticulture still relies heavily on gas and oil.

But horticulture is more than part of the fossil fuel based global system or a key contributing factor to millennia-old societal metamorphoses. Horticulture may best be thought of as a matrix of concerns situated at the heart of civilization: "the art and science of plants resulting in the development of minds and emotions of individuals, the enrichment and health of communities, and the integration of the 'garden' in the breadth of modern civilization", as P.D. Relf has framed it. Through the cultivation, consumption, and celebration of plants, in striking ways horticulture connects science, art, economics, and the social world, and this relationship has been particularly poignant in the Netherlands. Of course, it's the social aspect of horticulture in the Netherlands that this book explores. One recent story helps illuminate some important facets of Dutch horticulture and suggests its diverse contemporary impact on Dutch society.

Somewhat misleadingly referred to in the press as a modern-day tulipmania, the story also touches on many of the themes in this book: the tulip as a symbol, male networks, economic bubbles, traders, and the Dutch Golden Age.

The story centers around two shady companies, Mark van der Poll's Sierteelt Bemiddelings Centrum (SBC), a Dutch market-making company that specialized in new tulip varieties, and Marco Vrijburg's Novacap Floralis Future Fund, a Dutch investment vehicle established to identify and support profitable tulip varieties. Before it went bankrupt, SBC's job had been to find buyers for bulbs whose cultivation had been funded by investors via Novacap. Between 2000 and 2004, the companies created a scheme in tulip bulb trading that eventually bilked rich investors of over 85 million euros. The cast of characters in this absurd affair includes corrupt flower bulb producers, multi-million-euro players from the upper echelons of Dutch society, government bureaucrats, and even Hell's Angels. And through an even more unusual turn of legal events, the two figures at the center of the controversy have escaped prosecution.

Van der Poll and Vrijburg grew up in Lisse in families in the bulb business, and both achieved early financial success. To high-power Dutch investors, the young men must have seemed reassuringly familiar – shrewd, rakish, and prosperous (like many of his financiers, Van der Poll drove a Porsche). Through their networks of entrepreneurs, they attracted over 100 well-heeled and well-connected supporters from inside and outside the tulip bulb trade who were lured by the promise of a 30 percent return in 18 months, and were convinced by the young insiders' knowledge and brashness. In exchange for such huge and fast returns, these investors were required to contribute 100,000 euros each. Vrijburg took the money and invested it in new tulip varieties from the harvest of 2003, which Van der Poll identified and in turn purchased. The idea was as follows. The bulbs would then be planted, and their flowers would be severed from the bulbs and sold at the flower auctions. Because tulip bulbs typically divide once they flower, the bulbs would multiply before the next season. In this way, the 2004 harvest would consist of more tulips, which would be sold in the 2004 auctions, as would more bulbs (which would divide and flower again in 2005, and so on): the more bulbs sold at the high prices would cinch the 30 percent profit. Novacap ensured that the buyers of the harvest of 2003 were protected against the risk of failing to find buyers for the harvest of 2004 because Van der Poll would have already identified the 2004 buyers. With both buyers and sellers guaranteed in advance by these charming fellows, the plan seemed quite promising.

Novacap Floralis quickly attracted people to contribute a whopping 120 million euros – 85 million from external investors and 35 million from within the tulip bulb trade. They included some powerful figures of Dutch society: Cor Boonstra, the former CEO of Philips, invested 200,000 euros; media mogul and publishing scion Willem Sijthoff invested 800,000; Blumex's[2] Peter van der Velden contributed 11 million; and the de Rijcke family (former Kruidvat owners, with a net worth of 1.7 billion euros) put in 12 million. ABN AMRO offered credit to potential participants through a subsidiary, the Hollandsche Bank Unie (HBU), which supplied 60 percent of the 85 million euros. HBU's director himself, Pascale van den Boogerd, invested 200,000 of his own money; HBU account manager Bas Welling set aside 100,000 in his father's name; and Jan Maarten de Jong, a former ABN AMRO board member, ponied up 300,000. Even a former researcher in fiscal fraud at the Ministry of Finance and previous director of the de Rijcke family's Hoge Dennen Holding, a man named Sushilkumar Ong-A-Swie, threw in 200,000. The caliber of investors inspired confidence, and financial regulators saw nothing amiss (and since Vrijburg himself had once been a tax inspector, the whole business seemed impeccable). In 2003, the Netherlands Authority for Financial Markets (AFM) approved Novacap Floralis, and set in motion 'the money making machine' (as the *NRC Handelsblad* called it).[3]

At first, the machine ran smoothly. When Novacap closed the fund to new investments in September of 2003, it had bought bulbs worth 75 million euros (with real money) and had managed to sell them for 160 million euros (in unsigned contracts or promissory notes). But since the bulbs had to be planted in order to multiply, the 160 million euros could only be claimed in cash once the bulbs had been harvested. Until that point, Van der Poll maintained he was content with the promissory notes. He trusted that the model would pan out, and anticipated handsome commissions from the purchase and sale of tulip bulbs, as planned.

But then, something curious began to occur: one by one, in very similarly phrased letters, the potential buyers began to cancel their purchase orders. It turned out that, lo and behold, none of the buyers had actually signed the promissory notes in the first place, so they had no binding legal power. SBC declared bankruptcy. This is where the parallel to the seventeenth-century tulip bubble seems most apt. Then and to some limited extent now in the tulip bulb trade (but not in cut flower auctions),[4] gentleman's agreements and individual honor and reputation could seal agreements; they did not require signatures. But then, a much broader swath of society was included in the bulb trade than now, with the hundred or so rich investors involved in this scandal, and the vast sums supposedly lost in the tulip bubble of 1637 turn out to be a myth,[5] unlike the very real 85 million euros that vanished in 2004. When the purchasers defaulted in early 2004 and SBC went bankrupt, Novacap was left with many tons of unsold bulbs. The real money contributed by those wealthy investors was now gone.

According to lawyers, the funds had been siphoned off and secreted away through other shell companies to Lugano Switzerland, post addresses in London, and trusts in the British Virgin Islands. It turned out that the prospective buyers guaranteed by SBC had come from among Van der Poll's tulip-growing friends. Between themselves they had bought and sold certain tulip bulb varieties in what is known in bulb business slang as 'kasrondjes', 'tussenstationnetjes', or 'heen-en-teruggies' – a carousel of buying and selling that drives up the market price of the bulb but which none of the buyers will ever actually purchase.[6] When first rumors, then investigations, and then newspaper articles exposed that this had occurred, some condemned the unethical behavior in language that sounds like it was lifted from seventeenth-century popular pamphlets. "De 'bollenboefjes' zijn er met het geld vandoor"[7] (the bulb-scoundrels made off with the money), said Bert Oosthout, an investigator critical of both the bulb dealers and the Dutch financial regulators (the FIOD, the Fraudedienst of the Belastingdienst, and the OM, the Openbaar Ministerie). In a ludicrous twist on the scam, even Hell's Angels seems to have heard about the investment opportunity, and contributed a hefty sum to Novacap, though through a third party, since they are barred from investing in the Netherlands. When SBC announced bankruptcy, Van der Poll reportedly received certain threats – the sort of 'gentlmen's agreements' Hell's Angels is known for.

Though the incriminating evidence was overwhelming, both Van der Poll and Vrijburg managed to elude jail (and death) through a peculiar and even more unlikely chain of events. As in a Hollywood thriller, some laptop computers contained volatile information and held data key to the whole affair. One recorded the history of all of Novacap's transactions. At some point in 2007 during investigations it was discovered that the hard disk containing Novacap's records had been irrevocably damaged, had been replaced with a clean disk, and that regrettably, the back-up copy also somehow had been ruined, so there was no reliable way of knowing what Novacap's assets actually were. The administrators concluded that the Novacap management had deliberately mishandled the records of the fund: and this suspicious record keeping is what alerted the authorities to investigate SBC and Novacap in the first place... But there was another wily computer involved in this story.

Joost Tonino, the chief public prosecutor in the case against Mark van der Poll and SBC, had saved a lot of the information regarding the investigation on his laptop, which he misplaced one day in The Hague. It was lost but not gone: a taxi driver rescued Tonino's computer, and sought to return it. But while looking for information about its owner, he came across official government documents *and* child pornography stored on it, and turned it over to a television crime reporter, who had a field day. Tonino unconvincingly claimed the porn had been downloaded by mistake; the incident cost him his job (though he was later reinstated) and discredited the state's case. Possibly worse from a legal standpoint were Tonino's files containing illegally recorded conversations between Van der Poll and his lawyers. This caused the entire case to unravel. In March 2009, after almost a decade of official investigations and legal procedures, the court had reluctantly to conclude that the confidentiality of the lawyer-client relationship had been so severely compromised that the evidence presented against Van der Poll and his associates had to be dismissed. Mark van der Poll walked away scot-free, and the much weaker case against Marco Vrijburg also collapsed. In 2009, Vrijburg said "[after this whole affair] personally, I've resumed a normal life in a flower export company in Lissebroek. Because finally, flowers are what I do best."[8] Van der Poll eventually published a book called *Tulpenmaffia*.

This story seemed worth recounting here for several reasons. In an outlandish way, it illustrates that horticulture in the Netherlands encompasses a number of themes and sectors of society: it evokes some similarities and differences with the famed tulipmania, and demonstrates how references to the Dutch Golden Age and financial bubbles remain in circulation; it also exposes the small world of male power networks in the Netherlands and shows how easily and naturally they can overlap with the horticultural world. Though both national and international news organizations covered the story, it is notable that very few industry publications discussed it.[9] And while some had heard about it, no one I met claimed to know more than what was reported. Nevertheless, the unusual episode seems in keeping with Dutch horticulture.

Tulipmania is a perennial subject, inspiring several books (fiction, non-fiction, and historical) over the past decade alone, and it is frequently invoked in the press regarding the internet bubble of the late 1990s, the housing bubble of 2008, and the ongoing financial scandals today. But already a hundred years ago, Dutch horticulturalists were complaining about tulipmania's undue attention. In 1913 Ernst Krelage was bemoaning the continual uproar over tulipmania, and in a short, probably ironic article, he even warned of a 'gladiolamania' taking hold and threatening the incipient industry's reputation; but this leading bulb grower and President of the Dutch Gardening Council went on to write an entire book on tulipmania (called *Bloemenspeculatie in Nederland*) in 1942. The subject continues to tickle people in and outside the Dutch horticultural industry, and this latest scandal is sure to unleash further commentary. It occupies a sort of niche motif within Dutch horticulture and views of the Netherlands.

As much as the rose gardens of medieval European monasteries or contemporary marriage rituals involving flowers, the sorts of social and financial aspects of Dutch horticulture revealed in this latest installment of 'tulipmania' also belong to what anthropologist Jack Goody called 'the culture of flowers'. The concept has widespread application. The phrase refers to "the complex social and cultural organization of cultivation", the language, emotion, and meaning we assign to flowers, as well as the association of such meanings with the rise of civilizations and a modicum of affluence and leisure, particularly since the nineteenth century. It's broad enough to encompass the commercial activities in today's horticultural auctions, ancient Greek flower cults, and seventeenth-century botanical experiments in Leiden. Similarly, these pages cast a wide net over the Dutch culture of flowers, especially its contemporary commercial practices in a central institution, FloraHolland Aalsmeer. Throughout, tulipmania occasionally appears as metaphor, historic incident, or cultural symbol; the culture of flowers, though rarely named as such, permeates every section. The aim is to convey a full, well-rounded account of Dutch horticulture, and to situate it in our historical moment.

~

With systemic threats to our survival – wars raging around the planet, economic crises, gendered violence, environmental devastation – how does the Dutch flower industry even matter? Again and again between 2008 and 2010 I found myself asking this sort of question as I did fieldwork, partly in Ethiopia but primarily at the premier Dutch horticultural auction located in Aalsmeer, about twenty kilometers from Amsterdam. It's the largest flower auction in the world and remains very much a local institution, although it's central to the global industry. Of course, FloraHolland Aalsmeer does not hold the key to our grave environmental, social, and economic troubles. But unexpectedly, I found that the Dutch flower business does in fact correspond with some of the world's foremost issues in direct and indirect ways. Because the agricultural sector uses more oil and gas than almost any other part of the global economy, for instance, the organization and management of the flower industry epitomizes both problems and possibilities in the ways we grow, sell, and distribute basic necessities. Also, at the heart of our global economy and the horticultural system sit auctions, this curious method of assigning price and value for everything from government bonds and oil, to paintings, corn, herring, and tulips. That's not all. Dutch flowers also crop up in several prominent contemporary political controversies, from the Israel-Palestine conflict to the land grab in East Africa and other aspects of globalization. And more generally, our use of flowers is strongly associated with values of beauty and aesthetic practices; flowers themselves (particularly roses and tulips) have been and are powerful tropes for emotion and ethics; the incipient Dutch flower industry of the Netherlands' Golden Age helped to launch the world's first modern consumer society; and cut flowers are today a key luxury commodity, with a mysterious power.

Crucially, what links these larger issues to the Aalsmeer auction is not merely a facile association or thematic overlap; often, through personal networks, the industry is never more than one or two degrees of separation from national policies, ranging from foreign affairs to infrastructural planning. This was the case as the industry took root in the seventeenth century and it has been even more so for the Aalsmeer institution's founding at the beginning of the twentieth century until today. While I focus on the background and daily workings of a contemporary Dutch institution, these ongoing intersections and convergences nevertheless seem compelling, as they illustrate historical continuities in the Netherlands and suggest lessons for other contexts, and other industries. The general issues that underlie contemporary Dutch horticulture remind us of the remarkable connections and correlations of our era. But besides these sometimes explicit, sometimes oblique relationships between local practices and values with Dutch national policy and broader topics, the global flower industry and FloraHolland fit into an even larger story about the role of flowers in the evolution of human life, into what one might call the really *longue durée*. Ultimately, I'm convinced that the operations of Dutch horticulture gesture to this wider scope, a blurred horizon of economic, cultural, and social issues somewhere in the distance.

After all, the use and cultivation of flowers is one of the oldest and most enduring of human activities. Flowers have turned up in Iron Age grave sights in Northern Europe and Mesopotamia, and have been a part of most communities and societies around the globe for as long as agriculture has existed, and probably much longer. From our earliest existence, our relationships to flowers and to each other have been intimately bonded, and suggest a lot about our values and civilizations. And when conceived of as more than merely ornamentals, flowers have performed and continue to serve widely ranging and essential functions for human societies and the development of the planet. Botanist William Burger reflects that "[f]lowering plants have been central to the evolution of primates and swinging apes, to the origin of bipedal humans, and to the origin of agriculture. Today, flowering plants provide a bit more than 90 percent of our caloric intake; and they are the primary food of our domesticated animals as well. In 1990, it was estimated that we humans were raising 1,294 million head of cattle, 856 million pigs, and 10,770 million chickens – mostly fed with flowering plants. Clearly, flowering plants are the foundations for larger human communities over the entire planet. Putting all these observations together, one can easily claim that without flowering plants we humans and our grand civilizations simply wouldn't be here".[10] Fifty years earlier, the naturalist Loren Eiseley put this sentiment in even starker and more poetic terms. He concluded his essay, 'How Flowers Changed the World', with these words: "Without the gift of flowers and the diversity of their fruit, man and bird, if they had continued to exist at all, would today be unrecognizable. Archaeopteryx, the lizard-bird, might still be snapping at beetles on a sequoia limb; man might still be a nocturnal insectivore gnawing a roach in the dark. The weight of a petal has changed the face of the world and made it ours".

Our world today, facing threats as well as possibility, continues this enduring relationship with flowering plants, not only through agriculture and medicine, but in our ceremonies and rituals around love and death, as well as our more refined sensibilities around class in consumer society. The Dutch horticultural industry invites us to wonder at this, and to ask: how should we manage resources, and how might we sustainably cooperate and compete? And fundamentally, what are the values, practices, and organization behind our economic institutions? Emily Dickinson wrote: Tell all the Truth, but tell it slant. That's what I attempt here, to look at the world through Dutch flowers, from that slant or vantage point, how the horticultural system plugs into contemporary Dutch life and our sphere at large.

Specifically, the book explores how the Dutch horticultural industry is built on a few fundamental things that intersect and complement each other in various ways. Male networks is an important one: social, artistic, scientific, and economic, this

Dutch variety of old-boy system launched the industry and has made it work at every stage. State planning and funding account for other huge aspects of the horticultural system's growth and success from its beginning until today. What makes these points characteristic of the Netherlands has to do with the size of the industry relative to the country (no one is far removed from the industry), and the prominence of horticulture in a lot of what the country has done, from colonial exploits in the seventeenth and nineteenth centuries to its legendary water and land management, from its models of economic success to its artistic achievements in still-life painting. In other words, horticulture has been integral to the modern nation. Another argument here relates to how this successful 'market system' works in actuality: it's not about only the strong surviving and the individual entrepreneur or company fighting it out to win and dominate. It's also about values and practices not usually associated with capitalism and contemporary industry: namely, cooperating, distributing risk, sharing knowledge, and pooling resources. The book explores how this cooperative institution actually functions in a dynamic global sector. One of the chief lessons is that economic practices do not really run on the basis of abstract principles, disinterested values, and other hackneyed but standard beliefs about 'the market'. When you look closely at FloraHolland, it is clear that beyond bottom-line profit, its daily working owes more to social mores, sentiments, loyalties, and historical patterns than to laws about the behavior of markets, or the ingenuity and character of entrepreneurship and capitalism.

Also, besides what they imply or suggest, the history and practices of the Dutch flower industry are themselves intriguing. In FloraHolland Aalsmeer's auctions and across the industry, I met quirky, passionate people with visions of the world that sometimes seemed charmingly off kilter, sometimes banal, but often insightful and steeped with implications. I learned a lot from them, and do my best to let them speak for themselves and to describe what they do and how their activities fit into larger contexts. I spoke with hundreds of people involved in the industry at every step of the value chain, including breeders, growers, importers and exporters, FloraHolland officials, auctioneers, workers on the floor, office staff, and florists. Beginning in 2008, I spent many early mornings at the Aalsmeer auction observing, asking questions, and making notes, and befriended traders and workers on the floor. I attended industry events and meetings in the Aalsmeer auction and at venues around the country. I also spent six weeks in Ethiopia visiting flower farms, interviewing Dutch growers and officials, as well as people from Ethiopian civil society and Ethiopian commercial horticulture.

Through my interviews with growers and traders, and observations in greenhouses and at the auction, certain themes recurred. And as I read about Dutch history and the background of flower culture in the Netherlands, although the situations differed considerably from the contemporary world, I found a sort of family resemblance with these themes, a rhythm or echo from previous centuries. The connections are easy to overstate, but they nevertheless struck me as significant, and helped to structure the book. These leitmotifs run through each chapter, which is organized around a question or series of related questions. The questions are straightforward, but the leitmotifs deserve some explanation. Though this book looks at the Netherlands and the larger world through the *slant* of horticulture, the institution of FloraHolland Aalsmeer remains the focus.

~

I began my research just as the global financial industry collapsed and have made sense of Dutch horticulture in the seismic turmoil it has triggered in the years since. To be sure, financial elites accelerated trends well under way for decades in shaping the contours of this continuing catastrophe. Among its pernicious effects so far, it has bankrupted entire countries, impoverished millions of people, led to speculative frenzies, and driven up the price of commodities that have in turn devastated populations and inspired riots (among other places, in Haiti and in Egypt in

2010). Although not on the tips of the tongues of horticultural traders in Aalsmeer, these events have affected their business, and influence many seemingly distant and disparate institutions, policies, and economies. A recent report by the Institute for Agriculture and Trade Policy at Tufts University concluded that "[a] paradigm shift is underway, caused by the deepening integration of agricultural, energy, and financial markets in a resource-constrained world made more vulnerable by climate change."[11]

In late 2008 and 2009, many executives in the Dutch horticultural industry still saw the crisis as brief and contained, and they predicted continued growth and prosperity for the horticultural sector. But although the horticultural industry may have fared better than other parts of the economy, it soon became clear that they had not grasped the depth of such events. It's not yet certain if these global events represent part of the end of a long cycle of what's sometimes called 'the world system',[12] and the beginning of a more sustainable and just system, but it seems clear that the collapse and the official response to it represent the failure of the ideology of markets, of a range of economic practices, and for better or for worse, probably signals still more dramatic changes to come. As events unfolded week by week and month by month, I came to see the auction as a small system with its own logic, but embedded literally and ideologically in the mutating global system. The Aalsmeer auction is connected to state policies, to Dutch national discourses, and historical legacies in ways that conform to and also challenge how we understand business. The crisis made far more urgent the links between the auction and larger policies, and between the horticultural market and 'the market'. One market is a specific place for buying and selling that is managed by institutions, and the other is abstract, disembodied, deterritorialized. But the ways many in the Dutch flower industry conceptualized markets, they often amounted to the same thing, even though in practice it was plain that FloraHolland did not work according to the espoused market principles.

Feminist economist and historian Nancy Folbre described the issue like this: "If we use the word 'capitalism' to describe the world we live in, rather than some idealized abstraction of economic texts, we should recognize that capitalism is not equivalent to 'the market' but to a complex combination of markets, families, communities, and the state". But while 'capitalism' certainly encompasses more than prices and records of transactions and ownership, 'the market' is also a vague term, something both literal and figurative. Outside of technical jargon to delimit specific definitions, this fuzziness seems inevitable. If one accepts that both 'capitalism' and 'the market' involve cultural and social factors, the broadness and overlap of both terms necessarily follows. That said, whenever relevant, I do my best to distinguish them. When they speak in general terms about how and why Dutch horticulture works as it does, people in the flower business tend to use the term 'the market'.

It's also helpful to point out a general truth about wealth and poverty, because these categories are too often taken as given, the invisible parameters of market logic. Rich and poor are relative designations and are caused not merely by individual decisions, fate, or even specific policies, but result from the very structure and institutions of an economic system. In his landmark *Stone Age Economics*, Marshall Sahlins argued that "the world's most primitive people have few possessions, but they are not poor. Poverty is not a certain small amount of goods, nor is it just a relation between means and ends; above all it is a relation between people. Poverty is a social status. As such it is the invention of civilization". This perspective was (and remains) controversial, especially among market ideologues who insist that our current economic order is a meritocracy, value-neutral, and has produced unprecedented, widespread prosperity. But Sahlins' view was prefigured by several popular Enlightenment figures. For instance, in *Agrarian Justice* Thomas Paine made the same point in nearly identical words: "Poverty, therefore, is a thing created by that which is called civilized life", he wrote. "It exists not in the natural state. On the other hand, the natural state is without those advantages which flow from agriculture, arts, science, and manufactures". Similarly, Rousseau reasoned that "as there is hardly any inequality in the state of nature, all the inequality which now prevails... clashes with natural right... a distinction which sufficiently determines what we ought to think of that species of inequality which prevails in all civilized countries; since it is plainly contrary to the law of nature, however defined, that children should command old men, fools, wise men, and that the privileged few should gorge themselves with superfluities, while the starving multitudes are in want of the bare necessities of life". These strident words are remarkably apposite when considering the place of luxury commodities like flowers in the contemporary world.

~

More than merely working together toward a shared goal, cooperation refers to the various processes and institutions in which relationships, resources, information, and activities are shared within and between social groups for communal advantage. Cooperative behavior and practices have been around as long as human societies, very likely formed a decisive part of our pre-human evolutionary past, and have been observed not only in our closely related primates but in elephants, dolphins, rats, and other mammals. Cooperation and cooperative activities can also be understood as a variation on or compliment to practices of gifting and reciprocity that have been observed among indigenous peoples as well as peasant societies.

Around the world today, cooperatives are big business, but their place both in agriculture and the global economy are sometimes underappreciated. According to eRNAC (the electronic European research network of academic researchers of agricultural cooperatives), a third of world food production passes through cooperatives. To put this in a global perspective: the European Union has 132,000 cooperatives with 83.5 million members and 2.3 million employees; the US has 47,000 cooperatives with 100 million members; and China has 94,771, with 1,193 million members. Because of their prominence and emphases on working together, small farmers, and sustainability, the UN declared 2012 the Year of the Cooperative, and in the Netherlands, the NRC (Nationale Cooperatieve Raad voor land-en-tuinbouw) sponsors events and regularly publishes material on the achievements, potential, and appeal of cooperatives. In a recent NRC report, ICAO (International Cooperative Agricultural Organization) president Won-Byung Choi articulated a key reason why cooperatives today are especially valuable: "cooperatives are an alternative that can alleviate the negative effect of laissez-faire," he said, since free-trade agreements often destroy small farmers. Though integrated in the global economic system, coops represent an appealing and vital model that can provide a buffer from the ravages and vicissitudes of market forces. They offer a different way of doing business. Membership is open, and members own and govern their institutions, collectively managing their affairs and collectively benefitting – instead of decisions taken by a board of directors and profits merely enriching managers, CEOs, and shareholders. In theory, coops are organized by and run for the membership; in practice they hew closer to or further from this ideal, and exist in many sectors (including retail, consumer, housing, and agriculture).

Of the 300 largest cooperatives in the world, 15 are based in the Netherlands. For over a hundred years, cooperatives have occupied marked positions in the Netherlands, particularly in the agricultural sector, and within the financial institutions that support agriculture. In the Netherlands in 2001, for instance, cooperatives processed 84 percent of all milk and 63 percent of all sugar beets; they supplied 54 percent of all compound feed, provided 87 percent of all credit to farmers, and sold 95 percent of all flowers and potted plants. According to the NRC, the total profits of the forty largest cooperatives in the Netherlands in 2010 was just under 37 billion euro. (For an arresting perspective, note that the non-cooperative Royal Dutch Shell's profits for 2011 were 31 billion).[13] All told, cooperatives in the Netherlands employ about 74,000 workers (and if one includes related services, the 4,000 Dutch cooperatives in existence employ about 150,000 people and account for 85 billion euro in profits.)

In addition to the prevalence and profit of coops in global and national terms, within the Dutch horticultural industry, *cooperation* is also a prized value. The pleasure of success is often attributed to *samenwerken*, working together. Nevertheless, it should not be assumed that all Dutch trade communities will automatically form cooperatives. In fact, in many cases they have not. Anthropologist Jojada Verrips investigated the community of Dutch bargemen to understand why, of the many barge-master's associations that have formed and then dissolved over the decades, only a few have enjoyed much longevity.[14]

These men would seem to share a lot in common with horticultural entrepreneurs: a masculine occupational culture, a tradition passed down in families and communities, regional and national values that support and encourage working together, and some favorable legislation that does not present hindrances to forming occupational and professional institutions. There may even be a parallel between male grower's attitudes toward their flowers and bargemen's affinity for their boats, since both objects tend to be conceived of as fragile, curvaceous, and feminine. Verrips found that men often named their boats for women and expressed an emotional attachment to their ships ("with ribs, a belly, flanks, a face, and a rump... [bargemen said that] 'a boat feels like a woman'"). And there is another comparison with the flower industry. As a country criss-crossed with canals, the Netherlands hosts the world's largest national inland fleet that employs many skilled people, so as national figures, bargemen could be said to be as notable as flower growers, although in the public imagination bargemen may be less yolked to national identity, even if as cultural types they predate flower growers. But crucially, unlike horticultural growers, bargemen display a sort of stoic independence; they tend not to see themselves as part of a collective, and lack the necessary fellowship. Verrips concluded that the comparative weakness of their associations is due to this quality of individuality, of ambivalence toward valuing and maintaining organizations.

Among other communities of Dutch watermen, the patterns of disunity are similar, but for different reasons. Rob Van Ginkel sought to discover how and why fishermen in Texel formed cooperatives, unions, and collective organizations between 1870 and 1930. He found that the values of cooperation were strong and that there was often an eagerness to establish trade cooperatives and other associations of solidarity, but that few lasted. The frequent effort to create unity demonstrated that one common explanation was false – that fishermen were too solitary, individualistic, and independent to think collectively. So why, again and again, did their trade associations peter out? Van Ginkel argued that the group loyalty expressed was real but limited, based on extremely local affiliations that were not broad enough to sustain much power, and that ultimately, economic and institutional forces encouraged fishermen to see one another more as competitors than potential partners with shared interests and concerns. Remarkably, this remained true despite the fact that the fishing industry, like the horticultural business, sells its commodities via auctions, and that one of the functions of auctions is to stabilize a community and encourage collectivity. In the early 1990s Alex Strating studied the *lijnrijders*[15] (traders and wholesalers) of a small-town horticultural auction, in Rijnsburg, and found a mixture of cooperation and competition: as community members, *lijnrijders* stuck together and were loyal to their local identity and institutions, but as businessmen, they were often fiercely competitive and individualistic, engaging in serious but somewhat affectionate rivalries.

What do these similarities and differences say, finally, about the practice of horticultural cooperatives and the ideology of cooperation in the Netherlands? In keeping with Van Ginkel and Verrips, I found that the cultural value of working together is necessary but in itself not sufficient to build and maintain a cooperative institution; in addition to camaraderie, structural considerations must also be in place (market advantage, shared interests, a legal framework, physical and financial infrastructure). But the two sides (psychological/social and material/economic) are also closely related. For example, the very structure of collective interest in cooperatives may foster powerful feelings of solidarity and stimulate a social norm of communality, as several studies have found. But also, when and if the material advantages and incentives of working together shift – due to market changes or legal or political power dynamics – cooperative structures can quickly break down. Some variation of this is what took place in the 1990s with the Dutch fruit and vegetable cooperative auctions. Before explaining what occurred and suggesting what it might mean for FloraHolland and Dutch horticulture, there's more to say about the local context.

The co-op movement in the Netherlands began in the late nineteenth century, at a time in Western Europe when industrial capitalism was coming to dominate production and social life. Work was brutal, low-paid, and unregulated. Individuals and communities began to understand that they could protect themselves to some extent from an exploitative system by forming collective organizations. From the beginning, enthusiasm for the Dutch cooperative was social and spiritual as well as economic – religious groups, for instance, advocated for the cooperative movement at the turn of the twentieth century, particularly in rural cooperative banking. During this same period of cooperative development, a range of social theorists began to grapple with the structure and meaning of the economic system and its relationship with societal development, articulating concerns relevant to Dutch cooperatives and society. Fruit and vegetable auctions, and slightly later the Aalsmeer flower auctions, were founded in this milieu of agricultural cooperatives, industrialization, and a sense of egalitarianism. In pre-cooperative auction days, agricultural growers had an isolated and weak position, facing a buyer's market that regularly undercut their prices and fostered a precarious existence. It's not hard to understand that cooperatives enjoyed strong practical as well as ideological support.

At this time as well, although social Darwinism was increasingly celebrated by the powerful, some theorists argued that human society was based more on mutual aid and concern than on cut-throat competition and individualism. When Peter Kropotkin investigated a range of societies as well as animals in their natural environment, he found a sort of cooperative instinct, which he concluded is "of the greatest importance for the maintenance of life, the preservation of each species, and its further evolution". Rejecting social Darwinism (but not Darwin's theory of natural selection), he reasoned that "[i]t is not love to my neighbor – whom I often do not know at all – which induces me to seize a pail of water and to rush towards his house when I see it on fire; it is a far wider, even though more vague feeling or instinct of human solidarity and sociability which moves me". It was equally this sort of friendly and practical sensibility that helped stoke the early cooperative movement. (On the other hand, some of this collective thinking and values led to disastrous policies in the twentieth century when states pursued centralized hierarchical programs in the name of the collectivization, industrialization, and peasant development in places as diverse as the Soviet Union and Brazil. Though such programs were promoted as democratic, socialist, and cooperative, in fact they were part of a rigid, top-down form of governance.)

During the depression of the 1930s, many countries passed legislation to encourage cooperatives. The Federal Credit Union Act (1934) in the U.S. ensured credit was provided to farmers and "people of small means"; it was specifically intended "to stabilize an imbalanced global financial system". European laws did likewise. The Netherlands enacted an 'auction law' (also in 1934) which favored cooperatives and was meant to mollify the severe effects of economic crisis; it mandated that all growers of fresh produce sell their goods via cooperative auctions. Auctions were established as grower-owned cooperatives, and they proliferated until the mid-1960s when the auction law was repealed. Between 1970 and 1995, the number of cooperative auctions in the Netherlands shrank from 88 to 6, and those that remained were in the horticultural sector. Today the structure of the fruit and vegetable market in the Netherlands is different: they no longer sell via auction, and although most growers remain part of a cooperative, since 1996 (when 20 cooperatives merged into one) they're part of a single, centralized, wholesaler called The Greenery, which supplies 70 percent of Dutch grocery stores.

Why did this happen, and could flower and plant auctions be going the way of fruit and vegetable auctions, toward extinction? Chapters two and three offer some perspectives on the latter question, but here it's possible to comment briefly. In the early 1990s, many Dutch fruit and vegetable growers felt pinched by the regional auction system primarily because it didn't seem to interface well with the market: the auction seemed to introduce a lag time between buyer's changing needs and grower's adaptation. The solution pursued was first to merge all Dutch fruit and vegetable auctions into one new cooperative, in order to take advantage of economies of scale, prevent inter-auction competition, and establish countervailing power. Next, the new auction cooperative would become more of a marketing cooperative specializing in direct trade with major food retailers. Today The Greenery is by far the largest marketing cooperative for fresh produce in the Netherlands, enjoying annual profits of 1.5 billion euro, and selling about fifty percent of all vegetables produced in the Netherlands. In 1996, out of the 20 extant auctions, nine came together to form the Cooperative Voedingstuinbouw Nederland (VTN) and combine their assets and activities into one central marketing firm, The Greenery BV, which is connected to but autonomous from the VTN.

These structural changes and particularly the schism between The Greenery and the VTN have been celebrated as a great success. But it is also commonly conceded that "...the separation was intended to give management more freedom to operate". They sound familiar, these two highlights – merging all auctions to one and increasing management power. They were complaints I heard from Dutch grower-members of FloraHolland in the first several years after the merger of Bloemenveiling Aalsmeer and FloraHolland, which left just two horticultural auctions, the smaller and more local Plantion, and the internationally oriented FloraHolland, with its six auction locations. But the flower and plant auctions don't exactly mirror the fruit and vegetable auction, and because the changes were approved by the membership, the fruit and vegetable growers understandably did not vote to ruin themselves. Nor have they reverted to nineteenth-century, pre-cooperative days. In fact, The Greenery remains a cooperative, though it is a less democratic institution than what came before. One big difference now is that the structure of decision-making changed so that the authority and strength of management has been greatly enhanced. Likewise wholesalers are sitting in the catbird's seat: now just 25 percent of fruit and vegetables are sold via the auction clock because The Greenery provides wholesalers with another option and they prefer direct negotiations for better price control and a stronger competitive position.

But small growers have not been eliminated and replaced with one super grower company that has a monopoly, along the lines of Monsanto in the U.S., for example, continuing a long established pattern there of centralized and hierarchical practices in agriculture. In the U.S. over the course of the twentieth century, agriculture's high equity, low-variable cost structure turned farmers into little more than indentured servants of the big centralized industrial producers. As different as this history is from that of the Netherlands' agriculture and horticulture, there are some parallels worth noting. Already in the 1940s, one response in the U.S. to the comparative weakness of small growers and local cooperatives in the face of the staggering power and wealth of the big companies was to create 'orderly market cooperatives'. Different agricultural coops would pool resources to do joint marketing campaigns before and after the growing seasons, thereby lengthening the sales period, augmenting profits, increasing their visibility, and gaining some autonomy. Well-known brands today like Sunkist, Sunmade Raisins, and Ocean Spray all began as agricultural cooperatives that adopted this strategy. Their marketing power provided an 'extra bid' against the authority of the regional monopolist, and the pre and post cooperative price difference was known as 'the competitive yardstick', which could compensate for market exploitation and protect farmers by providing fair prices in exchange for members' production and loyalty. If there's a lesson for Dutch agricultural and horticultural cooperatives, it's that 'small d' democracy and cooperative structures engender greater local control and a fairer distribution of profits. Also, management structures need to allow for flexible policies and quick decisions, but not at the expense of majority interests. Though cooperatives vary in design and practice, their essence is a representative, egalitarian approach.

In the Netherlands, cooperative values enjoy a strong pedigree. Though sometimes exaggerated or debunked as myth, popularly celebrated values of political compromise and consensus building must be acknowledged, and they seem directly related to the values of the cooperative. Probably the most conspicuous area to underline in this regard involves the policies and discourses of the polder model.

A polder is a chunk of low-lying land reclaimed from the sea or a river, and depends on dykes and levees for protection and maintenance. Up to seventy percent of the country today consists of such reclaimed land, so the well-worn saying 'God created the world, but the Dutch made the Netherlands' is more than a fanciful bit of national pride, and what the Dutch call the 'polder model' also occupies a renowned space in Dutch civic affairs. An accurate topographical designation, a metaphor for the founding of the country, a characterization of the political system, a description of widely held social values, a depiction of the historical framework that led to great wealth and widely distributed prosperity: the polder model is all of these things. Like many concepts with political cache (globalization is another), the polder model is rooted in both myth and reality.

Since this lowland and river delta region regularly floods, inhabitants have long perceived the common threat of deluge, and already in the Middle Ages they set up water boards (*waterschappen*), local institutions to manage water and land, which they did in a number of ways, including the creation of polders. The argument goes that this response to the lay of the land determined social structures and practices over the centuries, in which small, local democratic councils emerged and gradually evolved into more modern political arrangements. There are direct and indirect connections to these early modern cooperative *waterschappen* models, including the fact that today twenty-seven water boards around the country determine water policy. Pointing out the importance placed on collective decision-making and the state's ability and popular mandate to regulate the economy, the polder model has often been invoked to explain contemporary institutions, political practices, and more. But this is less true today than in recent decades. And in fact, historians question their political legacy and dispute how democratic the practices of early modern water boards really were. Some argue it was less the water boards and more the early urbanization of the country that led to the small cooperative processes that characterize 'the polder model'. Yet regardless of its historical accuracy in describing the development of the modern nation, the polder model remains a potent national trope, and spacial planning continues to depend on the management of water and lowlands.

In the second half of the nineteenth century and for much of the twentieth, the different social polders were often divided along religious lines or pillars (Catholics and Protestants), each with different schools, social institutions, and political parties. But by the end of the 1960s, the importance of religious affiliation had decreased considerably. From the 1980s onwards, three polders (trade unions, employers organizations, and the government) comprised the anatomy of the body politic, and together they reached agreements on wages, work hours, and industrial policy. In these and other ways, the polder model encapsulates some of the common features of what is sometimes called 'the Netherlands' business system'. Bargaining, finding a consensus, forming coalitions: these common features of collective decision-making in social, political, and economic realms of Dutch life are perceived as part of the polder model. And these broadly held communitarian and cooperative values have informed the development of Dutch horticulture.

~

Flower growers in the Gaza Strip have had an especially difficult past several years. In the 2009 Gaza War, the Israeli military targeted civilian infrastructure, including agricultural land and production facilities as well as schools and hospitals.[16] But even before that late 2008-early 2009 bombardment, Israel caused severe problems for the Palestinian flower sector by cutting off export routes. In non-violent protest of the blockade that kept their flowers locked in Gaza and rotting, in February 2008 Palestinian farmers hauled and dumped their roses and carnations at the borders held closed by their captors. Those flowers had been destined for sale in Aalsmeer as part of the Valentine's Day boom. According to Mahmoud Khalil, the President of the General Land Owners in Gaza, berry and flower exports constitute important commerce for the Strip, each year earning about thirteen million dollars for flowers, and about eight million dollars for strawberries. Combined, in 2008 the two sectors employed over eight thousand people, including production and secondary services. As part of the General Agricultural Cooperative, a spokesperson for Shafi Ahmed rose farmers warned that "if the problem of exporting agricultural products is not solved, the Gaza Strip will face yet another catastrophe."[17] Trying to prevent the total collapse of the main export industry, Gaza's Minister of Agriculture, Dr. Mahmoud Hebbash sought to provide immediate assistance to farmers in the agricultural, floral, and berry sectors, and joined a host of farmers and agricultural organizations in demanding Israeli compensation, though they did not expect to receive it.

In early 2008 Dutch news broadcast images of Gazan-grown flowers wilting by the thousands in heaps, representing for many viewers heart-wrenching scenes that brought home the harsh realities of the Israeli siege and blockade. Quickly but quietly, Dutch diplomatic pressures mounted, likely motivated more by financial interest than communal values or humanitarian concerns. In addition to impinging on the profits of Dutch import and export companies, the Dutch stood to lose on their investment in Gazan horticulture. According to the *Agrarisch Dagblad*, from 2007-2009 the Netherlands loaned seven million euros in support of the Gazan flower sector. In March 2009, Dutch Foreign Minister Maxime Verhagen met with his Israeli counterpart Tsipi Livni in Brussels to negotiate opening the border for Palestinian exports to the Netherlands, but at the time Livni would give permission only for flowers, no berries. Though drastically weakened and impoverished by Operation Cast Lead and the enduring blockade, a dedicated group of Palestinian farmers resumed work. Today they continue to operate under extreme duress.

Prior to the Israeli blockade, Gaza was a valued source of flowers and strawberries for European markets. According to the Oxfam-partnered Palestinian Agriculture Relief Committee (PARC) which manages Gaza's cash crop exports to the Netherlands, before the blockade Gaza used to export about sixty-five million flowers annually (fifty million of which were carnations), along with 1,500 tons of strawberries. By 2011-2012, five years into the blockade, total flower exports had been reduced to nine million, and strawberry exports had shriveled to 447 tons. In addition to the devastating material consequences, this continuing collective punishment has caused frustration, sadness, and outrage toward Israel first and foremost, but also toward the European Union and the Palestinian Authority for permitting the policy. "Shame on Israel," Mohammed Hijazi told the Palestinian Center for Human Rights. "But shame on the Palestinian Authority, too. My father represents many local flower farmers in southern Gaza, but no-one from the Ministry of Agriculture has even contacted us during this crisis. And shame on the European Union, because they have done nothing either. Why are they standing back in silence and allowing this to happen to us. Tell me–what is the security risk in exporting flowers?"[18] Throughout the blockade this father and son hung on. Along with a sense of despair, these flower farmers expressed remarkable restraint, humility, and humanity. Watching female workers packing flowers for the negotiated export, Hejazi commented, "My flowers will be a means to spread peace in the world, this is a message to the whole world that peace and love start from Gaza."[19]

As the plight of Gazan farmers vividly portrays, the flower industry is embedded in international politics and trade, as well as moral economies. FloraHolland Aalsmeer imports from over sixty countries, and the global panorama of production and trade dynamics of this horticultural commerce are explored in chapter five. But it's also valuable to frame the issues more generally, in terms of a moral economy, commodity chains, and global economic patterns and trends. This gives some deeper background to the issues and locates them in historical and institutional contexts – which is another way of saying that the messages from flower growers and lessons from development policies seem urgent and broadly applicable.

Economic practices seem inherently connected to morality. In support of this idea, one might point to Weber's observations about the associations between ethics and economic development, but the relationship goes back much further. In Roman mythology, for example, it was commonly perceived that 'the market' (even this precapitalist one) should be regarded with skepticism. It had a quality of strangeness, suspicion, possibly of not belonging. Mercury was thus the god of a triumvirate: the market, eloquence, and thieves. That those three types were grouped together reveals a common logic and critique that there's something innately unfair and distrustful about commerce. There are numerous examples of such implicit values embedded in the words and phrases of many languages. In Dutch the noun 'afzet' simply means 'sale' or 'market', but the verb 'afzetten' means 'to overcharge, cheat, or swindle'. Similarly, in many languages, the vocabulary around lending and owing money overlaps with words for judgement and ethics (in Dutch 'schuld' can mean both 'debt' and 'guilt', for instance). So if economic relations inevitably pose ethical problems, the term 'moral economy' may seem redundant. But in fact it has a more specific meaning, one especially suited for approaching the Dutch horticultural industry, since the concept's origins are explicitly linked to people's response to the sale of commodities in a capitalist market.

In his 1971 study, "The Moral Economy of the English Crowd in the Eighteenth Century," E.P. Thompson explored why people remained divided and accepting of difficult, exploitative circumstances for much of history, but sometimes public anger would explode and people would spontaneously revolt and demand change. In eighteenth-century Britain, as the country moved out of feudalism and reformed its market, bread prices shot up; people could no longer afford to buy their basic staple, and began to go hungry. They rioted, demanding lower prices. Thompson argued that British peasants rose up not merely because their stomachs were empty, but because their sense of the social compact and natural rights had been grossly violated by the emerging 'free market.' The new economic relations offended accepted notions of fairness, seemed an affront to basic decency, and so could be resisted with violence if necessary. In Thompson's words, "... these grievances operated within a popular consensus as to what were illegitimate practices in marketing, milling, baking, etc. This in turn was grounded upon a consistent traditional view of social norms and obligations, of the proper economic functions of several parties within the community, which, taken together, can be said to constitute the moral economy of the poor. An outrage to these moral assumptions, quite as much as actual deprivation, was the usual occasion for direct action". This was written at the dawn of the neoliberal age, when Adam Smith had not yet been launched into full apotheosis. In a prescient critique of neoliberal values Thompson wrote (against Smith's acolytes), "[i]t should not be necessary to argue that the model of a natural and self-adjusting economy, working providentially for the best good of all, is... superstition...".

It's important to underscore that the moral economy is *communal*, widely shared, and not based on or emerging from supposedly male assertiveness and violence; on the contrary, "[i] nitiators of the riots were, very often, the women. In 1693 we learn of a great number of women going to Northampton market 'with knives in their girdles to force corn at their own rates'", while men stood on supportively, vowing to destroy ships and cargoes if the women were threatened or harmed. Nor is this logic peculiar to centuries-old English sensibilities. Since 2008, as commodity prices have skyrocketed, food riots have erupted around the world – again because implicit social pacts have been trounced. Of course, as Marcel Mauss keenly observed, the transactions and relations around all sorts of commodities have been the focal point of values and reveal the logic of systems in vastly different societies with a range of social and economic institutions. Today's market legitimacy depends on it seeming, on the one hand, to promote efficiency and general prosperity, or on the other, at least to represent a neutral and disinterested system. If the economic system or institution doesn't seem natural and ineluctable, it lacks legitimacy and authority, will likely be challenged, and may collapse. And in fact, although providing excellent mechanisms for extracting fantastic wealth for a few, capitalist markets are extremely destructive for the majority of the population. Even 'natural disasters' may be caused or exacerbated by markets (global warming today, disease and famine in previous centuries).

As the Nobel laureate Amartya Sen has shown, famines are primarily caused not by actual shortages but by rational market mechanisms of hoarding and rationing in the interest of price control and profit. This was the case for some of the twentieth century's worst tolls of starvation and malnutrition, whether in Bangladesh or Ethiopia. The lack of food had little to do with availability or the capacity to produce it, even locally. But the necessity for profits and the capitalist model of distribution ensure that people who are poor remain poor and food insecure, while the rich reap rewards and grow richer. These effects are as old as market-based world systems. The first international market in food in the modern era was the global market in wheat established by the British in the nineteenth century. It replaced traditional practices by imposing market-based rules, which led to vastly increased production, but mostly for export. Selling wheat on the international market meant that South Asians could no longer afford the fruits of their labor. For the two thousand years prior to the nineteenth century, small-scale famines occurred about once a century on the Indian subcontinent; in the British-imposed, market driven, 'world system' mode of production and distribution, there was a much greater scale of famine and they occurred once every four years, Mike Davis has shown. Although more food was being produced, many more people went hungry and died. During the second half of Queen Victoria's reign, between 31.7 and 61.3 million people died in holocausts of "truly planetary magnitude, with drought and famine reported as well in Java, the Philippines, New Caledonia, Korea, Brazil, southern Africa and the Mahgreb....". Summarizing this ghastly period, Davis writes "[a]t issue is not simply that millions of poor rural people died appallingly, but that they died in a manner, and for reasons, that contradict much of the conventional understanding of the economic history of the nineteenth century... Millions died, not outside the 'modern world system,' but in the very process of being forcibly incorporated into its economic and political structures".

Given the vastly increased (and increasing) global scope of industrial agriculture, these sorts of disasters are possibly even truer in the twenty-first century. And it is likely that today, as in the nineteenth century, the numbers of those affected will go largely unacknowledged, and the cause-effect relationship remain obscured between market-based, large-scale agricultural production and numerous deaths and other deleterious effects. A realistic assessment of such consequences would have to include everything from the massive small-scale farmer suicides in India in recent decades, genetic engineering, and shortages and diseases due to corporate monoculture, to environmental and public health crises that have emerged from farming and breeding – such things as the avian flu and hoof-and-mouth disease, for starters – all of which are ultimately caused by a market-driven, hierarchical model of development and agricultural production. And although the discussion of famine, wheat, and rice may seem removed from the world of a luxury commodity like flowers, it's not. The incentives, production, distribution, and moral economy of the Dutch-centered horticultural industry only make sense if understood, in part, through this commodity-driven world systems framework.

In the Netherlands, the intersection of international trade and commodities with the idea of a moral economy has its own powerful history. The 1860 novel *Max Havelaar: Or the Coffee Auctions of the Dutch Trading Company* exposed Dutch policies in Java and Sumatra and horrified the public, who demanded reforms. The book chronicled the colonial government's hallmark Cultivation System, which mandated Indonesian farmers uproot staple foods like rice in order to produce a quota of commercially tradable crops like tea and coffee, and levied an onerous and corrupt tax regime. This program caused abject poverty and widespread starvation among the population, and stoked shock and outrage in the Netherlands. The response of citizens at home to the production of goods they were consuming made it clear how they were linked and indirectly responsible for those truculent but geographically distant policies. *Max Havelaar* exposed what today are called global commodity chains, and commodities like coffee, chocolate, and flowers are now often thought of in these terms (as a result, today Max Havelaar may be best known as a Fair Trade label). Public response to the book also led to an era of reform policies, and one of the companies to appear during this period, a sugar business called HVA, eventually moved, after Indonesian Independence, to Ethiopia, where it indirectly helped to launch the Dutch flower industry there (a story discussed in chapter five).

~

One cannot discuss networks in the cut flower and plant trade without also talking about masculinity and aesthetics, since these networks are composed almost entirely of men, and everyone involved (from growers and traders to florists and consumers) is concerned with the beauty and presentation of the flower or plant. Masculinity was an important ingredient in the cultural familiarity that makes networking ties come easily and naturally. And these networks arose and continue through close personal interactions, which are sometimes reinforced by media (today with the telephone and internet; in the seventeenth century, tulip enthusiasts not only regularly met around gardens but maintained contact through letters).

These early networks engaged in several intimately related activities, ranging from spacial planning to commerce. Thirty-one of the forty-one members of the Amsterdam government appointed between 1600-1625 were involved in one way or another in trade, which through family and networks spanned the globe and encompassed sizeable interests. In those days, the purpose of marriages was to forge alliances between families, each of whom hoped to gain an advantage. Merchants preferred to have relatives as partners in their trading firms, and regents usually considered family ties when conferring offices. In fact, many practices and factors intersected, contributing to Amsterdam becoming the center of the global economy of its day as well as the forging and expansion of political, social, and trade networks. The sixteenth-century herring business with the Baltic region and Russia set the stage for the Republic's emergence as a major trade power. Fishermen needed ships and rope; to preserve their catch, they required salt, which they imported from Portugal, Spain, and France, along with wine, which they then sold to the Baltic countries – in this way, powerful trading networks began: in the service of commerce, well-organized herring fleets exploited the Lowland provinces' location, seafaring skills, and its small interconnected population. Horticulture, too, was an integral part of the launching of commercial and aesthetic Dutch networks. Gardening, tulip culture, and still-life painting became fixed in the cultural environment and helped to invigorate the networks.

Networks don't have an inherent ideology. They can be part of egalitarian cooperatives or elite, extremely hierarchical multinational corporations, as Swiss researchers recently demonstrated in examining control of the global economy. Mapping the architecture of international ownership, they analyzed about 37 million economic actors, both individuals and firms located in 194 countries; at the center of this web, they discovered a cartel or 'super-entity' of 147 even more tightly knit companies that collude to dominate total wealth. They found that less than one percent of these mostly financial institutions (including Barclays, JP Morgan Chase, and Goldman Sachs) control 40 percent of the entire network, and much of the global economy. And about 1300 corporations control 80 percent of the global economy. It turns out that public opinion is not far from the truth when it decries the oligarchical power of financial institutions and corporations. Another paper analyzed corporate governance networks in the 250 largest corporations of the Netherlands between 1976 and 1996, and found that although networks thinned between financial institutions and industry, overall such Dutch networks remained "compact and connected". I found that the flower business similarly prioritizes personal relationships in stimulating commerce and making policy – not as the conspiracy of a controlling cabal, but as linked institutions lubricated by personal relationships. This is illustrated by a number of practices, meetings, and institutions, including Horti Fairs, auction membership gatherings, and *bloemencorsos* or flower parades. Fealty, nearness, personal and cultural familiarity, kinship, and masculinity all bear on forming and maintaining connections in Dutch horticultural networks. The creation of horticultural beauty represents a profoundly felt impulse, one that in fact doesn't seem far removed from gardeners, flower breeders, and florists – or for that matter, from the traders, exporters, wholesalers and others involved in more pragmatic aspects of the industry.

Something that initially impressed me and that strikes many outside observers of Dutch horticulture is how this aesthetic industry is dominated by men. On reflection, given that horticultural occupations often provide the breadwinner's salary, this may not be so surprising – in the Netherlands these are traditional male occupations. One kind of male bonding has earned a colloquial expression, *ouwe jongens krentenbrood* (literally, old guy's currant-bread), which isn't specifically an old-boys network but more a general fraternity, which may or may not enjoy much power or prominence. It refers less to the exclusive male environment of elite institutions (bank executives, say, or the alumni of prestigious universities) and more to ordinary male groupings and culture (guys who get together to play soccer, go fishing, or hang out in a bar). It's a good expression to evoke the Dutch horticultural environment, and gives a sense of the tone of horticultural networks.

Early Dutch Horticulture

Why are the Dutch so successful with flowers? I don't know, really. But we have many generations, hundreds of years, of growing flowers and other things in these sandy, swampy little places. It's just what we do, I guess.

A trader at FloraHolland Aalsmeer

Throughout 2009, New York honored the four hundredth anniversary of Henry Hudson's arrival as captain of the Dutch ship, Halve Maen (Half Moon), on a journey sponsored, like many other colonial ventures of that era, by the Dutch East India Company, the Vereenigde Oost-Indische Compagnie, or VOC. Many celebrations commemorated New York's Dutch roots, including several tulip-naming ceremonies. In Manhattan's Battery Park, on the spot where the Half Moon landed, Princess Máxima dribbled champagne to baptize the bright orange 'Henry Hudson' tulip, and the royal couple presented the City of New York with a gift of 120,000 bulbs donated by the Flower Council of Holland, which Mayor Michael Bloomberg formally welcomed. Uptown, another tulip event honored the controversial former Netherlands parliamentarian, Ayaan Hirsi Ali. Born in Somalia, Ms. Ali obtained political asylum in the Netherlands in 1992 and made a successful career out of criticizing "Islam" as well as immigrants. In front of the Metropolitan Museum of Art, flanked by executives from Holland's flower bulb sector and Wim Pijbes, director of Amsterdam's Rijksmuseum, Ms. Ali christened a new black tulip, the Ayaan, which she herself helped select, and at the same time, one hundred Ayaan bulbs were commemoratively planted in front of the Rijks.

The tulip galas have hardly been confined to 2009 and New Amsterdam-New York related fêtes. Tulip naming ceremonies have become regular events sponsored by the Dutch flower industry, particularly the bulb-growing sector, and are heartily endorsed by Dutch elites and the political class. In connection with Queen Beatrix's 2008 visit to Lithuania, for instance, the Dutch ambassador, accompanied by Dutch tulip cultivar Jan Ligthart, presented a tulip named for the Lithuanian First Lady, the Alma Adamkienė tulip. In 2004, Ligthart had also bred a pink and ivory tulip in honor of then U.S. first Lady Laura Bush, and this variety was grown by Aalsmeer's Blumex and sold at auction (though it was not too popular). At the naming ceremony, Mrs. Bush gave a short speech and was joined by Hans Westerhof, the chairman of the Royal Dutch Wholesalers Association for Flowerbulbs and Nurserystock, who grinned with pride in the photo. In recent years as well, the iconic Dutch tulip was married to the iconic Dutch airline with a new hybrid called Tulipa KLM. KLM CEO Peter Hartman and former Dutch top model Frederique van der Wal presided at the ceremony held at the Keukenhof Gardens and attended by then Dutch Minister for Foreign Trade, Frank Heemskerk.

What's communicated through this elite participation, along with the language and emotional pitch of such events, is a familiar sensibility. As with a lot of marketing, the message is that this product, the tulip, offers access to a certain refined and elevated status. Tulips subtly reinforce distinctions of class and taste while at the same time offer to transcend them through purchase and consumption, which is the heart of what it means to give aesthetic judgement a name. It's not just THAT you might appreciate tulips, or other ornamental flowers. The crux of the issue is why you feel drawn to these aspects of culture, how you consume them, and what you feel you get out of it by participating in certain social activities in particular ways. That's an important message of these tulip events, one that helps frame a temperament of the horticultural industry both today and in the past.

It was during the seventeenth century, and largely through the tulip, that what would become the ornamental flower industry began in the Netherlands. The tulip is so familiar to us, and so much a part of Dutch vernacular, that it's hard to imagine it's not indigenous to the Low Countries. Today tulip bulbs are big business: the Dutch sector employs thousands of people, annual exports generate about six million euros, and over seventy percent of tulips purchased around the globe 'have a Dutch passport,' as is said in the industry. Though bulb cultivation and bulb auctions date back to the seventeenth century in the Netherlands, the space used to grow them was quite limited until the middle-end of the nineteenth century – as recently as 1860, the Netherlands devoted just 600 hectares to flower bulbs. This is about twelve times the area of Amsterdam's Vondelpark or slightly less than twice the size of New York City's Central Park. But in recent decades, according to the KAVB, the hectares devoted to flower bulb production have increased from 10,000 in 1960 to more than 23,500 in 2007. On the other hand, the number of growers has decreased. In 1960, there were 13,000 bulb growers, but by 2007 only 2000 remained. Even with its small land area, the Netherlands is the world's top producer of bulbs (tulip, crocus, daffodil, etc.): the export value is estimated at about $40,000 per hectare. Over 3,000 Dutch companies do business in hybridizing, growing, forcing, and exporting bulbs.

For another measure of the tulip's embeddedness, look at the Keukenhof, which hosts about three quarters of a million tourists each year and presents tulips to the world often with the blessing of the royal family. So natural is it these days to be involved with cultivating, buying, or selling flowers that even many locals not involved in the industry claim that "the trade is in our blood". But there was a time when a commercial market for flowers was scarcely imaginable, when the Dutch did not trade in flowers. How it came about is part of a matrix of other events and developments, some botanical, others economic, cultural, and political. Scientific ideas about the cultivation of flowers emerged with the tulip, and at the same time, values around aesthetics, class sensibility, and monetary worth. In this sense, the tulip was a touchstone for a range of modern practices and ideologies.

Dutch commercial horticulture took shape in several contexts, and each helps to establish the sorts of relationships, values, and practices that also distinguish the industry today. These seventeenth-century contexts involve tulips, the beginning of pleasure gardens, new management techniques for land and water, the formulation of enterprises like the VOC, the rapid expansion of scientific knowledge, including botany, and a distinctive aesthetic commercial sense. Though the specific contemporary institutions, including Aalsmeer's flower auctions, only emerged in the late nineteenth and early twentieth centuries, this seventeenth-century formative period demonstrated the effectiveness of male networks and cooperative structures informed by an ideology of shared values and goals. In this way, from the young period of the Dutch Republic, one can discern the contours of the industry that eventually took shape in the twentieth century around the cooperative, grower-owned Dutch flower auctions.

The contemporary flower auctions continually offer new varieties of cut flowers, which have been created by studying successive generations with the goal of manipulating them or their environments in order to produce particular aesthetic or biological effects. The tulip was the first flower in the Netherlands to be the object of such scientific and aesthetic scrutiny, and to be conceived of as a source of profit for the wealthy and aspiring classes alike. Also, because of the social upheaval known as tulipmania, the flower became associated with broader economic and cultural values. Because its story converges with the emergence of Amsterdam as the center of the world system, as well as male networks, new financial practices, botany, land management, and the popularization of pleasure gardens, the tulip is an appropriate centerpiece for a discussion of the beginning of commercial horticulture in the Netherlands. Only with an understanding of how the tulip became indigenized can the other pieces fall into place, and with them a fuller picture of the origins of Dutch horticulture.

Before looking into the history, though, it's useful to clear away some of the mythology cloaking the tulip, since fables of glory and folly surround the flower, and trendy publicity campaigns elicit a glib aura of the Dutch Golden Age. Part of the press hoopla surrounding the current tulip-naming ceremonies centers around entering the new varieties in The International Classified Register of Tulip Names, a ledger held by The Royal Dutch Flower Bulb Organization (KAVB) that contains every tulip name ever recorded in its four hundred-year history. These promotional events encourage the consumer to draw a connection between the contemporary high-tech industry and a wondrous Dutch past, linking flowers to prosperity, folkloric cultural roots, and the founding of the nation, which both is and is not the case. "Next year a piece of Dutch horticultural history is literally set to rise from the soil," announced a 2009 article in *FloraCulture International*. This sort of hype and the ongoing tulip-naming ceremonies attempt to arouse nostalgia for an imagined past and to invoke a horticultural and economic vision of the tulip trade. All of this is self consciously crafted by the industry, not least through the tulip-naming rituals themselves, which are an industry-invented tradition. The ideology of these events so closely follows Eric Hobsbawm's well-known formulation that one suspects tulip-sector promotional people have carefully studied his book. "'Invented tradition,'" says Hobsbawm, "is taken to mean a set of practices, normally governed by overtly or tacitly accepted rules and of a ritual or symbolic nature, which seek to inculcate certain values and norms of behavior by repetition, which automatically implies continuity with the past. In fact, where possible, they normally attempt to establish continuity with a suitable historic past...".

The industry conjures a mythic past, but one nevertheless based on a kernel of truth. It is valid to say that the origins of the contemporary tulip trade date from the seventeenth century, the era of the Dutch Republic, and that tulips, commerce, and culture around the tulip formed part and parcel of that time and place. It is also accurate to say that the Dutch colonies of New Amsterdam brought seeds of familiar and cherished plants to cultivate in their gardens, including many of the flowers featured in seventeenth-century Dutch still lifes, such as carnations, roses, crown imperials, and indeed tulips. But it's not true to claim that tulip culture was widespread across the seventeen provinces, that people of all classes got deeply involved in the trade, and that an obsession with tulips led to bankrupting an entire economy. Historian Anne Goldgar demolished these commonly accepted ideas in her groundbreaking book, *Tulipmania: Money, Honor, and Knowledge in the Dutch Golden Age*. Nor were tulip bulbs planted in a public naming ritual. Those are tall tales. And almost needless to say, never mentioned are the uglier aspects of Dutch Golden Age prosperity, like slavery, slaughter, and subjugation. The cultivation and sale of tulips and other ornamental flowers did not directly involve these practices, as the trade in nutmeg and cinnamon did, but colonial truculence was an essential part of the system in which tulips came to be cherished.

Also harkening back to a fabled history is the latest attempt to create a 'black' tulip. Sotheby's Amsterdam held a 'Tulip Mania' auction in 1998, featuring pages from various seventeenth and eighteenth-century tulip books, including one called *A Black Tulip With a Ladybird*. The dark maroon or indigo-brown Ayaan joins a long tradition of 'black' tulips in the Netherlands and evokes the centuries-old, legendary quest of Dutch hybridizers to create a truly black tulip, which is impossible to achieve, as this absence of color only exists in nature when something is dead or charred. But each attempt to create the sleek dark tulip draws on an appeal first stoked by Alexander Dumas's mid-nineteenth-century murder mystery set in Haarlem, *The Black Tulip*. Dumas's popular novel dramatized the attempt to breed an ebony tulip, which through his imagination became a symbol not merely of elusive beauty, but of justice, and this image helped fuel public interest in the flower. (However far from justice one might understand Hirsi Ali's politics – in the midst of Israeli war crimes in Gaza she called for Prime Minister Netanyahu to receive a Nobel Peace Prize – it's not hard to conceive of a 'black' tulip's appeal for her as both classically Dutch and representing a graceful integrity.) It may well be, as Anna

Pavord has argued, that the tulip "has carried more political, social, economic, religious, intellectual, and cultural baggage than any other [flower] on earth". And it must be stressed that that 'baggage' wasn't picked up in the Netherlands alone. While an important chapter of the tulip's history occurs in the Low Countries and the nascent Dutch Republic of the seventeenth century, tulips were already being cultivated from central Asia to the Iberian Peninsula a thousand years ago. How the Dutch first took to these flowers partly grew out of other cultures' reverence for them.

After the harsh winters along the central Asian steppes, Tartars and other nomads must have been struck by the bright tulip buds emerging from the bleak stony landscape. Some of their colors resembled blood, and the flower came to be associated with vitality and fertility; other shades like cinnabar, fiery orange, and the flush of intimate flesh evoked passion and preciousness. No one knows when the tulip first came to be cultivated, but as early as 1050 it grew in Isfahan and Baghdad, when both cities were thriving stops along the Silk Road that drew caravans of traders from the eastern Mediterranean and ships from as far off as China and the Horn of Africa. Poets sung their praises, and gardens with scented roses and multicolored tulips were said to create an earthly paradise.

Tulips were particularly prized by the Ottomans, who venerated both their vibrant hues and their shape, which vaguely resembles a turban. In fact, European names for the flower (tulp, tulipe, tulipan, tulip) do descend from the Turkish word for turban (dulband or delband), but that's a mistranslation, apparently originating with Ogier Ghiselin de Busbecq, the Flemish herbalist who served as ambassador to the Ottoman Empire for several Austrian monarchs. To the Ottomans, the tulip was *lale*, a Persian term, which is reflected in the names of Turkish places such as Laleli (Place of the Tulips) and Laleli Gecidi (Tulip Pass). In Farsi, Arabic, and Bulgarian, the tulip remains *lale*, in Romanian it's *lalea,* and empires such as the Mughals and the Moors have honored the tulip. People from

Central Asia to the Middle East, including Persians, Ottomans, and Arabs, exalted the tulip as the Flower of God, and *lale*, in Arabic script, is almost the same as Allah. People imagined the paradise of the afterlife as abounding with tulips. The Ottoman military sometimes brought tulips with them into battle as talismans, and they were similarly embroidered on clothes for luck and prosperity. By the sixteenth century, the tulip had become an integral part of Ottoman culture, regularly featured in the Sultan's gardens, and appeared everywhere as an ornamental motif.

No wonder the Ottoman's showed them off to Western visitors, or that they brought bulbs with them to trade when they traveled to Europe. Western emissaries and European visitors in ornate places like those in Istanbul were tantalized by and fascinated with what they saw as the exotica of the bazaar, and the sensuous allure of dark women and perfumes that inspired their burgeoning Orientalist imagination. The tulip figured prominently in this setting. And the local's reverence and enthusiasm for these ornamental flowers struck the foreigners from the North as quite appealing, if also puzzling and strange. Unlike the ordered symmetry of Renaissance gardens, the Ottomans kept their gardens unruly and lush, and rarely cut their flowers. For people accustomed to thinking of plants and flowers as things to consume or perhaps to refine into poultices or other medicines (like many places at the time, including the Low Countries), their cultivation solely to admire as living objects of beauty seemed peculiar. Everywhere in this region, it seemed to Europeans, people revered these flowers. Yet as prevalent and celebrated as they were in these Oriental cultures, no one had yet systematically bred, crossed, or otherwise modified the tulip for domestic cultivation. So when Europeans became interested in the tulip, it was still a 'wild' flower, though ornamental and already possessing a worldly pedigree. Prior to the tulip's debut in Northern Europe, roses and carnations grew in the Low Countries, but failed to generate much excitement or commerce. But arriving from the East, and with their unusual, compelling colors, tulips titillated people, and came to be associated with upward mobility and a flair for the new.

~

Although it is often conceived of as such, it isn't immediately obvious why the economy of the Dutch Republic might be considered early capitalism, since it precedes the Industrial Revolution by several centuries. Early Dutch horticulture, and the incorporation of the tulip in the Republic occurred during this socioeconomic juncture, so it's worth tarrying over the point. In *The First Modern Economy*, Ad van der Woude and Jan de Vries argue that the United Provinces had precociously developed markets for three modern aspects of production (land, labor, and capital), enjoyed high agricultural productivity, achieved through advanced techniques in land management and a complex social structure that enabled social mobility, a legal system that codified property rights, political and economic institutions that cooperated to promote prosperity, which in turn helped stimulate a dynamic consumer culture. Not everyone agrees with this assessment. Because of its dominance in and focus on trade and finance, and by cornering the market on certain commodities, the Dutch Republic may actually have done "a disservice to industrialization in the short run... Dutch concentration thus proved extremely important, but it should not therefore tempt us to exaggerate the 'modernity' of the Dutch. If the only 'capitalist' economies of the seventeenth century had been like the Dutch, we may doubt whether the subsequent development of industrial capitalism would have been as great or as rapid," wrote Eric Hobsbawm.

Others historians have drawn attention to the Republic's modern character by pointing out how Dutch social life of the period revolved around cities and their urban elite, in contrast to other societies in the region whose politics and economies were still defined by their aristocracies. Also, although far from formally democratic, early Dutch social character differed from other contemporary societies in the region in another important respect. Although local populations could not elect the officials making political and economic decisions and urban planning, the dimensions of the Republic made a difference, since in the intimate space and small social circles, many local people personally knew and had contact with officials making decisions, which had the effect of inspiring a kind of limited trust, although the division of wealth and power was stark and not fundamentally different in character from other parts of Europe at the time. (For instance, between 1600 and 1700, the wealth owned by the upper one percent of the population of Leiden shot from 20 percent to 50 percent.) Though not seen as representatives carrying out the public's will, there was enough integration, cooperation, and personal contact that decision-makers didn't seem quite as remote as in other contemporary societies. Furthermore, local authorities often followed the advice of merchants and investors, and in fact, many of the officials stemmed from these entrepreneurial ranks.

Karl Marx took for granted that the Dutch Republic was capitalist. In fact, Dutch trade and colonialism in the seventeenth century strongly influenced him and Engels in developing their critique and theory of capitalism, as art historian Julie Hochstrasser has pointed out. In Volume 1 of Capital, Marx wrote, "[t]he genesis of the industrial capitalist did not proceed in such a gradual way... The discovery of gold and silver in America, the extirpation, enslavement and entombment in mines of the aboriginal population, the beginning of the conquest and looting of the East Indies, the turning of Africa into a warren for the commercial hunting of black-skins, signalized the rosy dawn of the era of capitalist production... On their heels treads the commercial war of the European nations... It begins with the revolt of the Netherlands from Spain... [though already by the eighteenth century] Holland had ceased to be the nation preponderant in commerce and industry". Nevertheless, Marx goes on to make another blunt statement in which he quotes Sir Thomas Raffles, a British statesman and author directly involved in defeating the Dutch to take over Java during the Napoleonic Wars. "The history of the colonial system of Holland – and Holland was the head capitalistic nation of the seventeenth century – " he wrote, "'is one of the most extraordinary relations of treachery, bribery, massacre, and meanness'". Although its volume of colonial trade during the seventeenth century has been estimated at around 10 percent of total foreign trade, the incipient consumer culture in the Republic and the development of capitalism in Holland would not have been possible without the colonies. Marx described it, curiously, with a horticultural metaphor: "[t]he colonial system ripened, like a hot-house, trade and navigation... and, through the monopoly of the market... The treasures captured outside Europe by undisguised looting, enslavement, and murder, floated back to the mother-country and were there turned into capital".

It's only a slight exaggeration to say that the tulip entered the Netherlands through a single figure, Charles d'Ecluse, better known by his Latin name Carolus Clusius, who was born in 1526. But this man's importance extends beyond his role disseminating tulips and establishing a link between science and aesthetics in the new field of botany. Through his travels and extensive contacts, he also helped to build networks of flower enthusiasts. With contacts in the VOC out scouting specimens, and by urging collaboration between artists, collectors, businessmen, regents, and others, he installed a vital link between systematic botanical inquiry, colonial exploration, and wealth accumulation. These social, scientific, and economic ties established a pattern under which early Dutch horticulture developed.

By the sixteenth century, decades before they became popular in several Netherlands provinces, a sprinkling of tulip bulbs began to circulate, attract interest, and take root across Europe through trade with the Ottomans. Cultivars had sprung up in and around Antwerp, which at that time was the major commercial center for the region. But in the sixteenth century few in the northern provinces showed interest in tulips. That changed rapidly in the seventeenth century with the arrival of Clusius. He had a remarkable biography. As a young man, Clusius studied botany when it was still largely a branch of medicine concerned with identifying and cultivating herbs and plants; as the Inquisition raged, he converted from a Catholic to a Protestant; he was a peripatetic character, moving around Europe, driven by his curiosity for plants. He was appointed to establish the Vienna botanical gardens, and struck up a correspondence with Ogier Ghislan de Busbecq, stationed in Istanbul, who turned him on to tulips. Inspired by tulips and going against the ethos of the day, Clusius believed plants worthy of study in their own right, not only as sources of cures, and launched a system of classification for plants based on their characteristics, an enterprise later refined and elaborated by Carl Linnaeus. Tulips intrigued him for their aesthetic appeal, and Clusius harbored a belief that beauty was an important value in plants, independent of or in addition to any practical use they might possess. Through his elaborate correspondences with contacts across Europe, Clusius garnered a considerable reputation both as a botanical expert and as a connoisseur of tulips.

When he was offered the position as head of the Leiden botanical gardens in 1592, he was already an old man, but he jumped at the opportunity. This was shortly after the United Provinces had gained independence from Spain, but only in the very early stages of commercial acceleration for the northern provinces of the Republic. Among other sundry seeds, Clusius arrived in Leiden with a suitcase full of tulip bulbs, which at that point represented one of the most extensive European collections of this flower of rapidly rising popularity. Tulips adapted quickly to the environment of the United Provinces, since tulips are hardy, yield extraordinary colors and diversity, and after around 1600, when incomes began to rise, more and more people had the money and the leisure time to pursue hobbies and to acquire luxury items. People experimented with ways to create petals with different colors, shapes, and patterns, though with very mixed success, since little was yet understood about plant breeding. This led both to more experimentation and to the tulips' appeal.

Clusius wasn't the first to admire tulips in the United Provinces – from the sixteenth century, especially in the south, people had begun to cultivate tulips – but he was the best qualified to describe and catalogue them through careful attention, systematic reflection, and scientific reasoning. He also fomented considerable interest in the flower, and through gifts, began a wide distribution of bulbs. It's due to his various botanical treatises and copious letters (as well as contemporary authors like Pavord and Goldgar) that we know so much about the tulip's early history in Europe, and particularly in the Netherlands. Furthermore, the secret of the Netherlands' abundant arrays comes from the dissemination of Clusius's tulip collection. Under Clusius' direction, the Leiden botanical garden began to grow dozens of tulip varieties. His own personal garden began to attract attention for its multiplicity of beautiful tulips, some of which were stolen from the ground, and many of which he willingly shared. He sent tulip bulbs to friends and acquaintances often signed with the generous and affectionate gesture, "con amore."

This tension, between stealing and coveting tulips or sharing them in a spirit of mutual affection, captures the changing ethos of the age, one that broke down from trust and intimacy to selfishness and a more craven interest in wealth – and this was the central insight of Anne Goldgar's book. The transition was most visible, and plainly upsetting to many, precisely because the social values circulated in such small networks. Through those networks flowed various kinds of trade and talk – of many things, including tulips, other flowers, gardening, collecting, art, and investment. In Europe, but particularly in the Netherlands, the new science and new philosophy of that era "were constant with the values embedded in commerce. Merchants took a deep interest in natural facts because they were essential to business", according to historian Harold Cook. So of course in correspondence and casual conversation, people involved in business moved seamlessly from subject to subject, and perhaps they seemed merely like different topics under the same rubric.

Tulip collecting and eventually tulipmania emerged from a close-knit world of personal relationships and exchanges among *liefhebbers* (tulip enthusiasts), and Clusius formed a crucial link in this community. Clusius sat at the nexus of a botanical network stretching across Western Europe, the early information age when the emerging botanical science was part of that era's enlightenment humanism. Clusius' hundreds of collected letters suggest a map of male networks interested in the aesthetics and emerging science of plants and flowers. Similar contemporary collections of correspondence such as that of Erasmus or Grotius maintained a limited, closed circle of university-trained men who wrote in Latin. But less than half of those sending letters to Clusius composed in Latin; the rest wrote in the common tongue of people living across Europe: French, Spanish, Dutch, and German. His correspondents came from many backgrounds, from princes, aristocratic collectors and fellow humanists to printer-publishers, artists, physicians and apothecaries, and included some women. What united them was their enthusiasm and knowledge of the subject as well as an upward mobility. Literally through one man, a considerable amount of botanical knowledge circulated, ranging from growing and breeding techniques (such as they were in those days), social information about collectors, funders, enthusiasts, and the locations of new varieties. No single person knew more than him, and no one had a larger collection of tulips than Clusius when he headed the Leiden botanical gardens. He maintained an extraordinarily broad network of correspondents with whom he exchanged information about seeds and bulbs: members of the VOC, botanists, collectors, merchants, and enthusiasts all wrote to Clusius about the curious, the unusual, and the exotic.

As Clusius' diverse contacts show, the emerging humanistic botanical community was not a democratic cross section of society, as often depicted in recounts and images of tulipmania, nor did it represent a totally exclusive network of the Low Countries' upper echelons. It was a community where ambitious small-time businessmen rubbed elbows with noblemen, one that, partly through Clusius' influence, began to stretch beyond the bounds of land owning wealthy nobility and into the hands of classes of regents that emerged as prosperity accelerated. The danger and instability of this environment was that the horticultural world was getting too big, was becoming cheapened, was not exclusive or elite enough. It was an ideal, imagined community rather than a strict account or census of membership, a setting where honor mixed with deception, a passion for the new and the strange combined with a core toughness. Above all, the dream was for a community of shared ideals, for an open exchange of information, ideas of mutual support and a sort of genteel masculine comportment. In reality, the tulip trade operated within small circles, an intimate web of aficionados, and despite the fact that men besides nobles participated, the majority of the population, especially the poor, were not involved. Again, Anne Goldgar's brilliant research exposes as myth the notion that tulipmania wrecked the economy and devastated the population.

What's more, interest in flowers at this time was limited to Holland (a small but influential province), to places such as Amsterdam, Haarlem, and Enkhuizen. These powerful sectors helped to set trends, but the fact is that far more people came to satirize and mythologize tulips in the wake of tulipmania than were ever involved in the trade, in cultivating other ornamentals, or in gardening. The reaction to tulipmania and the integration of tulips to the Netherlands suggests several issues relevant to the foundation of Dutch horticulture. Not only did tulipmania reflect moral and economic values, giving a popular rebuke to the nascent capitalist system, but it lays bare the ways information and specialization influenced growth and invention during this crucial period in the Netherlands' history. Part of what enabled excellence in so many disparate fields – including botany, colonial exploration, and civil engineering – was the management and flow of information through emerging institutions and social structures whose lifeblood was networks.

Social networks are groups of people and institutions linked by one or more kinds of interdependency such as kinship, values, conflict, friendship, or financial exchange and other kinds of trade, and the webs of connections that Clusius spun were no different. Who comprised this network of early modern horticulturalists in the United Provinces? A relatively small and insular group – few noblemen, and no ordinary maids or masons, nor farmers, since in this period, tulip cultivation was an urban and not a rural practice, and the poshest pleasure gardens took place in the yards of wealthy regents. The vast majority of those involved in the tulip trade during the seventeenth century – initially and in the decade or so following tulipmania – were merchants and skilled craftsmen. And they DABBLED in tulips: it was not a bread and butter earning but a sideline trade, a hobby, something to bring in extra money and to divert themselves with something undoubtedly fascinating, captivating, and a labor of love, but hardly all-consuming financially. Their average age was 38-39, and they came from a stratum below regents, from city office holders and the like. Cultivars, buyers, and sellers (and there wasn't a hard distinction between them) often knew each other through webs of family connections, and many of them were Mennonites. But networks of buyers and sellers were not just characterized by religion or origin, but by overlapping networks of 'vrunden' (friends, family, and extended family) and also more widely those with shared interests. Families didn't sell to one another but to other families in the trade, and information passed through these intimate, trustworthy bonds, and it was communication that greased the wheels of trade, to know who had what, where to find it, how to arrange transactions.

The details of who participated in the trade, how the networks functioned, and the kinds of horticultural values crystallizing in this period are important for two reasons. They describe the origins of Dutch horticulture, but they also reveal the kinds of relationships, patterns of organization, values, and practices that find expression in today's horticultural industry. Naturally, things change over the course of four centuries, but in many ways, a general outline took shape then which has endured. Even some institutions evolved to forms recognizable today. Tulipmania brought about 'florist fraternities,' for instance, where men gathered to discuss growing techniques and exchange botanical and commercial information, and by the end of the seventeenth century grower's clubs were widespread. Dutch villagers enjoyed the delights of horticulture, and rapidly insinuated horticulture into their regular habits and relationships. These florist fraternities have clear descendants today in grower-owned auction cooperatives, and clubs and associations of breeders and growers who meet regularly to share information.

Intimately related to the formation of these networks was the lay of the land, the geography of what today is Westland. Westland is the main area of horticulture in the Netherlands, sometimes called the city of greenhouses, since about a third of the terrain is under glass. Westland abuts the highly urbanized *Randstad*, the densely populated region of connected towns and cities (including Amsterdam, Utrecht, Rotterdam, and The Hague) where over seven million people live. Several towns and municipalities make up Westland, and the Aalsmeer flower auction is located there as well. As in Clusius' time, space and topology influence networks. The proximity of towns and the propinquity of people within those towns via schools and other institutions incubates local outlooks and loyalties in ways that advance shared interests, cooperation, and the building of relationships.

Tulip enthusiasts in Clusius' orbit were not the only networks during this formative period. Networks and networking began to assume formal arrangements, to shape projects of colonial exploration and land management, and to beget institutions organized around shared financial interests. In addition to its informal connections, the tulip trade quickly became established with commercial companies, where authority over transactions was governed by 'normal' trading practices (trust, honor, and fairness) and by a semi-official board, the collegie, whose decisions were not legally binding or enforceable, but symbolic and moral. The collegie's purpose was to oblige a sense of propriety in the tulip trade, which broadly meant to effect values both cultural and economic, tacit values that also informed any number of endeavors and organizations. The Beemster project represents another important example of the way cultural values and loose formal regulation governed businesses. It was the Netherlands' first large-scale *poldering* project, which involved draining the seventy-one square kilometer Beemster Lake near Amsterdam, a venture undertaken in 1609 and completed in 1612. Notable for its innovative feat of engineering of both land and water, for its patterns of finance, cultural logic, and management of information, the Beemster helped to institutionalize gardening as a national practice.

Between 1550 and 1650, as the Dutch began in earnest to modify the land, they were also shaping a "moral geography" and a national ethos, according to Simon Schama. As prosperity rose, the population multiplied; Amsterdam grew from 31,000 in 1578 to 150,000 by 1648. Increasing population and wealth had direct consequences for resources, including land, and the Beemster project offered a number of advantages – as a place to invest, a way to increase arable land, to expand potential areas of settlement, and to aid protection against flooding. With projects like the Beemster and companies like the VOC, networks and mercantile values mutually reinforced one another. Networks of geographically and ethnically close groups of men with a shared outlook and common goals made commercial enterprises fruitful, and lead to innovations. New kinds of institutions based on the primacy of cooperation through dense social and commercial networks characterized Dutch economic behavior, and left important legacies for the horticultural industry in both values and practices.

The group who conceived of, financed, and built the Beemster comprised "a community of people... [all of whom] knew each other directly or indirectly. This was a social group forged of mutually profitable advantage," and further solidified through friendship and marriage, wrote Annette Fleischer in her study of the Beemster. This community enjoyed considerable wealth and power. Johan van Oldenbarnevelt, the chief minister of the Republic, enjoined dozens of businessmen to invest in the Beemster project, and upon completion, they quickly got a profitable return on their money, some via rent on the plots into which the land was divided and sold, and others via capital appreciation where some of the funds recycled directly to the local economy. Among the Beemster's first investors were the prosperous duo, Dirck and Hendrik van Os, highly educated and socially connected merchants and brothers who had moved from Antwerp to Amsterdam and had co-founded the VOC a few years earlier. Other initial investors included urban merchants and regents, civil servants, lawyers, and even a goldsmith, each of whom judged the drainage of the Beemster Lake a sound fiscal prospect. Even so, it was an entirely new kind of venture, on a scale that must have seemed immense. Making matters still more dubious, to carry out this ambitious plan, they would rely heavily on the recently developed and unproven technology of windmills. As with the funding of hundreds of ships sailing to the East for spices, where risk was divided between numerous investors, the prospective Beemster was sliced into lots and sold as stakes. With so many people looking for a place to invest their money, stakeholders quickly grew from an initial sixteen to one hundred twenty.

The Beemster project offered both practical and ideological appeal. Modifying the land and water, channeling and organizing them in the most efficient ways for agriculture and human settlement remain common features today in the Netherlands' spacial planning, which is carefully coordinated with the horticultural industry. An important part of the Dutch imaginary involves reshaping the landscape, creating arable land where before there was swamp and bog, or lake and sea. One hears this notion of parthenogenesis in the popular expression, God made the world, but the Dutch created the Netherlands.

Like the Beemster, the construction of the Republic was both physical and ideological. Certain kinds of networks were essential for efficient economic growth in the incipient capitalist world system, a system centered in Amsterdam, pioneered by the Dutch, and one that would depend on directing rapid currents of capital and knowledge. The reasons for Amsterdam's ascendency were largely structural. By the second half of the sixteenth century, the great era of European expansion had crested, and was moving into a different phase, a 'turning inward', as it's often called. Not that expansion entirely ended or ceased to be important, but there were "new skills required to run a financial and commercial focus of the world economy. It was the command of such skills that enabled the Dutch to seize control" of this emerging system, wrote sociologist and historian Immanuel Wallerstein. As with the VOC, the scale and complexity of the Beemster project demanded extensive bureaucratic infrastructure and paperwork. Such an infrastructure was required in order to handle the technical specifications of the lake, patents, property rights, legal and governmental policies and practices, minutes from meetings, charts, decrees, correspondences, and other such things. Keeping records and managing paperwork posed one kind of challenge, but to make decisions, all of the parties involved had to communicate and coordinate, so information had to be organized and it had to be able to move quickly. In addition to managing information and finances through a unique blend of values and networks, the Beemster embodied the young Republic in another important way.

It was to be a garden. Planners envisioned plots of land for both agricultural and horticultural production. A long tradition of representations on official seals and political prints had depicted Holland allegorically as a garden. Due to its innovative character and vision of creating a grand garden, the Beemster had a strong figurative meaning. Fleischer aptly described it. "The young Republic of the United Seven Provinces was often imagined as recreating the ancient 'Land of the Batavians,' envisioned metaphorically as the Hortus Batavus or 'Garden of Holland'. With the founding of the Republic, this horticultural typology became a symbol of peace and prosperity. Depictions of the Hortus Batavus show a seated Dutch Maiden, crowned with a spire, in an enclosed garden surrounded by flowers, globes, and an orange, the symbol of the ruling House of Orange... The Beemster was thus in principle a symbol both of the Hortus Batavus and the Dutch Maiden, and also of the young Republic." The contemporary image of the Beemster is not so far removed from this. It remains a major agricultural producer, the source not only of organics but of a wholesome Dutch patrimony, and continues to brand distinctive cultural marks. It's a world heritage site; today's Beemster cooperative agricultural producers association claims that the Beemster's original grid formed the template for the Dutch settlement in Manhattan; all the milk that goes to make Ben and Jerry's ice cream in Europe comes from Beemster cows. From the outset, the Beemster was to be an immense garden, its fruits sweetened by the richness of the Republic.

During the era of the Dutch Republic, not only poldering but creating a well-ordered and sublime garden became popular. Private pleasure gardens offered an opportunity to flaunt one's wealth and status in a similar way that accumulating worldly goods demonstrated one's righteousness in the Protestant sensibility of the time. Pleasure gardens provided a way to celebrate the glory of God, to cultivate a heavenly presence on earth in order to exult a higher power. Also, by creating a sort of paradise on earth, at the same time one asserted one's privileged place in society. The notion of gardening as a way to create a worldly paradise became widespread. Using the Latin of the elite and educated, some *liefhebbers* (tulip aficionados) and regents of the time even referred to the garden as a *paradisus oculorum*, a paradise for the eyes. Part of this sensibility is actually built into the word, since paradise is a synonym for the Garden of Eden, and (as with the Turkish word for tulip) the etymology leads back to the Persian, where paradise was a walled-in compound with a garden (from 'pairi', around, and 'daeza' or 'diz', meaning wall, brick, or shape). But while paradise may denote a garden, gardens did not always imply paradise.

In the sixteenth century Low Countries (just prior to the tulip enthusiasts' debut), gardens served practical needs, providing sustenance or medicine. They were not particularly for looking at, strolling through, showing off one's wealth or expressing one's identity. But in the seventeenth century, a new kind of garden began to emerge, influenced in part by the Renaissance gardens of Italy and France, yet with a distinct local character. Pragmatic gardens did not disappear, but now many Dutch gardens transformed along the same aesthetic sweep as Leiden's Hortus Botanicus under Clusius's stewardship, which is to say, delight, leisure, and beauty came to define the purpose, layout, and contents of these new 'pleasure' gardens. And in the early decades of the seventeenth century, some of the crucial improvements to agriculture came through the development of horticulture. Whereas fruit and vegetables were once only cultivated in the gardens of a few rich families, now entire towns began in earnest: villages in the Streek focused on onions and carrots, the Langedijk grew onions, mustard, and coriander, other places cultivated trees in nurseries. While pleasure gardens were once the province only of wealthy landowners and now became more widespread, they did not cease to be markers of distinction. The cultivation of flowers, and tulips in particular, became important to this new project, one that was as much social as horticultural, since these gardens showed off not only dashing hues sprouting from the soil but also a certain sensibility that was both refined and new. Now in addition to the ordinary garden for the apothecary or the kitchen, a special type of garden was intended to enchant and impress. More than mere showcases, gardens were also important places for social interactions, locations to discuss events of the day, horticultural news, and to meet people.

Gardening became a common pastime, but especially at first, it was a relatively elite activity, and its development is inseparable from colonial ventures, the emerging economic system, and the excitement over tulips. In fact, gardening came into vogue along the same route as tulips themselves, first in the south, then in the northern Netherlands, where members of urban elites would often tend one or more gardens. This trail of development was no coincidence. In the transition from the sixteenth to the seventeenth century, the financial center of the region shifted from Antwerp to Amsterdam, and along with it moved merchants in search of opportunity, and Jews and Catholics of various means seeking religious tolerance. These people brought with them not only their expertise, but their appurtenances and capital, including tulip bulbs.

Tulips and pleasure gardens (many of which displayed tulips) reflected monetary value, but even more significantly, they had entered the moral economy. Gardens fit in to a system of values sharpened by technical expertise that was literally redrawing the landscape. The popularity of gardening affected urban planning not only with poldering projects that took place at the edges of urban settlements, but pleasure gardens were primarily for city dwelling networks. Fashionable houses of wealthy regents along Amsterdam's canal belt were laid out and built with plenty of room for gardens in the backyard. Notable not only for the style's newness, but in a small country that claims nearly every square meter of land for efficient and functional use, the display of space for leisure and pleasure stood out conspicuously. These gardens were locations to plant and marvel at, to reflect on one's place in the world, to consider nature and feel pride in one's command over it, and above all to experiment with, admire, and ponder flowers. Gardening reflected and helped to develop networks, mutual economic interests, and to cultivate a refined, distinctly local sensibility. It also found expression in various forms of painting and writing.

Dutch writers of the age produced a genre of what has been called 'garden literature,' which included poetry, treatises, catalogues, scientific texts, and images. One mid-seventeenth-century example comes from classical scholar and botanist Johannes Brosterhuysen, as recounted by historian Eric de Jong. Inspired by a line from Virgil's Georgics, which celebrated the beauty and instructive properties of plants, he composed "In Praise of Plants," a speech to inaugurate the botanical gardens of Breda. "Who is not captured by the beauty of herbs and plants and the enormous variety of types?" he exhorted. With their fragrance and color, said Brosterhuysen, they please the senses, evoke wonder and merit tribute. But he reserved special praise for flowers, which he called "sydera terrena," stars of the earth. In this and other works, the garden was often specifically imagined as not only adorning or bringing out beauty, but leading to profit, and itself representing wealth and the good life.

All literature regarding plants and flowers wasn't celebration and encomium, however. In the wake of tulipmania there emerged cautionary tales and images – warnings against greed in which the tulip symbolized danger and corruption. Popular pamphlets were rife with this sort of thing. And part of this garden literature included tulip books, which were richly illustrated, privately commissioned manuscripts of up to 500 pages, with one detailed and colorful illustration per page. Since the actual flowers only bloomed during a few weeks of the year (depending on the variety, between April and September), these tulip books helped to fuel curiosity and popularity, serving like sales catalogues. These books gave images of tulips a wider circulation than the flowers themselves, but gardens were important venues to actually see them. Images and literature roused curiosity for the real thing.

A choice place to see the real thing was Adriaan Pauw's garden near Haarlem, which came about partly as the result of the draining and polderization of the Haarlemmermeer, a project in which Pauw had invested. Pauw was a member of elite networks: one of the seventeen VOC directors, the Keeper of the Royal Seal of the Netherlands, an avid tulip collector and gardener. His first cousin, Pieter Pauw, sat beside Clusius as a professor of botany at Leiden University. Adriaan Pauw's Heemstede garden estate included topiary mazes, footbridges, aviaries, and mirrored gazebos, in order to multiply the image of his tulips, and give the impression of still more abundance and prosperity. The elaborate setting featured the glorious Semper Augustus tulip. The Semper Augustus was the most prized tulip of the day, whose unique stripes (and rarity) resulted from an unusual virus, though this was not understood until the twentieth century. In Pauw's time, people only knew that they were scarce, precious, and peerless. Particularly in the ambience of Pauw's garden, this tulip demonstrated wealth and power, not only because of what people would pay for it but "because when people saw it they experienced, or could be taught to experience, or could be taught to pretend to have, certain pleasurable sensations; the sight elicited conversation as well as contemplation... [F]inanciers were able to share with other people their appreciation of the flower by exchanges of gesture and word, which were in turn associated with other cultural assumptions... in effect serving as experts on good taste and judgment" as Cook put it. So a reverence for gardens and a fascination with ornamental flowers comprised part of the Republic's cultural and ideological framework.

If the socioeconomic order found local expression in places like Pauw's garden, it was also situated in a global context that included the VOC and the emerging order of the European world system. Pauw's garden, the Beemster, and backyards along the Herengracht can all be seen as minor stages in the production of the world system, a system that came to be centered in the modern era in Amsterdam. In other words, Dutch gardening of that era took place in a cosmopolitan arena, and as such, also nestled in with local events unfolding on the global dais. The VOC was an important development both locally and globally. During the late sixteenth and early seventeenth centuries, pivotal Dutch institutions were developing, and while many organized around trade, and along similar precepts of networking and collective action, none were more powerful, more enduring, profitable, or left as pronounced a mark on Dutch national heritage as the VOC. Though the institutions differ in myriad ways, the VOC was founded on the same principals as Aalsmeer's flower auctions: cooperation through networking increases market strength and distributes financial risk. Also firmly involved in agriculture, the VOC traded cloves, nutmeg, black pepper, cinnamon, and other spices originating in the East. From its founding in 1602, and at Clusius' behest, the VOC issued a special bulletin to keep an eye out for "strange" botanical specimens, including flowering plants, to apothecaries, surgeons, and anyone on board its ships qualified to heed the call. In these ways, the company supplied Dutch horticulturalists (though Clusius was not particularly satisfied) as it became an important institution in the world system.

In the seventeenth century, Dutch in colonial outposts cultivated all sorts of plants for aesthetic pleasure, medicine, and commerce, often with a special interest to promote these plants and flowers for export, to attract covetous eyes. Dutch gardens in Cape Town and Java, important frontiers in the global trade, each served as horticultural warehouses and thruways for plants and flowers used for art and medicine, on their way to the national gardens in Leiden and Amsterdam. This international shipping network not only brought in new seeds and plants, but because they came from different kinds of soil and climates, and were transported for weeks or months on board boats, Dutch planters began to learn more about how and why things grow. The Netherlands became a sort of spigot through which passed all sorts of goods, knowledge, and wealth, flowing out primarily to markets in Western Europe in which flowers were a small but increasing part. In his study of the history of flower cultures, anthropologist Jack Goody found that the development of the economy in Europe in the sixteenth and seventeenth centuries was accompanied by a growth in the market for flowers and exotic plants, in the range of species, in the demand, especially for cut flowers, the shift from crown to bouquet, and the acceleration in the complexity of mechanisms of their supply.

The international context offers part of the explanation for how this small nation emerging from occupation was able to maneuver itself to the center of the world system. From a period beginning in 1590, the Dutch came to dominate the international system of interlinked economies, though the Spanish, Portuguese, and other European powers struggled for control and profit from links with the East and the new world. It seems an unlikely course of events for a small collection of provinces recently unshackled from occupation. In the sixteenth century, Spain and Portugal had controlled much of the European trade with the East, but their power was waning when the Dutch revolt took place (1568-1609). Free from Spanish taxes, and at liberty to develop commercial enterprises, an independent Holland immediately began to advance. And as a former part of the Spanish empire, Holland could finagle business in the Americas through established trade links to the New World. England was not yet strong enough to consistently break through the Spanish armada, but since the Dutch were already incorporated in the Spanish crown, and as a small country not perceived as a threat (unlike England and France), their fleets slipped through and they gained important footholds. This international situation combined with internal developments to allow an emerging class in the Low Countries to act autonomously.

The importance of the Dutch revolt was less ideological, less significant for the establishment of a model for national liberation, but amounted to a tidal wave in its economic impact on the European economy. In a crucial period of instability, through the middleman skills of organizing and directing the flows of information, the Dutch took control, and reoriented global trade. "Dutch world trade became a sort of precious vital fluid which kept the machine going while various countries were concentrating on reorganizing their internal political and economic machinery", as Wallerstein put it.

This talent for organization, for managing information and bureaucracy, combined with local characteristics, interests, and circumstances to give the Republic an initial edge in world system dominance. But those subtle effects, the small initial economic and strategic benefits, quickly accrued to a level of command. The United Provinces, with Amsterdam as commercial center, was soon at the helm of global trade. Wallerstein again: "Because of the Netherlands dominance in the Baltic trade (herring, fur, and other products) they became the main market for timber, which allowed them to be innovative in ship design and construction, which in turn benefitted further expansion.

On this basis Amsterdam became a commodity market, shipping center, and capital market, each intertwined and interrelated, and it's hard to say which one was preeminent".

This upheaval in trade both at home and abroad created the conditions that shaped early Dutch horticulture. Domestically, the Revolt involved a "defection of nobles from the established order" plus "radical currents from below", as it's typically described: the Netherlands revolution not only increased the flow of trade and goods, including fruits, spices, and other agricultural commodities, it also shook up patterns of authority. As it displaced the old order, a portion of the population outside of the traditional elite came to power. It was this class of people who constituted most of the tulip financiers and enthusiasts

Another important aspect of this growing international trade, an aspect the VOC exploited, was the deepening connection between Europe and the East. This junction was certainly commercial, but it was also far more than that. It's worth stepping back a moment to recall that for centuries, India and China were the world's commercial centers and were the most wealthy and technologically advanced areas on the planet, easily far more developed than Europe during the Middle Ages and through much of the European Renaissance. Europeans themselves understood East Asia as the source of stupendous affluence, exotic goods, and advanced technology. East Asia lured Dutch traders with promises of treasure and fantastic wealth, but Japan and China, in particular, were not just lands to pillage for their raw materials or exotic commodities. They represented the pinnacle of civilization, and were vital centers of trade. Though contact via the Silk Road and other routes had existed for centuries, the cultural and economic impact of such interaction was small relative to what came later. From the sixteenth century, trade opened doors between geographically isolated parts of the world, and forged links between East and West that for everyone involved would have drastic consequences, ranging from medicine and forms of knowledge, to aesthetics and objects of daily use, economic systems, the movements of population, and the development of world views. The relationship between East and West, the development of capitalism in Europe and the New World, represent vital parts of the increasingly global system.

Looking at the gradual emergence of European horticulture, Jack Goody argues for the long-term interconnectedness of systems of knowledge in East and West, especially at the time of the Renaissance, and the growth of the modern world. In his view, the ornamental flower market of the West owes its origins to the East, but he also generalizes the point to include many aspects of related economic and cultural practices. He is not alone in this view. David Graeber, for one, has noted the impetus for the formation of European nation-states came from a desire to compete with the East, in particular the centrally coordinated Chinese empire. Also Janet Abu-lughod, investigating how Europeans borrowed financial practices from empires to the East, has gone so far as to characterize Renaissance advances as the "Orientalization of Europe". Jonathan Spense and other scholars have shown the exchange of knowledge and the debt the West owes to the East.

What made those ties to the East so appealing was not merely the profit motive, though economic gains for the VOC were quite lucrative for a long time. It was also a way of seeing, and the East (near or far) seemed very exciting, generating spices, tulips, and other mysteries. Institutions, networks, government, and ordinary citizens alike all seemed to want to do whatever necessary to ensure trade with the East. Hugo de Groot (Grotius), who had written a history of the Dutch people, finding the roots of noble national characteristics in the ancient Batavians, turned his attention to many matters, including trade. As the leading jurist of his time and today considered the father of international law, Grotius pleaded at the VOC's behest for the right of the Dutch to trade with the Indies in a work called The Free Sea. The VOC also enjoyed considerable sway over the central governing body of the United Provinces. It was far more than an important private trading company. In fact, the company's activities basically were state policy, once the government granted it a twenty-one year monopoly on the Asian trade. One might say that the business of the Republic was business, to borrow a statement often made of the twentieth century's world hegemon. In addition to conducting trade, the VOC, which supplied its own army, enjoyed the authority to wage war, negotiate treaties, coin money, and to establish colonies. The VOC's territories became the Dutch East Indies, which eventually expanded to include the entire Indonesian archipelago. The VOC, with its mandate to search out new plants and flowers, suggests how snugly the emerging Netherlandish horticulture fit in the nation's colonial project. But the enterprise was also launched in a spirit of passionate and profound curiosity about the wider world that was opening up to Europe and the Netherlands on a lager scale than ever before. Motives for profit commingled with the desire for discovery in medicine, spices, plants, animals, new sorts of people and ways of living – what has been called "the search for useful medicines and beautiful creatures".

Flowers, and early horticulture must be seen in this context of a drive for the new, the exotic, the marvelous, and exquisite. The enthusiasm for both gardens and curiosity cabinets where exotic specimens could be grown and shown, and the wealth committed to their establishment and expansion, stoked the desire to finding things out and convey them and information about them back to the home country. Horticulture in the home country didn't develop uniformly, but tended to excel in particular areas, determined by individual gardeners and collectors, municipal gardens, scientific inquiry, wealth, and trade. And locally, this occurred within the context of a densely populated and closely integrated network of communities; globally, these networks operated in a burgeoning world system centered in Amsterdam. Ferdinand Braudel had this to say about the seven provinces of the Republic. "Since they had to live together, the Dutch towns could not escape the need for joint action. 'Their interests', as Pieter de la Court says, 'are intertwined with one another.' Quarrelsome and jealous, they were nevertheless subject to the law of the beehive, which obliged them to combine their efforts and cooperate in commercial and industrial activity. Together they formed a power block".

Middelburg, as one of the VOC's ports, helped to get Dutch horticulture going, especially igniting the passion for tulips. Centrally located, having plenty of investment capital, and with an upper crust eager to show off its fluency with the fashion of the day, Middelburg quickly became a center for floriculture. Some of this new enthusiasm for flowers was class conscious, some botanical, and some of it was aesthetic. An active group of horticulturalists, including the authors of books of exotic plants and medicine for apothecaries lived in Middelburg. These people interacted with groups of *liefhebbers* and many of them maintained correspondences with Carolus Clusius. Alongside this scientific and aesthetic appreciation for flowers emerged some important early still-life painters with a horticultural focus. Within a decade or so, Middelburg grew into an important center promoting Netherlandish horticulture.

Because of the high risk involved with voyages, investors often assembled to create a company for just a single journey. Their gamble involved the threat of tropical diseases, piracy and tempestuous weather, but also the volatility of the European market for Asian goods. But the VOC began to take a longer and broader view, both anticipating and helping to forge global trade links. To manage risks, a synod of directors, under the stewardship of the States-General of the Netherlands, formed a cartel to control the supply of Eastern products entering the European market. (The Dutch were also competing with the English, who had, around the same time, founded their own East India Company.) The VOC's strategy involved investors working together with state authority to monopolize markets. This was achieved partly through military strength, as well as considerable naval cunning, and financial ingenuity. One game the VOC played, for example, was to slightly over-supply the pepper market, in order to depress prices below the level where interlopers were encouraged to enter the market. As with today's horticultural industry, the goal was not short-term profit, but long-term prosperity through market dominance. And managing the market, then as now, required inventiveness, cooperation, and consistently seeking the new.

If some of the VOC's more benign business practices enjoy a legacy today in the Netherlands, so does the VOC itself. Today's horticultural industry isn't the only institution to invoke the Dutch Golden Age. In 2006, in a debate about economic revival, Prime Minister Balkenende urged the Dutch to strive to get back that VOC mentality, by which he apparently meant to recover a national spirit of optimism and entrepreneurship. ("Nederland kan het weer! Die VOC-mentaliteit, over grenzen heen kijken, dynamiek!" The Netherlands can do it again! That VOC mentality, borderless, dynamic!) His comment was embraced by some but more typically was greeted with irony and sarcasm. Several critics pointed out that the VOC committed what today would be considered crimes against humanity, so the VOC deserves to be the source of shame, not honor. But this wasn't a popular view. More likely, for many Balkenende's statement seemed an appropriate, if corny, appeal to national pride, and no doubt for others, mention of the VOC struck a familiar, sentimental chord.

~

Another potent though more ambiguous national trope circulated in 2009, on the five hundred year anniversary of John Calvin's birth, which concerned the significance of Calvinist heritage for the Dutch. As with the VOC comments that summoned a formative image of the Dutch past, Balkenende came forward to declare that the Netherlands owes a great debt of thanks to Calvin, that Calvinism proved a benevolent and sober guiding spirit for the Dutch nation. But as many pointed out, labeling someone or something Calvinistic today could mean hoary, stingy, and uptight, or pragmatic, frugal, and trustworthy, depending on who says it, and how the term is intended. It could convey compliment, insult, a little of both, or connote an unbiased assessment. The debate over recuperating the VOC's character, along with reverent talk of the Calvinist heritage in the

Netherlands, is of the same timbre as Weber's 'spirit' of capitalism. Each refers to a cultural and moral framework that fostered prosperous business practices. But to lump them together may make the discussion of the history and economics of Dutch horticulture seem rather more like metaphysical work than an exploration of the legacies of the past, and the past's current cultural meanings. Still, both popular discourse around these similar notions and Weber's use of the term invite reflection. Since Weber's thesis concerns the Calvinist 'character' and its relationship to the origins of capitalism in northern Europe, it also bears directly on the foundations of Dutch horticulture. And since the Dutch are famously Calvinistic, it's worth a moment's reflection.

The Protestant 'spirit' of capitalism refers less to religious doctrine than to the underlying feelings that transfer directly from religious experience to a more secular environment. After the Reformation and already in the early period of capitalism, wealth accumulation becomes righteous, or a just reward for righteous behavior. Weber described the broad mental and cultural qualities of Calvinism – utilitarianism, honesty, industry, frugality – and argues that they fostered economic prosperity. (Unfortunately, this sentiment continues today and isn't limited to the Netherlands, as we were rudely reminded in 2009 when Goldman Sach's chief executive Lloyd Bankfein claimed the bank was "doing God's work" and "creating a virtuous cycle".)

But what was of greatest economic consequence in the period of the Republic may not be Protestantism per se, rather what resulted from the environment of relative tolerance that emerged in predominantly Protestant areas. One important outcome for horticulture was that Catholics and Jews from Antwerp and other places in the south moved north, and brought with them skills and capital, in many cases also tulip bulbs and floral paintings. Their business and aesthetic sensibilities helped build momentum in horticulture. Weber's point isn't about the supposed religious tolerance of Protestants of course, but the anointed feeling that came to suffuse capitalism, valorizing hard work in a context of 'free' labor. It was a mode of thinking useful not only for the rich, but also for poor and working people. For one thing, it explained the whole system ethically, justifying people's social places in a moral-religious sense. Ultimately, what was coming together in the Protestant areas of the northern provinces was both an ascetic mentality and an aesthetic system of values. But there are inherent tensions in such a system, and not only between haves and have-nots. A moral predicament arises between the need to eschew ostentation but also to revel in the new beauty and exotica flooding in from around the world.

This was the crux of the problem of tulipmania – the actual historical tulipmania, and not the myth. It was not a financial catastrophe, in spite of how it is typically represented. Instead, what shocked and appalled so many about tulipmania was the bold rejection of wholesome, celebrated values for the competitive, back-stabbing, profit-driven values of the market that was just coming into being. Tulipmania embodied the anxiety of riches. But of course, even though wealth in this period began to spread, the majority of people were not rich. What was widely distributed was the anxiety over the kinds of changes this new period ushered in. By setting in motion a set of cultural values and potentially altering a long-standing social framework, tulipmania undermined the whole notion of how to assess value.

Tulips became a sort of metonymy, standing in for the greed and wild fluctuations that characterize capitalism. As Anne Goldgar puts it, summarizing the plethora of pamphlets and documents mocking tulip *liefhebbers*, "comments on tulipmania have been comments on capitalism, and they never speak of it with approval". Tulip culture began on the cusp of the era of the Dutch Republic, a time when cherished values like trust were called into question by avarice, hoarding, status and other undignified traits. Initially, among the regents that treated in tulips, these bulbs and flowers circulated in a world of men bound by codes of honor. Part of what this meant in terms of behavior was that bulbs and information about them would be shared freely, in a spirit of courtesy and hospitality. But a virulent system of values began to unravel all that, and in this sense the spirit of capitalism was a sort of vile infection. As Goldgar summarized it, "The appropriate behavior for dignified gentlemen pursuing a learned past time within the context of a humanistic community was to exchange willingly; gifts, not sales, were the means of prosecuting these interlocking intellectual and personal relationships. But exchange, and friendship too, becomes more strained when the objects in question are not mere tokens, but expensive and coveted. Market forces began to intrude on a world that otherwise (despite its many merchant members) was not of the market". Put more bluntly, the transgression and horror of tulipmania was that tulips moved from a gift economy to a capitalist one.

This transition involves more than merely different formal practices for exchanging things. A primary difference between these systems involves the values and emotions that underlie economic practices. Weber's 'spirit' of capitalism is about the cultural and moral dimensions of the world's economic system. His keen insight was to identify the emotional and social depth of capitalism, not the superficial links between prosperity and culture in a capitalist economic system.

But the idea that certain cultural values may promote or hinder economic growth remains common. It comes up in reference to the rise of India and China as economic powerhouses. Weber himself of course had concluded that Hinduism, Buddhism (in India) and Confucianism and Taoism (in China) each encouraged value systems incompatible with capitalism, and that this went a long way toward explaining why capitalism developed in the West and not in the East. Cultural and religious explanations for economic achievement abound today. To mention one case, for several decades in the twentieth century, economists commonly described India in terms of a 'Hindu growth rate' to explain its sluggish pace, a phrase that has more recently fallen out of favor with India's economic boom. Cambridge economist Ha-Joon Chang has shown the shortcomings of this sort of pervasive cultural logic in a chapter of *Bad Samaritans* called "Lazy Japanese and Thieving Germans: Are some cultures incapable of economic development?" Using a broad range of sources, he reconstructs the historical record to remind us how, until relatively recently, the prospects for economic advancement in Japan and Germany were widely understood as preposterous. In terms of economic development, these countries were generally considered hopeless basket cases. "A century ago, the Japanese were lazy rather than hard working; excessively independent minded (even for a British socialist!) rather than loyal 'worker ants'; emotional rather than inscrutable; light-hearted rather than serious; living for today instead of considering the future (as evidenced by their sky-high savings rates). A century and a half ago, the Germans were indolent rather than efficient; individualistic rather than cooperative; emotional rather than rational; stupid rather than clever; dishonest and thieving rather than law-abiding; easy going rather than disciplined".

Clearly, the causative role of culture and religion in economic performance has been overstated. The idea that some cultures are more receptive than others to economic development seems both chauvinistic and absurd. Weber at least partly recognized the problem, and hoped to avoid it by saying the connection between Protestantism and capitalist prosperity was not causal but rather loosely associative. But even an associative connection is sloppy, since categories like Protestant, Hindu, or Muslim are too vague to be analytically meaningful, much less rigorous, even with Weber's finer distinctions. These simple, pure, imagined categories are inevitably clouded by real factors such as the diversity within populations, the geographical distribution of populations, change over time, variations in language, forms of government, international institutions, and policies, to name a few. Furthermore, one can cherry-pick different traits and values to evoke fear, revulsion, or dislike, or demonstrate what one doesn't like if one has a political axe to grind, as in the case of adherents of the clash of civilizations thesis.

The point in all of this is not to assert or prove the irrelevance of Protestantism or Calvinism to the economic development of the United Provinces – or of Hinduism or Confucianism to India's and China's today. Religion and culture can and do influence development in many ways. But these ways cannot be reduced to a formula; nor should we pretend that categories like 'culture,' 'religion,' and 'the economy' are discrete things. For the sake of argument we may speak of them abstractly, but they're inherently more complex phenomena and intertwined with one another.

So the issue in terms of Dutch horticulture is not religion or culture per se, but to worry out the various strains of how commercial horticulture developed in this particular time and place. Today Dutch horticulture has become so naturalized as to seem inevitable, and though it might have occurred otherwise, it didn't. It was established and unfolded through particular relationships and general patterns connected to Protestantism, networking, masculinity, aesthetics, economics, and science. The development of institutions based on cooperative principals, joint ventures, distributing financial risks, coordinating financial policy between the government and private industry – these all fell into place in the United Provinces in the seventeenth century. And these characteristics have clear descendants in today's horticulture industry. This is not the same as saying 'the culture' made it happen; but certainly the values and practices that helped establish Dutch horticulture were part of the larger culture. The period of the Republic was an important starting point, and various practices and values annealed at this time, but the past is important in another way as well. It has become a feature of the imagined community of flower growers in the Netherlands.

~

Roses, carnations, and lilies all grew in pleasure gardens, but it was the tulip that really mesmerized people. It captured people's scientific, aesthetic, and civic imagination, and became the focus of speculative value. Through the tulip, Dutch horticulture became ingrained. The tulip inspired fraternities, a reverence for horticultural beauty, helped situate ornamental flowers as something lucrative, and via gardening, as a kind of expression of the nation. But they took on other meanings in their own right as they became insinuated into the Netherlands. These were both negative and positive.

When Claes Pieterszoon returned in 1614 to a thriving Amsterdam after studying medicine in Leiden, the tulip's prestige was well into its ascendency. Pieterszoon looked at himself and found his name rather undistinguished. So he adopted a new one to match his political ambition: he chose Nicolaes Tulp and inscribed the tulip on his family shield. In addition to being a doctor, Tulp would become the treasurer and later the city magistrate of Amsterdam. But he is best known for his place in Rembrandt's *Anatomy Lesson of Dr. Nicolaes Tulp*, which hangs in the Mauritshuis museum in The Hague, and shows Tulp dissecting a cadaver's forearm. Assuming a new surname like Tulp was not unusual in seventeenth-century Holland. "As with the names of tulips, Dutch people of this period were creative with their names," notes Goldgar; other examples included Pieter Dircksz Spaerpott (Savings Bank) and Pieter Alderwerelt (All the World, since his Herengracht home featured a globe on the roof). Though some of these self-chosen surnames may suggest irony or irreverence, as in Jacob Pieter Olycan (Oilcan) and Pieter Jacobsz Indischeraven (Indian Raven, or Parrot), many index important changes occurring in Dutch society. Elements of that period of Dutch history, such as the power of financial institutions, a cosmopolitan or global sensibility, and the renown of the tulip, left signposts in people's very names).

But what was it about the tulip that so captivated certain people? There's something missing so far from the discussion of the flower's appeal. Today tulips are familiar, and may even seem rather commonplace – you can buy a bouquet in the supermarket for a few euro. So it's difficult to get a visceral sense of the powerful emotional effect these flowers once had on people. But without that sense, an important aspect of the tulip's magnetism in that era is left out. It's impossible to fully recuperate the passion these flowers once excited in people, but one gets an inkling of it in the breathless annotations of well-known seventeenth-century botanist Joost van Ravelingen, published in Dodoen's Cruydt-Boeck, and cited by Anne Goldgar. The fervor comes through in the extensive details, the run-on sentences, and the sheer volume of description, which itself embodies the celebrated diversity and variety of the tulip.

"Every year one finds new varieties and sorts which no one has ever seen before. It is yellow, red, white, purple and (as some assert) blue: or two or three of those colors are mixed within one flower, that is in the middle, or on the sides, or one or the other side of the petals, with speckles, stripes, or spots, themselves beautifully embellished: sometimes the stripes are like flames, or winged, like bunches of feathers or plumage: Sometimes one color shines above the other: that is the white and the yellow have something red shining through: one seems like gold cloth, another silver cloth... [And the early red tulips are] thoroughly red, or reddish, that is dark red, beautiful light or high red, orange red, true red or vermillion red, blood red, carmine, incarnadine, or flesh-colored, sweet red and dead or unsweet red, or yellow-brown: sometimes all these colors are mixed with yellow or with white, or other colors, which tend toward violets or blues... For you see these sorts of Red Tulips, with gold-colored, yellow, white, or darker or lighter red, and also green and violet edges, stripes, rays, spots, and nerves, on the inside and on the outside, on the edges, on the back... These varieties are more easily wondered at than described".

Wondered at, indeed. Wonder is one of several useful frames that can deepen the way we might hear this quote and understand people's infatuation with tulips. But first it should be said that while those words might amuse contemporary ears, the point of van Ravelingen's excerpt is not to mock such enthusiasm or demonstrate how those sober, calculating Dutch burghers went gaga for tulips. First, that's only partly true. But one must ask, on reflection, is it so unfamiliar or so alien, after all, the emotional reaction to a thing that possesses both aesthetic and economic value, something new and colorful, with a distant and mysterious origin? Even if, as Goldgar has shown, the price swings and economic destruction of tulipmania have been exaggerated, is it so slippery a notion that a market for something both lucrative and beautiful could lead to price inflation, and inspire greed and back-stabbing? The delirious outpouring that tulips uncorked seems reminiscent of what former U.S. Chairman of the Federal Reserve Alan Greenspan meant in the 1990s when he suggested the dot-com boom was driven by "irrational exuberance." The emotional economy of tulips in the Netherlands of that era can be described as an exuberance, ebullience, or effervescence pushed forward by an urge to covet beauty.

Today, tulip symbolism and marketing have taken the flower to new heights. They often crop up in unexpected places and unusual ways. For instance, the European Space Research and Technology Centre in the Netherlands has been working with the European Space Agency to attempt to cultivate tulips on the moon. This is not as far-fetched as it might seem. Because tulip bulbs are hearty and carry their own nutrients, they offer promising possibilities in the search for plants that might be able to adapt and grow in extraterrestrial environments. It seems like more than a coincidence that the tulip proposal would originate in the Netherlands. Like wooden shoes and toy windmills, tulips appear on the shelves of airport kiosks and tourist shops alongside miniature canal houses, cheese wheels, and caps with marijuana leaves. But they're more than trinkets, symbols, or reminders of an imagined past. They're also part of a high-profile, profitable industry, and are prominent in Dutch vernacular and the national imaginary.

As global-warming-driven rising sea levels threaten low-lying countries like the Netherlands, people table new proposals for water management. One of the most exotic (or quixotic) plans is to construct a gigantic barrier island in the North Sea in the shape of a tulip, a civil engineering project that would dwarf the Delta Works system that took decades and massive resources to construct. Supporters of the ambitious plan, inspired by Dubai's Palm Island, claim the isle could also alleviate the problem of overcrowding in Europe's most densely populated region. The cause was advocated in the Dutch parliament in 2009 by center-right Christian Democratic Party (CDA, which represents many flower growers) member Joop Atsma. In pleading for the project, he said: "People live on top of each other in the Netherlands. We are hungry for land. A huge area is needed for building." The plan is unlikely to come to fruition, but in the course of its history, the Netherlands has carried out a number of ambitious civil engineering projects of comparative scope and complexity, from the Beemster to the Delta Works.

On one hand it's tempting, though misleading, to draw too close a connection between the present and the past. Today's flower auctions are in many important respects the products of recent developments, and evolved in nineteenth and twentieth-century contexts. On the other hand, contemporary values, practices, institutions, and traditions in the horticultural industry show provocative parallels with the past, and it would be equally shallow and misleading to present everything in the contemporary industry as merely the product of events in the last century and a half. Moreover, the horticultural industry actively cultivates its own version of the Dutch past. And the global context in which Dutch flowers are grown, marketed, and distributed demands a more careful reading of contemporary social and economic developments. In his introduction to the first volume of *The Modern World System*, Wallerstein discusses the imperative for incorporating many disciplines to understanding the world system, how notions of truth evolve, and asserts that "everything is contemporaneous, even that which is past", a principal that echoes William Faulkner's famous sentences: "The past is never dead. It's not even past." In looking at the marketing of tulips today, and the practices of Dutch horticultural auctions, one could hardly disagree.

The Rise of Aalsmeer's Horticultural Grower's Cooperatives

Bloem
Het is een bloem
om er met een vaantje om rond te gaan
en zacht te zingen.
Het is een bloem om niet meer burger te zijn,
maar een broer van een kinderhemdje in zonneschijn.

Flower
This is a flower
for wrapping oneself in its flag
and softly singing.
This is a flower to quit being a citizen,
but a brother of a child's T-shirt in sunlight.

Pierre Kemp

"This is the place to be," said Fedor Broers when I asked him why he had come all the way from his farm in Ecuador to the Aalsmeer auction. He cast his eyes across the five-hundred-plus-seated hall up at the triple screens of auction clocks, and then down to the trains of linked flower carts snaking along the floor. "I use the auction as a display for my flowers. That way everybody can get a look. This place is like a global showcase." On his balance sheet, Fedor doesn't earn much money at FloraHolland. Most of this Dutch grower's flowers head directly from his greenhouses near Quito to U.S. destinations in Florida and California. But because Aalsmeer enjoys a central place in the global market, Fedor sells some of his flowers here, promoting his product and getting feedback. And just as important, he maintains regular contact with the Dutch institution – keeping abreast with its innovations in breeding, growing, and marketing, as well as with its exporters, importers, and of course, its auctions.

Over fifty percent of all the cut flowers and plants sold on earth move through the Netherlands, with shipments arriving at Schiphol airport, a few kilometers away, from points as far off as Israel, Ethiopia, and Ecuador. But most of the flowers are still grown locally, amid the flat, patchwork distances of West Holland. Aalsmeer's auction is located right in the thick of things, close to Westland's greenhouses, and with easy access to air freight for imports and exports. Walking along the floor of this one million cubic meter space might feel odd to the newcomer, like you are inside an airplane hangar instead of a bustling commercial center, or, given all the gadgets and movement, almost like you are inside a Borg cube, albeit a cube full of flowers. Seeing Aalsmeer's auction, its statistics aren't hard to believe: with a daily turnover of more than twenty million flowers and two million plants, it earns about six point six million euros per day, four billion annually, and it directly employs forty-five hundred people, though between importers, exporters, and other businesses, over ten thousand people pass through the auction every Monday through Friday. It's a multinational company with a cooperative structure, which until early 2006 was owned exclusively by Dutch members. Since then, Ecuadorian colleagues of Fedor and other international growers have entered the fold as full-fledged members of FloraHolland Aalsmeer. This, the largest flower auction in the world, also takes place in the largest commercial warehouse in the world.

But the industry superlatives don't end there, since FloraHolland and the horticultural industry are part of a larger picture involving national and regional policies and infrastructure, which coordinate transportation, spacial planning, and other aspects of agriculture. In turn, these policies and practices are informed by family networks of men, a shared national culture, commercial vision, and an ideology of cooperation. Even given these favorable conditions, it seems astonishing that this small country is one of the world's top agricultural exporters, behind France and the United States, nations with considerably more land. Many Dutch companies in the sector excel. Avebe, in Groningen, is the world's biggest producer of potato starch; the VanDrie group in Apeldoorn leads the global market for veal; Stork tops the list in building conveyor systems to slaughter chickens; the Netherlands is the number one exporter of onions; and the Netherlands also has the world's most prodigious inland shipping fleet, with 8,600 vessels. And of course, the Dutch also export more bulbs, cut flowers, and plants than any other nation. Cut flowers are the most visible face of this agricultural sector, and are perhaps most clearly associated both at home and abroad with conceptions of 'Dutch culture.' Many areas revel in pride, local identity, and regional flavor. But among all the villages that grow flowers and places that host horticultural auctions in the Netherlands, Aalsmeer is probably the best known.

In less than a century, this little town with a cottage flower industry mushroomed to become the high-tech, powerful center of global horticultural commerce and innovation. Aalsmeer was quite a different place before the auction, and before residents began in earnest to cultivate roses and other flowers. Prior to its poldering, the area was best known for a shallow lake popular with eel fishermen (hence its name, Aalsmeer). Later, locals grew and sold strawberries on the land, and until the late nineteenth century, that's what the town was known for, a bit of heritage still reflected on its flag. But already in the nineteenth century there were flower growers. By 1860, a hundred growers in Aalsmeer were producing lilies, carnations, and above all, roses, but due to overproduction and competition between one another, business remained fragile and not very profitable. Growers delivered their blooms to market via canal boat, horse, and bicycle, a transportation system that continued into the first decades of the twentieth century. So what happened in Aalsmeer? How did today's fast-paced, prosperous, high-volume institution come from this?

It developed through grower's cooperatives, and they sell their flowers and plants at auction. If many of the important general features of Dutch horticulture emerged in the seventeenth century, the flower industry as we know it today really began to coalesce at the end of the nineteenth century. That was when flower growers first came together and organized to sell their flowers communally and via local auction. There were some structural factors that smoothed the way for this to happen, namely an agrarian crisis that caused deep rural poverty and migration to the cities. But this is only part of the picture, since it is generally agreed that the agrarian crisis didn't directly hurt the horticultural sector, and the areas where the auctions emerged were not strictly rural but a mixture of agricultural land and industry in Noord-Holland and Westland. Once the auctions began, agriculture and horticulture began to change. Horticultural cooperatives strongly influence the entire production chain, including breeding, growing techniques, transportation, and pricing. From the simple but elegant arrangement of grower-owned cooperative auctions, the entire industry took shape. The grower's organizations and their method of sale has made this happen. With their social and commercial organizations, they define the industry. Equally important to Aalsmeer's rise, and an aspect that seems most clearly tied to the past, is the industry's cultural logic, which is expressed in organizational patterns as well as how people in the industry talk about what they do and why they do it. Networks are a big part of that, both structurally and ideologically, as they process and circulate information on a local and global scale.

Many typical network characteristics make them an ideal architecture for the horticultural business, and a natural fit for Dutch horticultural cooperatives. Networks enable the industry to accomplish a lot. They distribute risk, by widely dispersing ownership and investment, and by encouraging and building in both cooperation and trust. They're adaptable to often rapid and subtle fluctuations in the market, they circulate information essential to innovation that allows the Netherlands to dominate the flower business, and they diffuse cultural information to the wider public about flowers and the Netherlands. In some ways, Dutch horticultural networks conform to ideas of how they supposedly function in the abstract, like the conception of small and large groups working together being characteristically Dutch, and in their modern form, growing out of pillarization. But in other respects, the horticultural business doesn't work the way theories describe. Some predicted in the 1990s and early 2000s that in the emerging information-based society, social and economic networks would become more loosely organized, informal, and virtually based, that technology would increasingly supplant the human base of networks. But in the flower industry, networks are shaped by physical proximity, cultural familiarity, and shared outlook. In the Netherlands, they are forged with groups of neighbors and local growers who meet regularly; among traders sitting elbow to elbow in auction halls; through casual contact in the supermarket or on the street; family connections; acquaintances from school; or through informal but professional contact at any of the frequent flower industry events. Standard theories also argue that a network has no center, but rather many different nodes, but in the global horticultural industry, the Netherlands clearly represents a center, and Aalsmeer, as the flagship auction, is situated right at the bulls-eye. Furthermore, in horticultural networks, place remains important. Above all, it's important to people who work in Dutch horticulture, but also, in a variety of ways, to the political and financial life of the country, and even to local and national identity. As Fedor's comments illustrate, the Netherlands occupies center stage in the global flower business, with Aalsmeer as one of the primary sales and distribution centers.

It's the initiative and practice of growers that launched the industry, and they're still a strong reason why it is so successful and works the way it does. In some ways, Fedor epitomizes the evolution of the Aalsmeer's auctions from a business held in a village pub to one located in a giant building with a cosmopolitan view. Fedor's father was a tomato farmer, and stayed close to his village near Rijnsburg his whole life, but Fedor has an MBA and studied agriculture for a year in the U.S. while in college.

He speaks Dutch, English, Spanish, and Italian, and his flower business has led him to East Africa, Japan, and South America. He's at ease discussing African droughts, Latin American politics, currency crises, hitchhiking in the U.S., Geert Wilders, flower breeding, and the place of FloraHolland in it all. Urbane, good humored, and with dynamic and practical views on business, Fedor may not represent a typical cultivar, but nor are these qualities especially unusual among Dutch flower growers.

~

The beginnings of Dutch horticulture in the seventeenth century follow a narrative of the emerging nation moving rapidly from an isolated, rural perspective to a more integrated, cosmopolitan one. Aalsmeer's auctions in the twentieth century reflect a similar pattern of growth. They both mirror and facilitate the transition from a provincial, insular, small-town business to a sophisticated, influential, worldly one. Though the foundations for Dutch horticulture were laid in the seventeenth century, and though horticultural auctions began only in the nineteenth, the Dutch flower market did not merely stagnate during the intervening two centuries. In addition to the ideological and organizational patterns established in the Golden Age, several developments in and outside the Netherlands made horticultural auctions an attractive option during the middle-end of the nineteenth century.

By the eighteenth century, Dutch tulips had gained international renown for quality and variety, and the Netherlands was exporting bulbs to neighboring Germany, France, England, and elsewhere. Tulip and daffodil bulb cultivation expanded around Haarlem and further south, as well as in Noordwijk, Uitgeest, and Lisse. Although transportation for moving cut flowers rapidly over great distances was still a ways off, there was an expanding international market for the more durable Dutch flower bulbs. Also, the practice of pleasure gardens continued, and gradually became widespread, which bolstered interest in ornamental flowers. Tulips remained prevalent, but by the 1730s, another flower of Persian origin, the hyacinth, began to captivate the popular imagination in the Netherlands. Hyacinths, roses, daffodils, tulips and other ornamentals joined with shrubs and small trees in creating beautiful gardens. The French revolution influenced social relations in the entire region with more demands for equality, and lower classes began to purchase flowers. Still, horticultural production remained largely focused on flower bulbs, trees, and shrubs for gardens, as well as fruits and vegetables.

An equally important development in the late eighteenth and early nineteenth centuries was the masculinization of citizenship in the Netherlands. In this era, ideas about manhood and the nation took shape, and informed one another as the country moved from a republic to a monarchy. An ideal crystallized of the new citizen as male, possessing military daring and mettle, and earning a wage. If growing flowers did not generate money, it seems unlikely many men would have taken up growing them – aesthetic appeal notwithstanding. Along with these social shifts of the late eighteenth and early nineteenth centuries, technological advancements started to change growing practices. In the middle of the nineteenth century, growers began to use greenhouses to cultivate grape vines. Soon, with some modifications and heating introduced, people were also growing flowers in them. Greenhouses allowed production of cut flowers on a comparatively massive scale, and extended the growing season.

A longer growing season, a new growing environment, and the increased volume of cut flowers led to several consequences. Aalsmeer growers began to cultivate lilacs and roses en masse, with many specializing in roses. Then, as more and new varieties flooded the market, prices fell. Flowers became both more plentiful and affordable, which was generally good for expansion of the market, making flowers available to a wider public and during more months of the year. But growers had no control over price, and felt pinched. In one way, greenhouses made their job easier, but it was hard for them to earn money, since the buyers, the flower traders, would consistently undercut prices. Traders set growers against each other in a race to offer the lowest price. It was a buyer's market, very unstable for flower growers. Another part of the buyer's strong position came from their distribution networks, which were important because the consumer market was centered not in Aalsmeer, but in Amsterdam. Flower and plant growers were frustrated.

But it was a different story for the fruit and vegetable growers. They organized themselves into cooperatives and sold their goods at auction, and they put together their own distribution services. Their initial goal was not to set up an auction per se, but to form an organization that would protect them as a group. The idea was for buyers to come to them and compete with each other on the market for the best price. And growers preferred the method of sale over some sort of collective shipping: it was "simple" and "required little or no market orientation" in their view. At auction, fruit and vegetable growers got better prices, and the buyers were assured a higher quality, because products had to meet certain standards to be sold. For mass-produced, highly perishable goods, the system proved fast and efficient.

After eyeing this arrangement with envy, in 1899 Aalsmeer flower and plant growers who supplied Amsterdam came together to found De Vereenigde Tuinbouwers, or United Horticulturalists. They opened an auction on the Marnixstraat in Amsterdam, and the main local market was along the Singel canal downtown, where there is still a daily flower market, though now primarily geared toward tourists. But this auction and market served only a portion of Aalsmeer horticulturalists. Other Aalsmeer growers thought it made more sense to auction their plants and flowers closer to home, and so in 1911 and then in 1912, they began two auctions in Aalsmeer. The first, which began in Welkom pub, was called Bloemenlust, or Flower Passion, and the second, which opened business in De Drie Kolommen pub, was called Centrale Aalsmeerse Veiling, or Central Aalsmeer Auction, CAV. In addition to the local market, they especially focused on exports to Germany, sending boats with small trees and shrubs by sea to Hamburg and Bremen as in the seventeenth and eighteenth centuries.

The decision of Aalsmeer's growers to organize production through cooperatives that sell at auction has had far-reaching effects: cooperative auctions have shaped the anatomy of the industry. This is true in two basic senses. Aalsmeer's horticultural auction, as the largest in the world, influences many aspects of the industry world wide, from setting prices to setting trends, standards, and innovations. Plus, due to its sheer volume of trade, Aalsmeer's auction is unignorable. But Aalsmeer is not the entire industry; many towns began to have flower and plant auctions, and today FloraHolland has six auction sites, and Plantion, the second remaining independent horticultural auction, is located in Ede. Horticultural auctions have directly shaped growing and selling in the Netherlands, the fundamental segments of the supply chain. Other aspects of the chain, like breeding, wholesaling, and retailing, have fallen into place around the cooperative auction structure. These two related but distinct parts of the story of Aalsmeer's rise merit separate attention, though in reality they intertwine. One focuses on the evolution of Aalsmeer's auctions from these small-time, pub-centered businesses to what we see today, and is about an institution; the other describes the development of a national industry, which entails explaining the supply chain and its intricate webbing of supportive horticultural organizations, institutions, and policies. In addition, especially in their first decades, Dutch horticultural auctions formed organizations such as the Groep Bloemsterij and the Kring Bloemenveilingen, which linked cooperatives around Westland (which has a high density of greenhouses) and beyond. This did a lot to both stabilize prices and strengthen the position of growers.

Although Aalsmeer growers were the first, they weren't the only, to organize Dutch flower and plant auctions. Within five years of the two Aalsmeer auctions' founding, growers in Rijnsburg began their own, and other areas in Westland followed suit. But from the beginning, in many ways Aalsmeer led the industry.

From early on, it had not only the largest market share, but also excelled with the best established export position, mainly to Belgium, Germany, Luxembourg, Britain, Scandinavia, and Switzerland. From their inception, Bloemenlust and the CAV enjoyed tremendous success in both domestic and international trade, earning in their first year 110,000 and 80,000 guilders, respectively. Already in those early days they had a strong market position, partly because the preceding horticultural auction in Amsterdam had ironed out some of the kinks in the system: namely, attracting the exporters to buy at auction rather than independently. By 1950, profits in Aalsmeer had ballooned to 10.5 million guilders each, and by 1960 they had soared to over 25 million guilders. Among other effects, the auction's success helped to stabilize flower growing as a reliable and suitable profession for a male head of household. During the same period, a near identical process was going on in nearby Rijnsburg, where the flower trade provided the key to social mobility.

From discussions with older and retired growers, it seems that even during these decades, masculine norms may have been slightly freer and more flexible than in other male-dominated institutions. The industry gestalt was certainly rugged and agricultural, but also entrepreneurial and allowed space for flair and eccentricity. In other words, the environment probably had less stolid conventions than among, say, potato farmers, but on the other hand, masculine styles were likely more rustic and spirited than among business owners and independent professionals. These shades of distinction helped to define insiders and outsiders to horticultural networks, and contributed to the cultures of Aalsmeer's two auctions. On a more general level, grower's customs and behavior reflect a familiar dimension of male domination, which shines through in ritual, habit, and language. Equally important to this conceptual relationship are the arenas in which it takes place, where in this case, men are producing ornamental flowers. The social spaces and the flowers themselves aren't the only gendered aspects of the grower's environment. As the grower cooperatives expanded and dug in to the local terrain, they joined institutions of church and state in perpetuating gender differences where men maintain economic power and legal authority.

And expand they did. By the mid-1960s the Central Aalsmeer Auction on Cleefkade, squished in between the village and a flank of greenhouses, had run out of room to enlarge, though booming business demanded it. At the same time, several other fortuitous factors nudged the CAV and Bloemenlust toward a merger. Auctions in nearby Beverwijk and Vleuten began to draw business from Aalsmeer growers, and some new Aalsmeer growers did not want to honor long-standing agreements about where they should auction. Though by the mid-1960s pillarization was in decline, differences between the two Aalsmeer auctions were not trivial, so the merger had other dimensions. Bloemenlust growers were Dutch Reformed Protestants and Catholics, while the CAV group were Baptists and socialists, and each circulated in their own social circles, pubs, schools, and sports clubs. But fusion made sense. With the combined strength of both auctions, Aalsmeer could cement its position at the center of national and even international flower trade. Bloemenlust didn't sell plants, but only flowers, mostly roses and carnations, while the CAV did sell plants along with flowers, specializing in lilacs and tulips. Both cooperatives voted overwhelmingly in favor of merging as the Cooperative Society Verenigde Bloemenveilingen Aalsmeer, VBA, or United Flower Auctions Aalsmeer.

The Aalsmeer municipality strove to keep the auspicious business within its boundaries, and negotiated an attractive deal on land where the new, improved, much larger auction structure would be built. In this way, the auction expanded along with local infrastructure, or vice versa. In either case, Aalsmeer's auctions have been integral to regional planning over the past century. When building highways, intersections, traffic lights and so on, planners have had to take into account the route and schedule of thousands of trucks coming from and going to the auction. Such volumes of traffic also affect quality of life issues for local residents, especially air pollution levels. This has been true as well for nearby Schiphol airport, on which the auction relies as a primary export platform. Since Aalsmeer from the beginning served both the local market and the international one, Schiphol and KLM played a vital part in horticultural distribution. With land transport, the cooperative growers voted to commission their own modes of distribution, partly because, prior to the auctions, the buyers controlled distribution, and that was one reason for the grower's weakness. But they didn't do so with air freight, and some growers feel that the auction made a big mistake. Fedor Broers thinks the cooperative lost a good opportunity by contracting KLM ("they kind of had their heads up their asses," as he put it) instead of commissioning their own planes, which would have enabled them to have more control over costs, given the volatile prices of oil and that airlines buy fuel in bulk, ahead of time (and also via auction). Coordinating distribution with KLM, conferring over both internal plans for auction construction and the auction's infrastructural needs with public officials, as well as negotiating financing with banks points out the complexities and intricacies of the institution's growth. Politically, the negotiations on development were sometimes tricky because as the auction grew, it overlapped with four different regions, each with separate governance. From this alone, one can see the value of networks and cooperation. Without them, here in this densely populated region, it would be hard to get anything done.

The auction occupies not only a sizeable plot in the regional geography and economy, it is and has been a part of the cultural landscape. One sees this in a variety of ways, from its relationships with schools and organizations to sponsoring local events such as flower parades, or bloemencorsos, and charity events. The old Bloemenlust building became a warehouse for the Vroom & Dreesman department store, while the CAV was converted to TV studios. Far more than a site where flowers and plants are sold, the Aalsmeer auctions are insinuated into the popular culture and imagination. Examples abound: a reality dating show in 2008 featured auction employees and was shot on site; a 1977 film, *The Amsterdam Kill* starring Robert Mitchum, climaxed with a chase scene across the Aalsmeer auction floor. But common references to the auction go beyond modish commercial media. Leaders in banking and finance as well as local and national politicians advocate for the industry, especially the industry's largest auction in Aalsmeer. It's also important for flowers to maintain their stature with the public, which is accomplished partly through marketing. But another key way that the industry maintains the flower's power of distinction is through periodic endorsement by national and international leaders, and the Dutch royal family. After the Bloemenlust/CAV merger in 1964, over several years they constructed a new, vastly larger building to house the United Flower Auctions Aalsmeer, and when it was ready to open in 1972, Prince Claus and Princess Beatrix came forward to inaugurate the world's largest flower auction. In 1946, Winston Churchill toured the CAV, then just resuming business after the war; in 1958 Queen Juliana guided Queen Elizabeth through Bloemenlust; in 2000 Chinese Prime Minister Li Peng visited the VBA; in 2010 former U.S. president (and peanut grower) Jimmy Carter dropped by with Rosalyn, exclaiming "I've been a farmer so this makes us feel comfortable"; and in 2011 at the centenary celebration of FloraHolland Queen Beatrix made an appearance.

After the 1972 opening, the Aalsmeer auction made several evolutionary leaps forward, reflecting important trends and changes in the industry. Men who were around during that time explained that this felt like a turning point, and compared it to the mergers of 2008. By the early 1970s, the auction had reached a size where old ways of doing things were no longer efficient, and so the auction developed a number of internal practices and devices that made business easier, faster, and more reliable. Some of these advancements related to the greenhouse and were developed by growers, and some came from people working in the auction and related to storage, as cut flowers require refrigeration to maintain freshness. One advancement involved devising an aluminum cart with many trays. These carts made transport from greenhouse to auction safer and allowed far more volume per truck, and once at the auction site, transport became smoother from truck to storage, from storage to the auction halls where buyers sit, and then on to the buyer's lots parked across the warehouse floor. The carts were also a boon for local business, since they could be produced right in Aalsmeer by the Verhoef Aluminum Scheepsbouw Industry. The auction continued to expand throughout the decade, both in sales volume and reach, and by leasing the considerable auction building space to importers, exporters, and other businesses.

The first major energy crises also took place in the 1970s, and they affected Dutch growers in several ways. The industry depends on oil and gas for the production of fertilizers, for heating and cooling, and of course also for distribution by plane and truck. The Aalsmeer cooperative was fortunate, though, in that the majority of trade was still regional and by truck (much less costly than air freight), and because of the Netherlands' natural gas reserves, which had been discovered a decade earlier in the North Sea, and which growers used generously due to the government-sponsored discount rate. Nevertheless, the volatility of oil prices and supply signaled a warning shot both to the Aalsmeer cooperative and to the industry. Dutch growers began to feel concerned about where and how their flowers and plants would be grown and distributed in the future. Also, the oil crises occurred around the same time that the Aalsmeer cooperative voted to allow for the first time flower imports to be sold at their auction. The international growers, mostly in Israel and Spain, remained only a small part of turnover (eight percent in the first decade), and they were hit hardest by the oil crises.

In spite of this, in the 1980s and 1990s the auction tended toward increased international growth and sales, though internationally produced horticulture remained under thirty percent of turnover until the new millenium, and even now it constitutes only around thirty-five percent. In 2006, the cooperative voted to allow foreign-based growers into the collective as full voting members. But perhaps a more dramatic trend during these decades involved the consolidation of auctions themselves though mergers. Although nationally, overall growth and sales continued to rise, the number of horticultural cooperatives shrank. In 2005, the VBA, which was the Netherlands' largest horticultural auction, voted for fusion with FloraHolland, the second largest, resulting in FloraHolland Aalsmeer, and five other auction locations (in Naaldwijk, Rijnsburg, Venlo, Bleiswijk and Eelde).

This merger was disputed in court on the grounds that it represented a monopoly, but the challenge was struck down on the logic that the merger strengthened the Dutch position internationally, and that differences and objections among unaffiliated Dutch growers were essentially irrelevant to the business. Although the initial court decision found that the merger did not violate anti-monopoly laws, in 2010 the Aalsmeer merger was challenged again by the VGB (De Vereniging van Groothandelaren in Bloemkwekerijprodukten, The Association of Wholesale Trade in Horticultural Products). But this time, the focus was on the auction's internet auction, TFA, which Dutch wholesalers argued put them at a disadvantage from FloraHolland Aalsmeer growers located in East Africa, since their products are produced more cheaply but are considered 'Dutch' and thus not subject to import tariffs and laws. The Nederlandse Mededingsautoriteit (NMa, the Dutch Competition Authority), the government division of the Dutch Economics Ministry that examined the case, eventually ruled in favor of FloraHolland Aalsmeer.

The merger signals the Dutch horticultural industry's trend toward consolidation. Not only have the auctions merged, so have other parts of the production chain: breeding companies have been merging, and in the past decade or so, new organizations (many with government funding) have sprung up. Once FloraHolland and Bloemenveiling Aalsmeer voted to merge, just two independent Dutch horticultural auctions remained – and they, too, quickly chose to merge in what is widely understood as an effort to avoid getting put out of business, to maintain a market position, or possibly to carve out a new niche in a market dominated by a single institution. But it was not a coincidence that the second merger, the one that created Plantion, directly followed that of Bloemenveiling Aalsmeer/FloraHolland: in fact, it was instituted two months retroactively, so that both FloraHolland and Plantion officially began in January 1, 2008. Ever since then there have been tensions between the Netherlands' two remaining auction institutions. Plantion has sought to distinguish itself by emphasizing green technology and little world impact – and since it is a smaller company/auction, it may be more successful or credible at that. In recent years, Plantion has refused merger offers from FloraHolland, occasionally stirring a legal row. Plantion's managing director André Kruisson stepped down in 2012 in a move that some suggested reflects controversy about the merger and internal debate about the future of the second remaining Dutch horticultural auction. It's notable not only that he left, but where he went – to become the director of Veiling Holambra, Brazil's rapidly expanding horticultural auction. Founded in the mid-twentieth century by Dutch farmers, this auction suggests something of the Dutch flower system's global reach: here it's worth merely pointing out both the fluidity and international character of Dutch horticultural networks.

FloraHolland and the VBA described the merger along rather different, if also familiar, lines. Working together (*samenwerken*) in the cooperative has been "rediscovered" after the 2008 merger, according to Aad van der Knaap of FloraHolland's advisory council and Eric Persoon, FloraHolland's treasurer in FloraHolland Aalsmeer's monthly magazine. According to Van der Knaap, "the government always seeks a balance between commerce and cooperation." Nor does Persoon understand the merger as creating a monopoly, which anyway, "makes you lazy." Instead, "the world is changing, and together we're building a giant network economy." The language may be hackneyed, but there's some truth to the statement.

The Aalsmeer auction has gone from Bloemenlust and the CAV to the VBA, and is now FloraHolland Aalsmeer. Aalsmeer's

3,500 grower members have joined with the grower-members of the other auctions to become a 5,200 member-strong collective. Glossy promotional materials tout this 'bigger, better' Florahollland as the institution Where Beauty Meets Business. In addition to the controversial merger, FloraHolland has expanded by opening an auction in Germany, the Rhein-Maas auction, which has strengthened the Dutch horticultural position with its biggest trading partner and largest consumer of Dutch horticultural products. As the auction has consistently expanded, the institution's cooperative structure has shaped that expansion. But in spite of the merger's corporate mien, the cooperative's growth has not been a simple story of big fish eating little fish. Unlike strongly hierarchical franchise industries that swallow, drive out, or bankrupt small, independent businesses, the horticultural cooperative thrives with small and mid-size growers. They're members of a larger structure, and so cocooned, their businesses remain profitable, and no grower gets too big. At least, that's the general idea. Though the growing power of the institution of FloraHolland worries some small and medium-sized growers, it remains true even today that the average Dutch flower farm is between two and three hectares, and while annual profits rise and fall, most growers continue to earn a modest, middle-class income. This too helps maintain the ongoing culture of the Aalsmeer auction, the industry in general, and to characterize networks, class values, and other aspects of a horticultural weltanschauung. Nowhere can you get a better feel for a Dutch horticultural outlook, and Aalsmeer's changes over the century, than with Mr. Van Akker, a grower I met unexpectedly one October evening in 2006, who cultivated flowers from his childhood in the 1940s until his retirement in 2000.

~

We met in a squatter's cafe in Amsterdam Oost called Joe's Garage, around the corner from the squatted apartment of an acquaintance of mine, where Mr. Van Akker[20] had come to visit one of his six daughters. In contrast to the Aalsmeer auction, attendees touted this as an 'anti-capitalist space,' a place that operates under a different ethical and economic code than the outside world. Named for the 1978 Frank Zappa rock opera, it was an ironic venue to talk about the flower industry. A handsome sixty-eight year old, with white hair and a Clark Kent style cowlick across his forehead, Mr. Van Akker did in fact seem both ordinary and oddly heroic. He summed up his life with a wry smile and an unabashedly romantic statement. "I was born into flowers, worked with them all my life," he said, "and I hope one day to die in flowers."

Born in 1937 in Vleuten, his career spanned a period from the Second World War and the occupation, when there was no flower market, to the European Union, the euro, and FloraHolland. 1940-1943 were deep crisis years for the Dutch horticultural sector. Because of fuel restrictions and exorbitant fuel costs, up to 50 percent of flowers, fruits, and vegetables had to be grown outdoors (not using greenhouses); due to high production costs, lilacs, carnations, and roses were banned from auction in 1942; partly because Germany was (and is today) the prime consumer of Dutch horticulture, the market collapsed in the war years. "During the war, you know, the Germans wouldn't let us grow flowers. We had to grow vegetables for food. For them." Though it must have been harrowing that his family greenhouses fed the occupying army, recalling it, he remained calm and composed, the only hint of distress in the rhythm of his sentences. "Yes. For them. So officially there were no flowers. But my father and some others used to grow chrysanthemums and poppies between the rows of potatoes and other things."

Gesturing down at our 'people's kitchen' plates of potato cauliflower curry, cumin rice, and a dal with fresh tomato and cilantro, he said, "we grew everything we're eating here, except the rice. But of course our meals were very different. And during the war we had less food."

It seemed curious that his father and other men would defy the Germans by growing flowers, especially when there was no trade, so they couldn't even earn money by taking such a risk. "You know, even in war – especially in times like that – people have to have something Good," Mr. Van Akker explained. "They must have something Good, something Beautiful. Beauty is very valuable, very important." He spoke in English and enunciated the words Good and Beautiful.

This was the lesson he took away from the experience as a boy, and in both conscious and unconscious ways, he reflected, it has shaped his views on flowers. Clearly, growing flowers entailed something beyond employment and an opportunity for upward mobility, and represented far more than a stable identity. Though a livelihood and a business, cultivating flowers inspired a kind of wonder, a devotion to something outside of the world's cruelties and indignities, but also intimately connected to the earth. After the war, at fourteen he left school to work in the family business, as in a lot of flower-growing families. "I never went to university, though I wanted to go, but my parents told me: you have to work. Eventually I liked it, but not at first." After fifty-five or sixty hours a week in the fields and greenhouses, Mr. Van Akker went on to part-time jobs in factories or repairing farming machinery. There was so much work that "you didn't even think about finishing," he explained. He described how one day just bled into the next, time was governed by natural cycles of seasons and daylight, by the long arm of the auction clock, and by a steady though not insatiable public demand for flowers. Flowers, hard work, and family were running themes in our talk. In the postwar years, it was not unusual to have illegal or semi-legal immigrants doing this hard work in the horticultural sector. It has been estimated that at it's peak use of foreign labor (from the early 1970s to the early 1990s), as much as 20 percent of the greenhouse workforce was composed of immigrants, but since then, the introduction of fines and stricter enforcement of the law has dramatically reduced that number. In the early 1980s some growers were complaining that the only way they could earn a profit was to hire underpaid illegal immigrant workers, which they did in spite of the 10,000 guilder fine introduced in 1979.

Though born into flowers, Mr. Van Akker didn't push any of his children into horticulture: "I wanted them all to pursue their own goals... None of them chose my business, but I'm proud of them all." In the 1960s, a cousin did start a flower auction in Vancouver. Most of the investors were not Canadian but Chinese, and the flowers came from Colombia. But his entrepreneurial cousin didn't stay in the flower business, and no other family pursued a career in horticulture, which is somewhat unusual among Dutch flower-growing families. His youngest "is the wildest, in to singing and dancing and performing, you know." The eldest daughter, in her forties, is an anesthesiologist in England; another daughter, married and a homemaker, has a passion for gardening and is his only child to maintain any involvement with flowers; another daughter "loves South America." She was working toward her Master's in Latin American studies, speaks fluent Spanish, and spent a year in Ecuador, "where they also grow many flowers."

He added, "I also have one daughter who dedicates herself to studying the Bible. Yes, I believe that religion is very important. I believe in God. But except for one girl, none of my children are really religious, at least they don't go to church. I wanted them to, you know, but you can't force it, and I've decided it's okay because each of them has very strong moral beliefs, and that is very good, too."

As one of Mr. Van Akker's daughters chatted beside us with her boyfriend, a photographer who works in a homeless shelter, someone slid a flyer for an anti-war demonstration onto our table. Of the wars in Iraq and Afghanistan, Mr. Van Akker commented, "I think they're terrible, huge mistakes." He took a deep breath and composed himself before continuing. "You know," he said, "I also think that flowers have to do with peace, and not just in a hippie way, but the spirit of flowers is peace. Imagine if the whole world were covered in flowers, blooming everywhere... Flowers are Good. There should be flowers everywhere, as there are flowers in heaven...Yes!"

If one day there were to be flowers "everywhere," it seems likely that a good proportion of them, in fact, would be cultivated by Dutch growers and sold via Aalsmeer's auction. What began a century ago among rural growers spawned an enormous cooperative institution and made Aalsmeer the center of world trade. But it has shaped the industry in other crucial ways as well. Almost everything that occurs in the horticultural value chain happens the way it does as a result of the grower's cooperatives. Today, this begins with breeders and propagators. Then growers take over, and sell their flowers and plants at auction, which are bought by import and export companies, wholesalers, and retailers, who then distribute and sell to the consumer.

For views on how this works, and the joys and complaints of Dutch growers, few are more articulate or insightful than Hans de Vries, who cultivates evergreens and cactuses in Aalsmeer. De Vries began working in the business when he was fifteen, and by his mid-twenties, after a brief stint managing an "eclectic electric bluegrass band," he took over his father's business in the mid-1960s. In addition to managing the business, he writes a lively and unorthodox column for FloraCulture International, 'Dust'. On a cloudy June afternoon in 2009, we met in his office and toured his greenhouses.

"As you know, it's common to have cooperatives in the Netherlands," De Vries began. "The flower auctions are just one of them. The auctions are the backbone of the cooperative, and also what makes it work – but, it's far from perfect." As one might expect, the system offers significant advantages for those who organized it, the growers, but the business is hardly easy, and smooth sailing, and for most flower and plant growers, profit margins are narrow. In fact, many growers feel their position is precarious. Since the price of products in an auction is a negotiation, and the market can perform erratically, growers constantly fret over finances. So why would such a fluctuating and unpredictable system help producers, and why would they collectively organize themselves and specifically choose to sell their flowers and plants via auction? One might suppose, on the contrary, that a grower would seek to develop relationships with particular buyers, in order to be able to rely on more constant and stable prices and firm contracts. As in other industries, contracts might be negotiated between individual parties.

The special advantage this system offers growers is not the unstable aspect of auctions; rather, it's the auctions' location in the structure of the production chain, and the protection of a cooperative institution as a mediator. The auctions neatly split vital, and very different aspects of the horticultural industry. "If you disconnect sales from production," explained De Vries, "as a grower, then you can focus wholeheartedly on the production system. You don't have to worry about sales, not so much, because the auction takes care of that. You don't know the clients, who's buying your product, so you don't view other growers as competitors. You're not fighting each other to win a contract with someone. This is the genius of the grower's auction system," or at least as the system works in combination with the cooperative, and other cultural, financial, historical, infrastructural and policy-related factors in the Netherlands. In some industries, individual businesses sell on the market and compete directly with one another. They work to develop relationships with clients, with businesses who will buy their product. But because of the grower's cooperative auction "you don't know your clients, not really. You don't know, or necessarily care who's buying your crop, [even though] you're selling in the same place, and for about the same price. So your business becomes about being the most productive you can be, because that's how you can perform well."

"If I compare this with my American colleagues," continued De Vries, "I mean, it's pretty dramatic. They're secretive, threatened by other growers, and competitive with one another. And in the end, while some individuals may have this or that advantage in the short term, the cut-throat approach doesn't really help the business." In the Netherlands, growers work together: they form clubs and share expertise on the best growing techniques so they can grow greater amounts, and do it faster, cheaper, and more efficiently. In these grower clubs, as they socialize, they discuss and share growing techniques, tips on heating, lighting, or fertilizer, and relay other kinds of market information. In some industries, individual businesses sell on the market and compete directly with one another. They work to develop relationships with clients, with businesses who will buy their product. But not so much in the horticultural industry, or at least, not in the same way. As a cultural value, and as rhetoric in almost any circumstance, the Dutch prize working together. But, as De Vries points out, "*samenwerken* only makes sense if [it allows you to be] more productive, if it's to your advantage." Otherwise, it's just a lofty goal and an empty phrase. Although in recent years the line between growing and selling has somewhat blurred, since it's inception the modern industry's structure, the sharp demarcation of growing from selling has fomented cooperation.

Maybe it's not strictly correct to describe cooperation as an explicit function of the grower's institution, but it is certainly an effect, intentional or not. As De Vries elaborated: "Most of this works out by accident. I mean, it was meticulously planned, the auction. Sure. But when you look at how it actually ended up functioning, I mean, the growers and planners had no idea what was going to happen, really. A lot of the benefits come from hard work and foresight, but a lot of things just worked out by luck – circumstances, trial and error, and chance." The cooperation and sharing of knowledge also has social and psychological consequences. To an extent it fosters an 'all-for-one-and-one-for-all' sentiment among growers, and, because many of them regularly come together via industry clubs, associations, meetings, and other social events to confer on the (global) market, this communitarian sensibility may also breed a certain urbane and cosmopolitan outlook.

I reflected on this when I noticed that many of De Vries's neighbors also grow plants or flowers, and that the surrounding landscape can seem misleadingly rural. Westland appears rural, but flower fields and horticultural greenhouses are integrated in this highly urbanized region, the Randstad. The day I interviewed him, I stepped off the bus as a fleet of swans was gliding through the canal between the highway and "J. de Vries Potplantencultures," and I scanned the panorama. Goats in someone's front yard were staring at the traffic, and at the end of the road, in a wide field, cows were ruminating under a low sky, with FloraHolland Aalsmeer in the distance. The landscape may seem bucolic, but De Vries is no country bumpkin. He's sophisticated, worldly, and very fluent in English. He boasted of being different from his neighbors, but also imagined himself equally as part of the same tradition. "A hundred years ago, guys like me were selling our stuff down the street at Welkom pub, you know."

While the auction's global reach may have spurred local growers to widen their horizons, and although the auction's position in the production chain encourages cooperation, that does not mean that business is always hunky-dory from their perspective, even when FloraHolland is thriving. There is of course a down side – growers are not uniformly and universally pleased with FloraHolland's performance. Created to protect the interests of growers, the auction has taken on a life of its own (another unintended consequence), a new institution with its own needs and its own bureaucracy. FloraHolland seeks to protect and defend its interests, which don't always necessarily coincide with the interests of Dutch growers. De Vries put it bluntly, if hyperbolically: "the co-op works not for the growers but for the co-op." In other words, as the institution has expanded, it has acquired its own needs and priorities. The institution's board, planners, and executives steer the institution's course, though the membership elects them and votes on the agenda. But the membership isn't tied into the institution's day-to-day operations, nor is it active in setting the agenda for the future. Most growers focus on their own business and trust that the cooperative takes care of their interests, though increasingly, as growers have less and less to do with the auction's daily operations, this may be changing. Grower's interests and the institution's interests aren't always identical. Dutch rose growers are a case in point.

De Vries is not optimistic about the future for Dutch growers, and ironically, he sees their ultimate undoing resulting from the fantastic success of their system. Growers have supplied a steady diet of high quality inexpensive flowers, and by now consumers have come to expect low prices. For over a hundred years, due to superior growing techniques, cooperation, the auction system, and excellent marketing, Dutch flowers sold at the lowest prices and beat out all competitors throughout much of Europe. But De Vries characterized the situation rather pessimistically in a prominent industry magazine: "the current financial crisis and recession have intensified the search for lower prices. Prices this low can only be achieved with free heating and dollar-a-day labor. Dutch growers with their costs still rising cannot keep up. They are at the end of their cycle. Their hundred years are over. They are finally closing down, beaten by their own strength." De Vries may exaggerate: the Dutch flower grower is far from dead. But increasingly, in many areas Dutch cultivars cannot compete with products from lands where labor and resources are considerably cheaper. Even so, the situation is not a simple story of global competitors uprooting local business, because these internationally grown flowers are often produced by Dutch men, and they are still sold through Dutch auctions, though many Dutch growers do suffer as a result. Flowers have never been more plentiful and rarely cheaper than in today's auctions. So FloraHolland remains vibrant and continues to expand, but through the same process many local growers struggle and straggle.

At a rose nursery called Kwekerij de Singel, a manager named Puk told me that flowers "are like bread. You don't think that someone got up at two a.m. to make this, and kneaded this dough in their hands. You don't really care where it comes from, only that it's good quality." Though some consumers do care where and how they're grown (e.g. Fair Trade flowers), the point still stands. More and more foreign-grown roses are sold at Dutch auctions. "We take pride in these roses," said Puk as we strolled through a greenhouse, the air rich with a nitrogen mist and a faint aroma of velvety red roses. "Each stem represents hard work, investment, and care." By 2007, the average price at the Dutch auctions for the lighter colored tea hybrids grown in the Netherlands was 36 cents, compared to 18 cents for those imported, primarily from Kenya and Ethiopia. (It was noticing these trends, as well as through conversations with people like De Vries and Puk that eventually convinced me of the need to go to east Africa, visit some flower farms, and see what was going on behind the figures I kept hearing about.)

Couldn't the auction have foreseen this trend? Wouldn't the Dutch growers, who constitute the co-op, and thus vote on major decisions, choose not to allow, or to limit entry of foreign-grown roses to their market? Though some saw the potential for competition, the idea that the East African rose market could one day come to dominate the Aalsmeer auctions did not seem likely. Traders, of course, don't necessarily have a stake in the flowers being grown in the Netherlands, per se – although, due to networks, kinship, personal background, taste, or even a national loyalty, some traders may prefer locally grown flowers. But if importing roses made long-term sense for the strength and viability of the institution of the auction, which it did, it wasn't in the long-term interest of Dutch growers. And the auction management might find ways to play down or muffle the voices of local naysayers. According to De Vries and some other growers, this is typically the case when growers express doubts or raise questions about policy. But "because most growers are simple and trusting and don't always see the big picture," said De Vries, "they're not that hard to fool. And management has used every trick in the book. They even use mass psychologists to get what they want, to sucker growers who don't know any better... But I also used to promote a pop band, so I also know about propaganda and how to stir things up!" Whether or not growers have been duped, it can't be easy, even with the vote, to oppose the organized will of management, as any member of an institution can attest. But by the same token, the fact that the institution may sometimes work to further its own ends at the expense of local grower objectives, that doesn't mean that in most cases the institution does not help them.

Much of that help, though, doesn't come from some form of advocacy by the cooperative on behalf of growers. It comes from how the cooperative and the auction sever cultivation from sales, enabling growers to focus and excel at what they do, and similarly, for breeders, propagators, and others to shine in their niche. The auctions help to structure cooperation among growers, and at the same time, it creates and maintains communities of buyers. But this basic picture of the value chain is incomplete. Without the webbing of interrelated organizations, plus the support of government policy (as well as infrastructure, which makes efficient logistics possible), and low interest loans from banks, the Dutch cooperatives and the Dutch horticultural chain could not work as they do. These multiple organizations, ranging from financial institutions to quasi state promotional boards to national planning and even foreign policy, together are what makes the sector particularly strong and dynamic.

~

A good deal of the contemporary horticultural business funnels through FloraHolland in one of its six locations, with most of the Netherlands' floral exports taking off from Aalsmeer. FloraHolland is a major center in a transnational flow of horticultural commodities, capital, information, technology, and labor. It plays an important role in national planning and infrastructure in the Netherlands, and plugs into and intertwines with other businesses, urban development, agricultural policy, as well as other institutions such as banks and universities. Many in the industry consider FloraHolland in Aalsmeer the nexus of Netherlandish floriculture, since it hosts the gigantic flower auction and is situated in the abundant Westland region. And it's more than local fame: Aalsmeer is often called the flower capital of the world. But Aalsmeer's cooperative grower's associations operate in a broader context of horticulture and agriculture in the Netherlands, and without an understanding of that context, the institution's rise and ongoing success makes less sense.

Horticultural networks include a vast array of interrelated groups and institutions. It is among the complex interplay of Aalsmeer's many supportive organizations and practices that one can see the social networks of men, the institutional exchanges, the nation's developmental policies, the dense overlap of small and large players in the production chain, and all of it, in its variety and range, informed by a sense of collective enterprise.

In policy and industry literature, as in casual conversation with people in the horticultural industry, one detects a sometimes subtle but still noticeable nationalist spirit, which in part is a response to the increasingly global trade. A recent report published by the Ministry of Agriculture, Nature and Food Quality, for instance, opens with these words: "In recent years we seem to have begun searching for our national identity again: what kind of country are we, what do we want it to be, and how do we relate to the rest of the world... Is the Netherlands, with the ongoing European integration, losing too much of its identity, and how do we maintain our economic competitive position when countries like China, India, and Brazil are coming into the global market?" These anxieties can be partly resolved, implies the Minister, through ambitious and effective promotion of Dutch horticulture and agriculture. Dutch flowers, plants, and other agricultural products are markers of distinction, and can serve as a sort of national brand, providing both economic security and cultural identity.

In the industry structure and in participants' reflection on it, there's a sense of fellowship, as though they see themselves as members of an all-star team in a world tournament. In some ways, this perspective keeps the industry humming, for the coordination and cooperation at work emerge from tacit values and ideology about trade, national unity, and a kind of small-town familiarity flavored with male camaraderie. FloraHolland's monthly magazine recently devoted an issue to precisely these themes. Titled *Regarding Economics and Cooperation (Over Economie en Cooperatie)*, a number of important players in the horticultural industry weighed in on these topics in several roundtable discussions. Two of those interviewed include Bert Heemskerk, who began his career auctioning narcissus in Aalsmeer and eventually became Director of the Netherlands's Rabobank, and Art van Duyn, who also started out in the flower business and is an executive in the powerful investment corporation Dutch Flower Group. Each describes their institution as a "family business," which despite how it may sound, comes to seem, as they elaborate, like more than a corporate motto or the rhetoric of a TV commercial. Van Duyn explains: "In our business, [throughout the hierarchy] people share tasks and this increases their bonds. I find this a strong common point in the agricultural sector..." The social and cultural bonds formed by working in close proximity and cooperatively are essential to financial success. Similarly, Heemskerk talks about the important sense of teamwork that emerges from lots of small businesses, many of them family run, and how Rabobank offers numerous risk management programs to those in the horticultural industry. In fact, he says that Rabobank extends loans to small horticultural entrepreneurs because "family businesses are the motor of our economy."

Heemskerk and Van Duyn are not alone in this observation. As anthropologist Alex Strating discovered in the 1990s, one of the strengths of the Rijnsburg flower industry is its kinship or affinity system (*verwantschapssysteem*), where a kind of family loyalty and pride pervades commercial practices in local businesses run by blood relations. Again and again, industry participants as well as industry literature bring home the value of kith and kin to the horticultural industry. But in slight contrast with the sense suggested by executives like Heemskerk and Van Duyn, in Strating's analysis, these business values emerged less from a spirit of cooperative unity and more from family pride, loyalty, and reputation. In Rijnsburg, the strong ties to the family also helped to define insiders and locals from *buitenlanders*, those foreigners from outside the region, as well as from outside the Netherlands. But this high appraisal of fealty in the horticultural sector is not the only characteristic worth noting.

"In addition," Heemskerk goes on to say, "there are those cooperative working relationships." The cooperation between individuals and families, between institutions, and between large and small firms all have contributed to the construction of the Netherlands horticultural economy, and continue to provide muscular resilience and depth to the related industries. Timo Hughes, the Executive Director of FloraHolland until 2013, also took part in the Regarding Economics and Cooperation conversation. He emphasized that people in the horticultural industry cooperate because, in the global economy of "today's world, most individuals are too small to make it on their own." Hughes stressed "the financial value of standing shoulder to shoulder" in the production chain. "[In the cooperative structure] of the auction, you see the commercial solidarity between growers and traders." His comments point to one of the key advantages of the Dutch horticultural system, and FloraHolland in particular: the distribution of risk. That's what the cooperative system, with its sinews of networks, does so well.

But if cooperation helps to disperse risk, that's not its only purpose, nor its only value to Dutch horticulture. According to Gert van Dijk, a former professor at Wageningen University, agricultural cooperatives offer many advantages from environmental safety to higher food quality, but he stresses the financial benefits for growers, who can get "the highest price for their products at the lowest cost of production." Like many in the horticultural industry, Van Dijk held a variety of positions within the industry before taking his current position as the Director of Cogeca, the General Confederation of Agricultural Cooperatives in the EU, which represents forty thousand farmers' cooperatives (including FloraHolland), or six hundred sixty thousand people. Many of these individuals are small and mid-size producers, as with Dutch flower growers. The Aalsmeer growers, and their institution, are thus loosely connected to many other kinds of growers, to policy, and to related sectors.

Though an impressive and singular institution, FloraHolland is clearly not an island. It is ensconced in the Netherlands' horticultural industry, in planning and development projects, and in Dutch social and economic life. FloraHolland is also firmly rooted in the country's agrarian infrastructure, which supports not only the Netherlands' horticultural industry, but the nation's agricultural sector, which includes the dairy, meat, and fruit and vegetable industries. The agricultural sector has been carefully planned and organized to achieve a number of goals. Through a steering policy (*bestuurlijk beleid*) that reflects the general governmental approach of central planning that still leaves a lot of room for local autonomy, imaginative variation, and public-private partnerships, the Netherlands has for over a decade pursued an ambitious agricultural project called Greenports, which is a title given to a set of policies which predate the name. These infrastructure and development practices have been coordinated and organized through steering policies to create massive 'agriclusters,' densely overlapping framework and planning between related industries. FloraHolland is nestled in this panorama, which helps explain both the success of the institution and the leading place of Dutch horticulture on the world stage.

Greenports are designated agricultural areas organized to maximize efficiency by coordinating transport and infrastructure, and grouping together associated industries and businesses, and to save energy through new technological advances in horticulture. Greenports encompass economic networks of companies, organizations, and institutions related to agriculture and horticulture, such as flower and plant breeding, the supply of equipment and products, primary production, sales, auctions, imports and exports, transportation and logistics, processing, research and development, and education and financial services. As both social and economic architecture, their objective is "to serve as the drivers for the horticultural and greenhouse complex throughout the Netherlands;" these clusters are grouped in Westland-Oostland, Boskoop, Duin en Bollenstreek, Aalsmeer, and Venlo and have several specific directives. They aim to produce valuable knowledge and innovation, to use space strategically in order to increase efficient economic practices, to provide shrewd and productive infrastructure and logistics, and to advance an increasingly interlinked European agenda. This last goal should not surprise anyone, given that the EU provides the biggest market for the Netherlands' agricultural goods. In the trade literature and discussions of Greenports, again and again people highlight the need for cooperation, for *samenwerken*. Recognizing both the structural and the social, the steering policies and the propinquity of the sector, planners single out the special role of the potted plant, bulb and cut flower enterprises in the overall Dutch economy.

Together the five Greenports employ a quarter of a million people and earn fourteen billion euros per year in exports, and garner high profile attention among policymakers and elites. One of the Greenports' special programs, the 'Innovation Platform' called 'Flowers and Food,' was chaired by former Prime Minister Balkenende, which shows the level of priority and prestige given to the agenda, and offers another example of public-private integration in Dutch horticulture. As both practice and ideology, the Netherlands has a long tradition of collaboration between public and private sectors, in labor, academia, health care, and more. But considering the scale of the development project, and FloraHolland's and other private businesses' participation in planning, the phrase 'public-private partnership' seems inadequate, though frequently bandied about.

Both Greenports policies and public private partnerships have also led to valuable research. The horticultural industry supplies ornamental plants and flowers, as everyone knows, but it also advances scientific exploration in a number of fields. It provides vital research and raw materials to the cosmetics and pharmaceutical industries, for instance. Recent investigations of the chrysanthemum, one of the Netherlands' most popular flowers, has yielded some promising properties in the treatment of Alzheimer's. The green sector also pursues integrated high-tech growing environments, and has devised self-sufficient or even energy-producing greenhouses, using solar and wind power as well as natural underground reservoirs to pump water for heating and cooling. Some of the latest systems cultivate tomatoes or flowers above fish tanks. Many of today's greenhouses run on automated systems, with conveyor belts and robotics that respond to 'plant psychology.' In some ways, these cutting-edge investigations of flowers and plants bring the industry back to the Dutch Golden Age, where distinctions were not so sharp between agriculture, medicine, business, aesthetics, and nationalism. Similarly, in cultivating their products, today's flower breeding entrepreneurs carefully eye scientific advances as well as fashionable tics in the market. Much of both the freedom and incentive to do this comes from the multiple benefits in transportation, knowledge, and finance provided by the dense overlap of industry sectors.

The Greenports program sits within the Dutch government's Nota Ruimte, or National Spacial Strategy, guided by the vision of a changed governance model, or steering philosophy, the way national policy is elaborated at the regional and local levels through the participation of a range of actors, including "the public sector, private firms and the community of voluntary and non-governmental organizations." The National Spacial Strategy, directed largely by VROM, the Ministry of Housing, Spacial Planning, and the Environment, uses this decentralized governance model to allow for the participation of business and civil society organizations in development, and commits itself "to nature, landscape, cultural heritage and water management." In addition to pursuing these preservation goals, VROM works to link infrastructure between main ports, such as Schiphol Airport and the Port of Rotterdam, with the metropolitan areas in the Netherlands and abroad, including the Eindhoven/Zuidoost-Brabant 'brainport,' which produces research and knowledge, and the five agribusiness clusters which encompass the Netherlands' horticultural industry. Though Greenports show how carefully and deliberately the Netherlands' agricultural policy is planned and coordinated, long before the policy took effect, the principals of governance, the net of related organizations and institutions and the Dutch culture of flowers were well in place. And many of the horticultural organizations and institutions now grouped in the Greenports have long-standing relationships with each other, and with the Aalsmeer flower auction.

While these policies and organizational styles pervade the Netherlands, including its horticultural industry, their impact exceeds national boundaries. As in the seventeenth century, Dutch horticulture takes place in a global context. Both Aalsmeer's grower's cooperative and Dutch Greenports have attracted attention on the world stage. The reason is easy to understand. With more than half of the earth's population living in cities, and with many of those cities located in coastal, delta regions, countries face daunting infrastructural challenges, and barriers to agricultural production, since these crowded alluvial regions are the most fertile. Countries may increasingly choose, as China has, to seek the Netherlands' expertise in fields like water management, green planning, and metropolitan agriculture, exemplified by the Greenports.

Partnered with Greenport Venlo and the World Horticultural Exhibition Floriade 2012, Shanghai has embarked on an ambitious urban agricultural project to design and construct Greenport Shanghai, also known as Dongtan Ecocity. Those committed to the project include the governor of Limburg, the Mayor of Venlo, the Shanghai Agricultural Commission, the Shanghai Industrial Investment Corporation, the Dutch engineering company Grontmij and the Environmental Science Group of Wageningen University. The plan envisions a twenty-seven square kilometer agricultural park, a 'circular system' involving transportation, water infrastructure (canals), and waste management, alongside ample production facilities, all taking place in a sustainable environment in which refuse and by-products of one unit are used as the input of another. The park is designed to include safe and environmentally friendly provisions for three million chickens and eight thousand cows, as well as multiple fishponds, and copious fruits, vegetables, and flowers cultivated in solar-powered greenhouses, which would also help to generate extra energy. All products would be sold via on-site auctions, so most of the value chain would be centered right there. Thousands of people would also live and work in the park, and move around on elevated rails that connect locations like a 'floating pagoda' for research and education with plenty of green space for recreation. The master plan for Greenport Shanghai was presented to Chinese Minister Sun Zhengcai and then Dutch Minister of Agriculture, Nature, and Food Quality, Gerda Verburg, at the seminar 'Innovating Metropolitan Agriculture' in Beijing in October of 2008. There, Ministers Sun and Verburg also opened the Sino-Dutch Agricultural Center, an initiative of the Chinese Academy of Agricultural Science and Wageningen University, to support cooperation between China and the Netherlands on innovative agricultural research and projects.

But it remains to be seen how much of the futuristic Dongtan Ecocity/ Greenport Shanghai plan will be achieved. It has neither emerged gradually, nor from the grassroots; rather, it is a top-down, corporate proposal. Originally scheduled to open for the 2010 World Expo, the project has run into snags and is currently on hold, and there is no official date for completion. But if and when it is ever finished, it is unlikely to work like the Dutch Greenports, which are founded on cooperatives comprised of small and mid-sized growers and similar players, and whose infrastructure blends with male networks and cultural identity.

The Greenport project is not the only elaborate plan in China to reproduce or modify some aspect of Dutch horticulture. In the 1990s, a Dutch citizen of Chinese origin named Yang Bin combined a devotion to Dutch aesthetics with ideas about how to do horticulture, and carried it out to an absurd extreme. Known in China as the Orchid King, he built an empire founded on real estate and horticulture. Yang constructed his own 'Dutch' town on two hundred twenty hectares of land just outside the city of Shenyang, an industrial center in China's rust belt. His Holland Village featured tall, narrow, Dutch-style homes, a theme park, several enormous indoor gardens, windmills, and drawbridges, as well as replicas of Amsterdam's Central Station and the International Court of Justice, where he housed his office – a place that would seem to have more in common with Michael Jackson's Neverland estate than with the Netherlands. Along with Holland Village, Yang built a network of greenhouses around the country, where he cultivated tulips and orchids along with fruits and vegetables, and sold them through a multi-million-dollar business he founded called the Euro-Asia Agricultural Holding Company, once listed on the Hong Kong stock exchange.

Though orphaned at a young age, Yang excelled in school and managed to attend China's premier naval academy. From there, he gained admittance to Leiden University in the Netherlands, and while he was there he obtained political asylum, on the grounds that he faced persecution at home resulting from Tiananmen Square protests. After graduating in the early 1990s, Yang built a lucrative business marketing textiles and toys in Eastern Europe, and used that wealth to return to China as a Dutch citizen with a plan to start a commercial flower business. By the late 1990s, Yang had become one of China's new class of ingénues, or what people call the Yuan Billionaires. In 2001, Forbes magazine ranked him as the second-wealthiest person in China, with an estimated worth of almost a billion U.S. dollars. At 39, the brash, flamboyant Yang epitomized the kind of character journalists often celebrate in bullish markets. But like a fluorescent tie on a plain, button-down shirt, this flashy tycoon contrasts rather obviously with the modest, independent characters of Dutch growers. He concocted a scheme to enrich himself through flowers, and for a time it worked, but it's hard to tell how much of the business was a ruse and how much was legitimate horticulture.

By evading taxes and freely admitting it to newspapers, Yang eventually faced charges before Chinese authorities. Police escorted him from his office in the copied International Court of Justice, and despite supposed diplomatic immunity as a citizen of the European Union, in 2002 he was convicted of fraud, tax evasion, and illegal property ownership, and sentenced to eighteen years in prison. Dutch officials attended his trial, but the

Netherlands kept out of the Chinese government's case. Holland Village mostly vanished or was knocked down as new, much larger construction surrounded it, but a few landmarks remain. I asked many officials in the Dutch horticultural industry about Yang, and though no one could add much to his story, his name never failed to generate a smile. Like Fedor Broers, Mr. van Akker, and Hans de Vries, Yang Bin is a horticultural producer, entrepreneur, and a Dutch citizen, but there the similarity ends. Yang was not part of the Dutch male horticultural networks, and it's hard to imagine him as a member of an agricultural cooperative.

Among Aalsmeer growers, one rarely hears tell of Yang Bin or Greenport Shanghai, but in conversations with people in FloraHolland Aalsmeer, the theme of 'China' cropped up again and again. For instance, many people enmeshed in local Dutch horticulture expressed astonishment that entrepreneurs, politicians, and flower producers in China (and India) would show interest in the Netherlands's flower auctions. With this in mind, one can better appreciate some comments of Stef Griffioen. He has been involved in the industry for over twenty years, working in greenhouses, and holding down various jobs in the auction, including his current position in the complaints department. One morning as he was showing me around, explaining what he did there, and telling me some lore about the auction, he mentioned something curious I had heard before from both traders and guys who work on the floor. "Some Chinese came here one time to study this place. Just imagine! They went around in these white lab coats and wore thick glasses and inspected everything." While few knew these conspicuous Chinese visitors' exact relationship with the Aalsmeer flower auction, their presence left a strong impression, and people's stories showed provocative consistencies not only in how they imagine Chinese people, but in how they think about globalization, and how the Netherlands fits in the contemporary world.

Griffoen continued, "they wanted to see how everything worked, you know, probably so they could build something similar back in China. That's what the Chinese do – everyone knows that – they copy things." (We had not discussed Yang Bin or Greenport Shanghai.) "And you know what? They probably could copy this place, and maybe make something even bigger, but it would never be the same, never."

"Why's that," I asked.

"They can copy this place, and even this building, right down to the trolleys on the floor. But they can't copy us, or the Netherlands. They can't copy the Dutch culture, and so whatever they make, it would never be the same." It wasn't just pride speaking. If by "Dutch culture" he meant a certain density of social relations that find expression in networks, a particular historical legacy in flowers, and cooperative practices between growers, the auction system, and government policies favorable to the industry, Mr. Griffioen couldn't have summed it up better.

The Dutch Flower Auction: Traders

Like beauty, freedom of the market is in the eye of the beholder.
Economist Ha-Joon Chang

Dutch growers founded the horticultural auctions, they vote on auction policies, and they closely follow auction prices and trends. But they have little involvement with the auction's day-to-day operations, not even with the order their flowers and plants are sold, which is decided by lottery. Yet to the horticultural industry and to FloraHolland Aalsmeer, what happens here is no less crucial than cultivation, the grower's side of the cooperative. Events in the auction impact the whole horticultural chain. This is where the flowers and plants are sold. The auctions determine prices, and those prices reverberate through exporters, wholesalers, and retailers, and Dutch auctions establish a global rubric for floral value. Among other things, this means that even transactions far from the Dutch auctions are affected by their sales, since the sales set the standard for price, quality, and aesthetics. Dutch auctions are where you begin to see styles and developments in the industry, to note what is currently popular or losing favor. Dutch flower auctions are an effective barometer of horticultural trade in the Netherlands and around the world.

But of course, the Aalsmeer auction is also a place. The building has four cut-flower auction theaters and one for potted plants. Each weekday, through this gigantic structure that houses horticultural commerce, over twenty million cut flowers and a million plants enter and leave. So do ten thousand people, including several thousand traders, over four thousand FloraHolland employees in charge of logistics, movement, testing, bundling, and much else, plus hundreds more who work in restaurants, banks, insurance offices, and other businesses located in the complex.

It's a massive operation. Coordinating the reliable and efficient transport and sale of these perishable commodities requires a carefully calibrated infrastructure – a heating system for plants, a cooling system for cut flowers, storage for both, and conveyors, trolleys, and machines to ensure smooth, rapid, precise movement. All of this is done to maintain the optimal freshness of the products for the traders sitting in the auction theaters. Working individually or for import and export companies, they come to Aalsmeer between Monday and Friday to buy flowers and plants. The growers own this place, but because this is where the flowers and plants are sold, it's much more of the trader's domain.

Traders have their own networks, which overlap with those of growers, and share a lot with other parts of the horticultural industry, in terms of broadly accepted values, a shared sense of mission, tacit codes of behavior, and assumptions about economic practices. Like growers, buyers tend to be men. In the auctions, they frequently describe the environment as 'a man's world,' something clear enough to anyone visiting FloraHolland Aalsmeer, where on any given day you find hundreds of men and no more than three or four women scattered among the seated crowds. But the actual workings of the auction and what happens among the traders are more complicated than what meets the eye, and may also seem more mysterious than grower practices and strategies.

Given the common impressions of traders and auctions, it seems unlikely that they might work not on the basis of competition and 'market fundamentals,' but on tacit agreements and norms, ultimately on forms of cooperation and community. Yet in fact, this turns out to be the case. And while that conclusion is consistent with other aspects of Dutch horticulture, it's not unique to Dutch horticultural auctions. All auctions work like that, as sociologist Charles Smith demonstrated over twenty years ago in a book based on decades of research, the insights and conclusions of which apply directly to FloraHolland. Today, there's a broad spectrum of auctions in the world, selling everything from agricultural products to e-band width, though the exchange of goods is only part of the picture. Smith came to some curious conclusions about the role of community and cooperation in auction practices. Auctions have many outcomes, he argued, but only one or two of those are economic, and while determining price is certainly one function, it's not always even the main one. So why have auctions at all? If finding a price isn't their most important function, what else do they do, and how? Why are such different things as a Dubai condominium, a Van Gogh painting, a cosmonaut's space suit, Chilean sea bass, and a stolen car recovered by the police, all sold using the same form? Certainly, auctions are nothing new. We know plenty of other things sold at auction through the ages: objects ransacked from a village by Roman soldiers, an Ibo man in chains on a nineteenth-century Charleston slave block, the prized Golden Age Semper Augustus tulip... Is there something about flowers, or oil, art, or U.S. treasury bonds that necessitates that they be auctioned?

To varying degrees outside of auctions, the pricing of many items involves assessing quality, supply and demand, craftsmanship, and current taste; most people's expectation is that, above all, a fair price represents the cost of producing and marketing, plus a modest markup for profit. But this isn't always feasible. It may be impossible to determine costs if they cannot be reasonably deduced, or if the object was produced decades or centuries ago, as with antiques. Similarly, yesterday's supply and demand do not predict tomorrow's supply and demand when subject to unknown, uncontrollable, or natural forces, as with flowers, oil, and other commodities. Another problem with other pricing techniques is that of classifying the type of thing being sold. In Aalsmeer's auction, it is not at all true that a rose is a rose is a rose, because the grower's reputation, the condition of the product, and the location of its growth all effect what buyers are willing to pay. Not only is the price of roses, or oranges unclear and unpredictable due to fluctuations in supply and demand, but the price of Florida oranges will likely stray from that of Brazilian oranges because of differing transportation costs, labor, and wages, as well as factors like infrastructure, regulatory laws, and technology, not to mention environmental conditions and weather. A Florida honeydew and a Valencia blood orange differ in many ways, likewise a popsicle-orange Sputnik rose grown in Ethiopia and a velvety Red Naomi grown in the Netherlands. But because so much about each of these commodities is uncertain, they share in common something crucial, an unstable value. That points out one thing all auctions share: they take place around objects of uncertain value.

Finding a value, matching buyer and seller at optimum prices, cannot be arbitrary, and the process of selling must be acceptable to buyers. The seller must be accountable and the sales forum must seem disinterested. Auctions perform both functions, and this is where community and socially sanctioned rules and laws come into the picture. They provide the auction's authority and legitimacy. Auctions take place in open forums; they require a social, public environment (including the virtual space of the internet) to be sold and bought. More than finding a price, auctions stabilize value through a socially validated institution. Like ancient auctions in Rome or the slave-holding United States, today's flower auctions in Aalsmeer are profoundly social organizations. In fact, one of the reasons for the creation of many auctions is precisely this social aspect, but legitimacy is a two-way street. An auction also gives authority to the community that hosts it, which partly explains why so many charitable organizations turn to auctions for fundraising – the format justifies their collective power while it raises money, as Smith pointed out.

And via the auction, the community may assign ownership to certain things, and give them a new identity, which may be brutal, as Romans auctioning the booty from ransacked villages, but they also function as public ceremonies, even amid the violence of antebellum slavery, where people were recast, legally and socially redefined, as property. In both cases the public legitimized not merely the sale and new ownership, but the new identity of the person or thing auctioned. In doing so, the auctions lend an aura of objectivity, fairness, and even naturalness and inevitability, to wider values and practices, whether they relate to slavery, pillaging empire, or capitalist commodity culture. It's a rite of passage: auctions baptize, or brand, or forge, what passes through them. The community that hosts the auction, therefore, sits in a unique position.

In the Dutch horticultural industry, the auction community consists partly of the traders, the sellers (growers), the auctioneers, and others along the production chain. But the main dynamic feature of the auction community is the sodality of traders. The traders form a society of professionals, defined not only by common gender and nationality, but by shared interests and group identity, which is reinforced through trade publications and meetings, and expressed in styles of dress, codes of behavior, ways of speaking and moving, which other members of a group implicitly understand and respond to. Traders tend to be white men between thirty and fifty years old, and dress in jeans, flannel shirts, worn pullovers, or the occasional bright, button-down top. Many smoke, and the smoking rooms are also thick with voices. Conversations rarely exceed a few minutes because of the pace of trade, but there's enough time for small talk, jokes, and observations about business. This binds the traders and reinforces the shared collective goals of buying the greatest variety of flowers and plants of the highest quality at the lowest price. Their community is defined in terms of their connections to the place, traditions, and the institution, but also by their relationships to each other and to the flowers and plants. Their judgement and expertise draw them together in a congregation and sets them apart as a group. Their outlook tends to be upwardly mobile, good-humored, and while not ostentatious, traders don't shun expressions of financial success by referring to the cars they drive, or vacations they've taken. The status of flowers, companies, people, and the auctions are all aspects of what binds the community of traders.

~

With its multiple tiers of trader seating, auctioneer balconies, and stage inset with a calligraphy of plant-display tracks, Aalsmeer's plant auction has an operatic feel that's curiously appropriate for the trade that goes on there. It is the seat of economic and social dramas that unfold around fragile, exotic commodities. Because this is the only space for potted plants (about twenty percent of FloraHolland's trade), it's much bigger than any of the four cut-flower auction halls. One morning, amid the sounds of trade, I overheard a buyer speaking Spanish, which is unusual in this environment, and I wondered about his experience as a Spaniard among Dutch flower and plant brokers. We began a conversation about auctions, the role of traders, and the global potted-plant business. He had just made his final purchase for the day, so it was a good time to meet.

"I deal mostly with clients in Spain," explained Gonzalo, a handsome thirty-ish trader for a large import-export company called Las Palmas. After studying international marketing in Maastricht, he landed a job in the flower industry, since he was well-suited to do business in the Spanish market. Fanning my arm across the seated rows of traders, I asked him what he made of all these men involved in buying plants. "Ooeey, it's too macho, this environment," he groaned, and smiled. Shuffling beside me toward the door, he continued: "All these guys, you know, and all this money, our job can seem quite glamorous... But you know what? You think the Dutch are so sophisticated and with all this money moving in the auctions, they're so rich, but us guys, the people you see working here, most of us, we're the *campesinos*. We're not earning the big money. These guys are basically farmers, not big shots. Actually, we're a bit like the slaves of the market."

Referring to enslavement in the marketplace was a rich and provocative way of describing his own place, and the position of traders, in the horticultural industry. On the one hand, the notion of slaves of the market resonates strongly through the history of auctions, from Roman coliseums to the Atlantic slave trade, which ran simultaneously with the coffee-house art market auctions in European capitals. But of course Gonzalo did not literally mean that he and his fellow traders were chained to their desks and forced to perform for the market. He was indicating the hierarchy of power and profit, and at the same time, implied a kind of camaraderie with the other traders in this milieu. The behavior of humans performing economic rituals is often described as that of 'economic man' or homo economicus, which indicates a kind of dog-eat-dog perspective. But given the amount of tacit cooperation occurring in the auction, and the affectionate relationships among the traders, homo reciprocans may be a better moniker. Yet whether the emphasis is on cooperation or competition, the almost exclusively male ambiance attests to the homosocial character of the auctions.

Flavored with homosocial humor and camaraderie, the traders' idiom sometimes resembles a locker room. As flowers pass through the auction pit, typically female FloraHolland assistants in light green jerseys pull out bouquets from the passing carts to display them for the buyers; if she's deemed attractive, she may receive hoots and cat calls. If a trader goofs and mistakenly bids too high, his colleagues may mock his error by linking it to effeminate characteristics. One may hear shouts to bring your mother in for help or a female teacher to properly educate you. Frequent responses to my question of why there aren't many women traders included: because it involves money, the auction is just too complex, or simply because the work is too demanding. Auction participants don't consciously perform as men – they're there to buy or sell flowers and plants – but like Gonzalo, many do indicate an awareness of the fraternal environment, the *ouwe jongens krentenbrood*, influencing their behavior. Yet even in these cases, their acknowledgement seems to focus on things like shouting and other boisterous activities, and not on their own 'feminine' qualities like cooperation and trust, which are equally intrinsic to auction activities.

Trust is a kind of expectation, based partly on experience, and although in this sense it is usually unstated, it is essential in forging personal bonds, institutional credibility, and communal cohesion. Trust brings a level of comfort and predictability to all social life, it helps to foster a sense of community, and it facilitates people working together. Large-scale, diverse, and anonymous trade can and does take place in many economic environments without much critical evaluation or trust. But in economic scenarios dealing with credit, such as the financial sector or Aalsmeer's auction, you must be able to assess the trustworthiness of the individuals and institutions with whom you exchange commodities, money, or credit. Although trust takes the form of contracts and treaties governing transactions that involve such things as property, taxes, bankruptcy, and commerce, it is ultimately a psychological and social quality. When present, it's practically invisible, part of the normal civic landscape; when absent, it leaves a gaping hole, and may wreak havoc. Though it manifests itself in documents and rules, without these other, more basic but nebulous social and psychological aspects of trust, institutions, currencies, and systems collapse. And not only institutions and commodity markets hinge on it. Social networks, too, depend upon a kind of trust or confidence at least that others will do the 'right' thing despite incentives to the contrary.

Horticultural networks in the Netherlands thrive not only in the flower business, of course – they're also the backbone of the corporate elite. Eelke Heemskerk has argued that the social network of these economic power brokers represents the institutional configuration of the corporate regime and is "part and parcel" of the Dutch form of capitalism. Social networks are important for business governance, says Heemskerk, because they supplement the competitive nature of the market with structured coordination, and that these social networks are the foundation of formal and informal institutions that coordinate the economy. (Although the internet and other technologies have influenced the flower business, what remains remarkably consistent is the character of the trade, where personal relationships define and seal commercial agreements. This is not due to a stubborn luddite refusal to embrace technological innovation, only that the technology has not really eroded the strong social bonds that maintain the industry.) Heemskerk calls some of the most important figures in Dutch power networks "big linkers", who are corporate directors that hold three or more positions on corporate boards, and who often become spokesmen for the corporate elite. The networks of the horticultural industry have similar figures, such as the current president of Rabobank, who began his career as a trader in Aalsmeer, or Tjibbe Joustra, who left his position as Anti-Terrorism Coordinator of the Netherlands to head the Flower Council of Holland. Which is curious, but not inexplicable: with a degree in anti-trust law, Joustra has also chaired the Ministry of Agriculture, Nature and Food Quality. These sorts of characters in the horticultural industry provide important links to the country's finance, infrastructure, and planning. In and out of the industry, these kinds of figures in the Netherlands are also commonly known as *bestuurders*, prominent people who seem to have a hand in guiding and organizing everything. The structure and composition of these network ties also affect social norms in the industry. In the flower auctions, masculinity is so basic a norm that it's almost like a gravitational force, lending substance, validity, and weight to the work of the trade, their common enterprise. Both the horticultural community and the business elite seem to fit with the conception of the familiar old boy's network. By virtue of their eminence, reputation, prestige, and notoriety, many of these grand old men enjoy power and influence beyond their professional positions. In 2013 FloraHolland's general manager Timo Hughes stepped down "with pain in his heart" and was appointed by Dutch finance minister Jeroen Dijsselbloem as the new CEO of Nederlandse Spoorwegen (NS, the Dutch national train service). The new general manager, Lucas Vos, comes from a background in logistics as the Chief Operating Officer of Maersk, the largest container ship operator, based in Denmark. Vos has said that one day he would like to be prime minister of the Netherlands. (He is also openly gay and married.) The powerful positions of Hughes and Vos give you a sense of the kind of connected figures heading the flower industry. These poo-bahs, big linkers, or bobos, as the Dutch also call them, fill the ranks of the business elite and the upper echelons horticultural networks alike.

~

How do thirty-five hundred or so people buy over twenty million flowers and plants each Monday through Friday? Cut flowers generally arrive in the afternoon to be auctioned the following morning; usually, they have already been sorted, bunched, and placed in buckets, on trays and carts, and sit overnight in cold storage. Plants, which have a longer shelf life, also come in each day for sale, but there is more flexibility in timing and movement. Around five a.m., traders begin to show up to inspect the flowers, see what looks good, and note the condition of the types they're planning to buy. At six, the auctions open, generally to some fanfare: a bell goes off, lending a religious feel to the ritual. The opening minutes showcase new varieties, and trade moves quickly. Traders sit in one of the five auction amphitheaters, each of which has enough room for five or six hundred people. They may sit anywhere, but tradition gives the front and center seats to the biggest buyers, generally those working for big import-export companies like Zurel.

Not just anyone can walk in off the street and buy at the auction. You have to register with the auction, which entails an annual fee, and entitles you to make purchases through the clock, as well as other formats mediated by the institution and located on-site. These other formats include 'cash and carry,' which offers a warehouse of garden supplies as well as flowers and plants, and the *bemiddelingsbureau*, a sort of intermediary that negotiates fixed-price sales between growers and buyers. Buyers that use the *bemiddelingsbureau* tend to be large and buy in bulk. In spring, the supermarket chain Albert Heijn might buy millions of tulips through the *bemiddelingsbureau*, for instance, ordering them weeks before they're available. By not purchasing through the clock, they may manage to negotiate a cheaper price with growers; on the other hand, Albert Heijn might find that they paid more on the day of delivery than they would have through the clock. It's a risk, but it offers several advantages. The buyer is guaranteed the quantity desired at a negotiated price; growers are guaranteed to sell their flowers at a price they find acceptable; and the auction institution benefits by positioning itself as the intermediary in even fixed-price negotiations, thus discouraging trade outside of FloraHolland. It works as a sort of futures trade, since it's done in advance and both buyer and seller are gambling that they'll do better this way than through the clock, but the negotiated prices may be higher or lower than what buyers pay through the clock on the day the flowers are delivered.

Before the clocks begin, traders come in to the auction hall and plug in: they take a seat at one of the desks and insert their yellow plastic ID card to a slot on the side, which registers their number with the auction, and other buyers and the auctioneers can see them and follow their purchasing activities. This allows them to see the order the flowers will be sold and thus estimate when they need to pay careful attention. They also put on a headset, which allows them to hear the auctioneers, and to speak to them. When they want to buy, they must be the first to push a button located on the desk, and then say how much of the lot they want – five or twelve or whatever they wish. They follow what's for sale via the clock, which they can see on wide screens positioned above the auction pit, or on their own laptops. Most traders have a laptop for convenience, to see clearly the same clock above them, as well as to follow the clocks in other auction halls, and they carry a mobile phone for quick communication with whom they're buying for, and sometimes also to speak with traders sitting in other auctions.

The 'clock' that they keep such a careful eye on tells far more than time or price. It is a screen with a lot of information that they can process at a glance: the size of the lot to be sold, the price per stem, the name of the grower, the grower's location, a digital photo of the flower, and a quality rating assessed by a team at the auction. Taking up most of the screen, at the center of the clock is a circle marked with one hundred tics (each one eurocent) and a hand that spins past the tics, registering the price. This is a Dutch auction, which means descending bid sales. Prices start high and fall until someone buys the lot. Each purchase stops the clock momentarily, and then bidding continues until the entire lot is sold or until no one will buy. Descending bid sales move far more quickly than the British style ascending bid auctions, and with such a fragile, short-lived commodity, speed is essential. This is how, in a matter of four or five hours, over twenty million flowers and plants can be sold through about one hundred twenty thousand transactions.

In addition to the card and buying number, traders also rent a lot, a space on the floor of the auction warehouse where their purchases will be taken. Information on the product and the buyer are relayed directly to hand-held devices of people working on the auction floor, who move the flowers and plants from the auction hall to the appropriate spot on the floor. Once traders finish buying, they go to their allotted space to inspect and collect their flowers or plants. If there's a problem, they may go to the complaints bureau, which maintains records of all the sales and will help to sort out the confusion. By around eleven o'clock trade is over, and the clocks stop, but activity continues with logistics and transportation to finish the day's business and prepare for the next one.

How traders talk about all this is partly shaped by their conceptions of markets, and where and how the Aalsmeer auction fits in to a larger economic scheme. This circuit flows in both directions. Not only are local practices inflected by popular conceptions of the market, social identity, structural order, and historical memory, but FloraHolland Aalsmeer is also embedded in other institutions, infrastructures, and in the wide cultural diffusion of the horticultural industry. This dynamic helps give the Aalsmeer auctions a sense of place. Markets are, after all, both real places and abstract notions, traditionally distinguished with the terms 'marketplace' and 'the market.' One is somewhere you might go to buy sunglasses, a radio, or flowers; the other is sort of like dark matter in the universe, everywhere and nowhere at once, undetectable in itself, but causing observable effects all over.

But if Aalsmeer as a specific location has critically shaped the industry, as the industry evolves, will communities continue to be geographically defined, and how might this change the ways Aalsmeer and the Dutch shape the flower industry? As the horticultural auctions have begun to shift to the virtual market, we may already begin to answer these questions. As of 2009, forty-five percent of Aalsmeer's trade was already done via remote purchasing – traders bought their products through the auction, but were not necessarily physically on-site when they did so. And auction planners project increasing volumes of e-trade. In fact electronic commerce and information sharing already influence the flower trade in many ways, from digitized images of the product just prior to shipping, to tracking transportation, and online marketing and information. But it seems unlikely that the internet will ever entirely replace the Aalsmeer flower auctions for several reasons. First, the horticultural industry needs a distribution center, a single location where buyers can come to assess and purchase the great variety of products available, because most buyers – be they importers, exporters, wholesalers, or retailers – seek many kinds of plants and flowers. It would be inefficient, and a major step backwards, for traders to suddenly have to coordinate with individual growers across the Netherlands, in Italy and Ethiopia, India and Ecuador. So it's essential to have a single location where buyers can view and buy, and that place should be actual, not virtual, because buyers like to see and touch their product before purchase, especially with a new variety or a new supplier. And if there is a problem with an order, it's convenient to have a central bureau to coordinate complaints and resolve problems. Finally, Aalsmeer has already established itself as a vital commercial and social center for the horticultural industry. Place matters. For another location to replace Aalsmeer, it would have to offer a competitive infrastructure as well as the interconnected social, political, and financial networks that in the Netherlands coordinate trade and direct innovation. There's a popular idea that global business tends to erase or eliminate any traces of local distinctiveness, but in the flower industry, at least, the local space continues to direct the flow of capital and to define horticultural styles. Many plants and flowers 'debut' in Aalsmeer. It's an important commercial testing ground, and, though it's not the only space where networking occurs, it's an important venue for growers, buyers, and other industry people to rub elbows and bounce ideas off each other.

On the other hand, e-trade can dramatically influence the auction's working without necessarily forcing FloraHolland sites to close (although that may happen). Most Dutch growers today have websites and communicate directly with buyers. So for them in today's context the question is, what added value does the auction bring? The auction handles sales and banking, which are huge services, but what has been accepted traditionally, and reflexively, is no longer taken for granted. In an effort to facilitate the transition to more virtual trade, the Aalsmeer rose auction (one of the five auction halls) was the first to stop the practice of showcasing the flowers on carts across the buying theater, where traders can see the product not only in the digital image on the clock above them, but the actual blooms as well. Now that the roses no longer make an appearance, fewer traders physically attend that auction hall. We don't like it very much, some traders told me. "It's weird, there's kind of a cold feel in here without the flowers," said Salim, a rose buyer and one of the few remaining regulars. Others appreciate the speed and convenience.

But the auction's changes haven't led to a fundamental shift in how business is conducted. More buying takes place online, but FloraHolland remains the intermediary, and though the flowers don't move through the auction hall, they still pass through the same building that holds the auction. The traders still connect to the market via headset and computer screen, but now they can link to the market from outside the space of the auction hall. In theory, this opens the market to buyers far from Aalsmeer, even in other countries. But because the expertise is still local, and for the reasons already stated, electronic trade has not displaced local business. Not unlike the *bemiddelingsbureau*, e-trade will likely have the effect of strengthening the institution of FloraHolland over time, ensuring its strong long-term market position. Instead of displacing trade, virtual space just provides more room for it to expand.

Though it may not dramatically alter the trade, it does trigger shifts among traders. On one level, the buyers have a private relationship with the market. They develop a feel for its rhythms, which is based partly on savoir-faire and knowledge of the business, but not entirely. There's always a mysterious element beyond knowledge and experience that flower traders talk about with reverence. Some have described as a sixth sense the anticipation of precisely when to press the button that halts the clock for a purchase. This perspective on the individual's relationship with the market's grace has a religious feel that jibes with the views of traders in the Chicago Board of Trade and other cathedrals of capitalism. But if the market is perceived as a supernatural force, it is also in the trader's bodies, and its effect can seem magnetic. They plug in to the market, and buy electronically, whether they're physically in the auction or elsewhere. In Aalsmeer's auction seating, sometimes they resemble pilots zooming in on their target, tensing shoulders, gritting teeth, and jutting forward in their seat to hit the button.

~

One morning in late March I entered the auction as lot after lot of tulips flashed by for sale. Standing by one of the showcases in back, a group of men were talking passionately. They formed a crescent around the shortest of the group, who stood at maybe five foot three (about a hundred sixty-four centimeters) while the others towered above him. In his mid-fifties, with a jovial air, in a white button-down shirt, dark hair, and thick mustache, the man resembled Nintendo's Mario. He was speaking English with an accent I couldn't discern, and moved his hands in quick circles as he spoke. "You come to my house. You will see. We are going to make lots of money together!" Beside him a younger man who looked like a relative began to translate to Dutch for the two red-haired guys he addressed, but one raised his hand, cracked a grin, and said, "I understand." They continued to talk as they walked out together into the lobby, and down the stairway onto the floor.

After they left, a trader seated nearby looked over his shoulder, gestured with his lips at where the group had stood and smirked at another trader who was idling in the back with a cup of coffee. Both seemed amused. The man had clearly stood out, and not only due to his appearance and because he was talking in English. His élan and his histrionic gestures were like a parody of trader talk, and seemed campy to the regulars, the insiders. The market place has real cultural codes, and in all sorts of ways including this instance, traders express a kind of class consciousness, humor, and irony. Both traders recognized me, though we had never spoken. I approached the guy with the coffee, smiled, and said "We're going to make a lot of money together." He chuckled and replied, "Not around here!"

Perhaps above all in the Dutch horticultural business, manhood epitomizes the style of trade. The livelihood, values, social outlook, cultural and business sensibility all seem to connect to, or to be expressions of, a basic personal sense that many traders have of themselves as men, as Dutch, as members of the community, as breadwinners, and heads of family. But traders also occupy an enduring place in the cultural imagination, in the Netherlands and beyond. Especially in the contemporary world, ideas about market behavior are closely associated with these characters. And although Dutch horticultural traders have only appeared relatively recently, the cultural figure of the trader is much older and more profound, almost an archetype.

At the turn of the twentieth century – just when men in Aalsmeer began to organize their cooperative flower auctions – Georg Simmel was theorizing the main 'types' of characters one finds in any society. The most mysterious and eloquently expressed type was 'the stranger,' a figure he abstracted from the role of traders in nineteenth-century Western Europe. Interestingly, the template of the stranger describes well both the role of the trader and the anthropologist or cultural go-between. Simmel defined the stranger by his status as not having belonged to the community from the beginning. "He is, so to speak, the potential wanderer: although he has not moved on, he has not quite overcome the freedom of coming and going". The stranger is "near and far at the same time". He is at once at home and foreign, both insider and outsider, a traveler and a local, trusted and suspect. The trader-model of the stranger was, of course, Jewish, which also helps to locate him in the nineteenth-century social imagination as someone familiar but somewhat shifty, part of the social landscape but whose loyalty may not be taken for granted. As you say 'trader,' you might even hear the echo of its homonym, 'traitor'. Traitorous may be a hyperbolic characterization of the Dutch horticultural traders, but it is true that, as people who don't produce anything and who make money off of others' work, they are sometimes regarded with suspicion and disdain. Making money off of money is not seen as honest work. For centuries the church outlawed usury, which is one reason money lenders in Europe were often Jewish, and one more thing that marked them as shady or deceitful. These days, of course, traders are associated with Wall Street scams, pilfering and plundering the economy with impunity. Traders exist in this realm of sneaky and nefarious financial activity, or at least are tainted by it.

Clearly, traders do more than fulfill an economic function in society and in the horticultural industry. Flower traders' practices are imbued with a sort of local and national logic. Even without factoring in the advantages of social networks, kinship, or growing up in the industry, a potential trader possesses, merely by virtue of being Dutch and male, the important social framework to become a successful trader. Such a person has social and cultural fluency, an ability to negotiate local codes, to manage networks, to insinuate himself in structures of authority, and business, and is likely already linked to the industry through personal contacts.

Due to their connection to wealth and power, financial traders hold a special allure. A number of films, articles, and books have explored the worlds of these traders, often focusing on scandals such as that of Jérôme Kerviel, who in 2007 through deceptive trading nearly brought down one of France's oldest financial institutions, Société Générale, defrauding the bank of nearly five billion euros. Though fascinating and even seductive (as films like the *Wolf of Wall Street* continually show), financial traders have long been recognized as a destructive force, their greed and reckless behavior causing calamity. After losing a fortune in the financial catastrophe of the South Sea Bubble in 1720, Isaac Newton famously declared, "I can calculate the movements of the stars, but not the madness of men." While these financial traders differ from flower traders in the scale of wealth and power they wield, the two may well be more alike than not. When I asked growers and others not involved directly in sales how they viewed the auction and traders, many quoted their father, uncle, or grandfather saying things like "Never trust a Rijnsburger," (Rijnsburg is a hub for flower traders) or "They don't know what work is." These views tend to be generational, though. One reason for it might be that in today's horticultural business, people may not have career-long jobs – in a decade they could go from trading to marketing to a government-sponsored promotional board. Flower traders may still be seen somewhat as a clique, but less so than in the past.

A far more lucrative, close-knit, and insular group are oil traders. Oil traders seem to operate via a global network, people who know each other and who communicate regularly on mobile phones. In 2008, *Business Week* uncovered what it called "the ultra secretive informal network of traders who dominate global independent oil trading. [...] They are the Rich Boys. All operate in the world of one-time fugitive billionaire Marc Rich, the most-wanted white-collar criminal in U.S. history until his controversial pardon on President Bill Clinton's last day in office in 2001." (His crimes seem almost quaint, however, by comparison with today's climate, where HSBC admits to laundering billions for terrorists and drug cartels and escapes criminal sanction, where sleazy figures like Jamie Dimon are openly admired by officials in charge of prosecuting them.) Rich, who in the 1970s and 1980s was the world's foremost commodities trader working at Phillips

Brothers, has spawned the most powerful informal network of independent commodities traders on earth. Companies run by the Rich Boys span the globe, and include the Netherlands-based Trafigura Group, one of the world's top trading companies. Not all of these powerful, male, financial networks operate conspiratorially, surreptitiously, or on the edge of the law. But like the Dutch flower traders, they have in common this gender element. Lately, there has been an effort to blame 'irrational exuberance' and the formation of economic bubbles not on corruption, lax regulation, or systemic contradictions, but on the male traders themselves. Their hormones, it seems, poison their judgement. A spate of biological studies have purported to examine the role of hormones in financial practices.

In recent years, neuroscientists at Cambridge University and MIT have studied professional securities traders during their normal workday to learn how biochemistry affects financial decisions. They concluded that cortisol and testosterone may cause traders to make wild, outrageous gambles, because of the potential rewards, both financial and emotional. Dr. John Coates, one of the studies' authors, calls it the 'winner effect,' which is when successive victories boost levels of testosterone higher and higher, until the winner is drunk with success, so bullish that he can no longer think clearly, assess risk reliably, or make sound decisions. Dr. Coates, who was also a Wall Street trader during the dot-com bubble, concludes that risk-taking becomes addictive, causing traders to swoon on an emotional high, and this contributes to the formation of market bubbles. He believes that excessive testosterone makes traders foolishly overconfident, exaggerating a market's rise. Too much cortisol, secreted in response to stress, might in turn make traders overly shy of risk, nudging a market's downward slide even more precipitously. The solution he offers is basically to break up the patriarchal, boys club atmosphere. He suggests that a better way to lower extreme levels of testosterone or increase estrogenic effects on a trading floor is to hire more older men and more women. Regardless of its consequences for risk-taking activities, this would be a welcome change, in the interest of promoting more diversity and democracy in elite environments. But it's hard to take such studies too seriously. (One can imagine a trader's defense in court to charges of violating regulations: a temporary insanity plea, my hormones made me do it!)

Dr. Coates' observations and recommendations do merit attention, but not for their dubious revelations of 'male trader behavior' – though human activities may have measurable biological expressions, behavior and cultural patterns can not be reduced to biology. But what's interesting is how scientific and economic discourses gravitate toward the figure of the trader in order to explain how the economic system works, and to celebrate or censure the performance of 'economic man.' Although Aalsmeer is often referred to as 'the Wall street of flowers', buyers in Dutch auctions really are a different breed of trader, and they're not all men.

Kim

"It's a man's world in here," Kim told me the day I met her. She placed both palms on the desk, as though measuring vibrations on a car's dashboard. "Can you feel it? The fuel is testosterone... Vrrroooooom!!!" We laughed, glancing around at the traders; a balding guy within earshot wearing a red flannel shirt turned and playfully stuck out his tongue. Then Kim continued: "Sometimes these guys can get really aggressive, like animals, but you know, mostly they just act like guys buying flowers in the auction – maybe a bit rowdy sometimes, but just themselves, just normal." Just normal meant that mixture of competition and solidarity, locker-room rambunctiousness tempered by serious concentration and dedication, an *ouwe jongens krentenbrood,* a place where a woman's presence is curious and provocative, but tolerated. Kim is a familiar figure, and said she feels the other traders respect her expertise, but that she's not 'one of the guys.'

While Kim's experience as one of the only women in the rose auction is atypical, that may slowly be changing. While the auctions remain overwhelmingly male, more and more women are scattered in among the crowds. But if their appearance is new and unusual, their method of entry to the industry is traditional. I once asked Frans Kuipers why men dominate the flower auctions. A veteran of the Aalmsmeer auction's board of directors, an energetic retiree still active in the business, he looked at me, and raised his eyebrows. "Is that true?" he said. "I think there are a lot of women in the industry. In fact, my own daughter is an auctioneer of plants at FloraHolland," he said with evident pride, and picked up his mobile phone. "I'm calling her right now!" But she wasn't interested in talking. Kim was somewhat unusual not only as a woman, but as a trader open and willing to talk, and possessing the confidence and reflective cast of mind that often offered some significant and penetrating view of the auctions, or the values and practices of traders.

"I have enough money. I don't need to be like – what's that Microsoft guy? – Bill Gates, or like Michael Jackson or Britney Spears. I mean, what would you do with all that money?" Like most traders, Kim's profits are not extravagant. Traders' profits vary, but many of those three thousand people who buy at FloraHolland work for import and export companies, and they earn a modest salary. They're not 'slaves,' but they're also not earning the lion's share of profits in the industry.

"Do you compete specifically with each other," I asked Kim, "keeping an eye on particular buyers?"

"To some extent, yes. Like, people know if a large company is buying a particular flower today. But that kind of thing isn't actually a big part of what goes on here. I mean, do other traders pay much attention to who's buying what at any moment? Maybe, if they're interested in that lot, but otherwise probably not. Sometimes, guys might look at ME, that little lady trader in the back, you know. But Marcel [her husband] also has the same number [the FloraHolland registered buyer's number that shows on the public screen] and no one knows who he is... So it varies, I guess, when and why they pay attention."

Watching them, one might be curious as to how they develop these skills, and more broadly, wonder how they decide to become traders. Often, of course, it runs in the family. One day, I watched a man showing his son the ropes. Looking down at the red button on the side of the desk, the man puckered, winced, and in slow motion drew his finger toward it. He was mocking the physical aspect of the transaction, but at the same time, indicating that the choice of when to push the button involved effort and expertise. For the next purchase, the father-trader raised his hand, formed his index and thumb in the shape of a pistol, thrust his hand forward to the button in a Western 'quick draw' style, 'fired,' and then raised his make-believe gun to blow the smoke from the barrel. The boy beamed at him. Though unusually theatrical, this kind of scene is actually fairly typical. Men often bring their sons to the auctions on a sort of field day. Visits like this, talk over the dinner table, and other practices help to convey cultural and business knowledge, to transmit a 'feel' for the market. Women traders seem to get involved in the same way, learning the ropes through male figures in their family, as was the case with Kim.

Kim's father has for decades sold flowers from his shop across the border in Germany, and has always bought from the auctions in Aalsmeer, which is not far from their home in the Netherlands. Kim grew up tagging along with him, then selling the blooms from their retail store. After buying for a couple of years at the auction, she thought it might be interesting to work as an auctioneer, and did that for a few years before returning to buying for her father once again. This sketch of Kim's background captures the essence of the horticultural system in the Netherlands. Through her father, and growing up with flowers, knowledge and sensibility about the horticultural industry were just bred in the bone. Kim has worked in many places along the production chain – trading, auctioneering, and retailing – so her fluency in and command of the horticultural business is deep. Plus, having also worked outside the industry, she has forged professional links with other sectors of society. The only atypical aspect of Kim's experience in the Dutch flower trade is that she's a woman.

After she had finished her purchases one morning, I sat at an empty desk next to Kim, who has sharp blue eyes and short dark hair. I asked her views on the auction's day-to-day operation, and wondered about her experience that day as the only woman buying among the rose auction's occasionally rowdy men. "Well, what's the expression in English?" she began, and chuckled. "'Boys will be boys? That's what you get here. They call me 'that little lady in the back.'" On another occasion she commented that the attitude could be annoying, but "they're not really that aggressive, and I'm pretty tough." At any rate, they never ganged up to conspire against her buying. But did she ever feel gypped in the trade, and did she often lose money? How did she understand her role in the market?

Her concise, matter-of-fact response might have been lifted straight from an economics textbook. "It's a fair system," she told me. "It regulates itself."

The fair-system-regulating-itself is a familiar outlook that rhymes with popular economic discourse on the free market. On the one hand, the market should remain open and allowed to perform without tampering, and will supposedly stabilize itself the way an ecosystem or a body achieves homeostasis. But unlike nature, in order for this system to work and maintain equilibrium, its ideology must be rigidly enforced, and transgressions against its policies are punished, often severely. (I'm reminded of Eduardo Galeano's famous quip about the Uruguayan military dictatorship enforcing a neoliberal economic order, that people were imprisoned so that the markets could be free.) Though nowadays 'the free market' is sometimes questioned in the mainstream, alternatives are not taken seriously.

Erik

Although the patterns and prices in an auction are determined largely by the traders, there is one figure in an auction who has a uniquely guiding role. The auctioneer introduces the product for sale, sets the pace and rhythm of trade, and directs the bids. Probably we're all familiar with the incantatory qualities of certain auctioneers, who are like barkers. In most auction schools, an important part of the training is how to lead and direct what's known as 'the chant.' But in Aalsmeer, the auctioneer's voice is not important because of the descending bid format. The winner is the first to bid, so the auctioneer does not try to build suspense or drive up the price with his voice, as in other kinds of auctions. The auctioneer sits in a booth at the bottom or to the side of the theater, and business is conducted via headset, so his presence is really only sensed by the traders who are plugged in, and not by visitors or observers. Nevertheless, the auctioneer does play a key role in setting the tempo of trade, and decides the starting price for each lot. The auctioneer works for the auction, which is to say, for the growers, and makes a special effort to fetch the highest price possible, sometimes even testing trader's mettle by opening the bid at an outlandishly high price. A trader unfamiliar with the market value of particular blooms at different times of the year, or someone merely not paying close attention, might slip up and buy at the inflated price. If and when this occurs, it's the source of great jocularity for the group, and singular shame for the trader who screwed up.

Not all auctioneers are men, as both Frans Kuipers' daughter and Kim attest. But perhaps even more than the trader, the auctioneer is a consummately male role, symbolically presiding over the daily sales. In fact, Kim wanted to try auctioneering in part because of the gender challenge. She explained that both the vetting and training of auctioneers for Aalsmeer is grueling and intense. One trial that initiates have to pass involves a mock auction, under live, simulated trade, where you're tested under the speed and pressure of a real day's trade. They do everything they can to cause an auctioneer to trip up or break down. "It was pretty tough," Kim commented. "They really f – - with you, you know. There was another woman in the room with me that day, and they made her break down into tears. I was not going to let that happen to me." She didn't crack under the pressure, and for several years she was an auctioneer in Aalsmeer.

Like virtually every other position in the flower trade, auction-eers tend to come from a horticultural background. This was true not only for Kim, but also for Erik, who worked for fifteen years at the Aalsmeer auctions, first as a trader and then, since 2005, as an auctioneer. Auctioneering requires intense concentration, and so the auctioneers split their shifts, working only an hour at a time. One morning settling in beside Erik in the auction booth, I asked why more women didn't hold his position. "*Ik vind het wel lastig. Tsja, vervelend*," (It's a shame, really too bad), he said. "But there are some, and the ones we have, like Kim, have been really good." A woman was emptying the trash as Erik spoke, and we both looked over at her. She nodded and repeated the line so often spoken, "It's a man's world." Trading isn't a prerequisite for auctioneering, but it certainly helps, as both Kim and Erik said.

Seeing the auction from the booth offers a different angle on trade. I was surprised, for instance, to finally see the importance of the mental and digital aspects of buying, which is to say that the silence was even more apparent. You don't hear much over the headsets. Erik may occasionally roll his R's or exaggerate a vowel, but mostly his voice is even and measured; from the hundreds of the traders, you hear "four... seven... no sorry, six... two..." which is them indicating to the auctioneer how many they are purchasing, once they've pushed the button to freeze the clock, and have won the bid. So most of the trade is silent, hap-pening on the screen and in the minds and bodies of the traders. "Some of those guys wiggle around a lot in their seats," said Erik. "Just look at them moving around, it's like they're playing a video game, which in a way, I guess, they are." Watching the action on screen, they push a button in competition to win. And, says Erik, "It's fun. I like working here. The business is never boring." Though Erik is now an auctioneer, he still also buys, though obviously not at the same time he's auctioneering. The morning I met him, in fact, he had just returned from a trip to Moscow, where he met with some high-end rose buyers. In his dual roles as auctioneer and entrepreneur, Erik has a keen sense of what flowers, particularly roses, look like as a commodity.

Salim

One morning after the auctions ended, I struck up a conversation with a trader I had seen, minutes earlier, smash his fist on his desk and mutter "shit" after missing the price he wanted for some Vermeer Orchids. As one of the few non-whites among the hundreds of traders, I wondered about his experience at FloraHolland. Wearing a red-sleeved leather jacket I would come to recognize him in almost every day, Salim said he'd had an okay day trading, though yes, he missed his opportunity on the orchids.

"It can be stressful for all of us guys in there," he explained, and laughed. "But I just got some other orchids. Not a big deal, really. My buyer won't care," he said in English. Since he described himself as part of a group, I asked him if he became a trader, as so many do, through family connections.

He explained he'd worked in the auction for sixteen years, but did not begin as a trader. He worked for a Greek trader for several years before the man wanted to go back to Athens, and when he did, he asked Salim to buy for him at the auction. Salim went on to say, "My family never had anything to do with flowers, no way. They came here from Pakistan, but I was born here. I speak Dutch. On the phone, I am Dutch."

"So, you're Dutch? Or just while you're on the phone?" I asked.

"Yeah..." He laughed. "I am Dutch, basically, but to them sometimes maybe not. I'm the only black one around, as I'm sure you've noticed. But I never have any problems. I grew up here. I went to school here. Yeah, OK, I'm Dutch."

He went on to explain how, in the auctions, when you've got your mind focused and eyes on the clocks, "[who you are] doesn't really matter, you've just got to know how to push the button," which electronically signals the auctioneer that you're buying. (Some of Salim's clients are Swedes and Danes, others are German and French, and most are in Western Europe.) Similar to many other Aalsmeer traders, Salim is jovial and sometimes engages in pranks and antics. He's also easy-going, friendly, and occasionally cracks jokes about race and nationality. Once, while we were talking (in 2008), my phone rang. "Quick call from Bush?" he asked wryly, knowing some of my disapproving opinions of U.S. policies. He went on to say that he had family in New York, Atlanta, and Houston, "which really is Bush country." He groaned. I asked, "It seems like there's a lot of Pakistanis in Houston – why is that?"

"There are, right? I don't know why. Maybe Cape Canaveral. Maybe because we love to take off in rocket ships..." He cupped his hand to his ear. "...'Houston, Houston we have a problem!' There are a bunch of Pakistanis on board. Repeat: Pakistanis on board. Our ship's full of Pakistanis... Request advice on how to proceed."

One morning toward the end of trading, Salim and his colleagues were tossing wads of paper and packets of sugar at the traders making the final bids. One guy in a denim jacket with a sprinkling of gray stubble across his cheeks swiped Salim's pack of Marlboros off the desk, and raised an eyebrow. "Sure, go ahead," said Salim. A moment later, the three of us were standing in the glassed-in smoking area in the lobby. After some discussion of that day's prices, I asked them if they felt that the Netherlands is changing as much as so many contemporary news reports suggest, or as Wilders' supporters warn.

Salim's colleague confessed that he didn't pay much attention to the news, nor really, think very much about the country in general. His focus was more on business, he said, and then on his family and enjoying his free time. Those were his priorities. Salim said that he didn't spend a lot of time thinking about issues of integration necessarily, but that in the flower business generally and in his experience particularly, some reflection was essential. He also said: "I do think the Netherlands is changing a little. I can't say if I'm an example of it. But for sure, you wouldn't see a guy like me here in the flower auctions ten or twenty years ago." Salim's buddy had stubbed out his cigarette and left by then. The rose auction was closing down, and traders were filing out toward their lots, to the complaints bureau, for a quick smoke, or to the bathroom. Did Salim think this scene would look the same in five or ten years? "Yes and no. I had a fortune cookie once. It said 'Life is the Process of Many Changes.'" We both laughed. "Maybe there'll be more *allochtonen* like me, who knows. Maybe less trading here. Already they don't bring the flowers down there," he said. "I think it will be different. But basically the same."

'Death or Gladiolas'? On the Floor with Karl at FloraHolland Aalsmeer

After the 2006 Bloemenveiling Aalsmeer/FloraHolland merger, profits grew and the institution's market position strengthened, but FloraHolland employees weren't initially rewarded with those benefits. The people who trim flower stems on site, haul carts, work in offices, and perform dozens of other tasks that ensure smooth-running logistics actually got what amounted to a cut in pay. And they were asked to contribute a higher percentage of their salary for retirement. They were told that this was because of the economic crisis, and some felt that in this new deal they were being told, in effect: take it or leave it, be thankful for whatever we offer. Meanwhile, the auction's managers got "fat bonuses", as it was often put. CNV Dienstenbond and FNV Bondgenoten represent FloraHolland workers (as well as others in the horticultural sector, and many white-collar workers: they're the Netherlands' biggest unions). Most of my conversations with union representatives took place before this conflict, and no one indicated animosity toward FloraHolland management; in fact, among workers I spoke to, what most struck me was how dedicated to their jobs they seemed. The occasional frustration they expressed was that, if only this or that happened, they could increase efficiency. At least once I laughed in disbelief, not sure I was understanding what I was being told. My expectation, I explained, and I suspect that of many people, would be just the opposite: given that this is not full-time work for many and that they're not high-wage jobs, most people would try to do the least possible, not strive to work harder or devise ways to better organize movement or improve practices. Don't misunderstand,

I was told: we're not all happy worker-bees, plenty of people "don't give a shit." They show up for work with a hangover and just want to do the minimum requirements. Naturally, to the extent that it came up, people expressed a range of views on the subject. One guy who had worked on the floor for over a decade explained that in his opinion, most of his colleagues, particularly the younger ones, both worked hard and partied hard. It's not a 'career job' for many of them. But regardless of motivation or morale, everyone seemed aware of the global dimensions of the business, had some local connection with the industry (family or friends working in the horticultural sector), and more or less enjoyed a certain prestige in being associated with the institution.

FloraHolland employees have a strong position in the sale of flowers and plants given that each day they help move about twenty million cut flowers through the Aalsmeer auction alone. They do a lot to ensure the institution's reputation for reliability, and thus to keep steady the daily flow of millions of euros in profits. If the institution was still profitable and the higher-ups in FloraHolland were being rewarded, why should the workforce that is the least well compensated but that performs essential tasks be asked to sacrifice? The apparent double standard in responding to the economic crisis didn't sit well with employees. In April 2010, citing "kwaad bloed" (bad blood) between FloraHolland management and workers, they threatened a strike, something clearly worrisome for auction policymakers. The CNV representative made the announcement with brio. "In termen van de bloemen," he said "het is voor hen nu de dood of de gladiolen!" ("In floral terms, for them, now it's do or die, death or gladiolas!") Faced with the stark choice, FloraHolland opted for the gladiolas: they agreed to a two percent raise for the workers (to be implemented over the following two years) as well as some other concessions regarding scheduling and workplace management.

I went to several (not well-attended) union meetings in 2008, and over the course of fieldwork spoke with about two dozen workers on the floor about their experience at FloraHolland

Aalsmeer, about how, why, and when they got into the industry, and what they thought about the institution, flowers, and more. Most are under 40, and in contrast to the white-male world of traders, there are many so-called *allochtonen* (a derogatory term for non-white Dutch) on the floor, as well as many women. A number of people are religious and there have been discussions about making an area in the Aalsmeer auction available for prayer. The guy on the floor I got to know best had a long history in Aalsmeer and was well-known among his colleagues. Tall, handsome, blond, and gay, Karl was also gregarious and eccentric. And, unusually for someone in his position, he is the son of a grower. According to Karl, his father made a lot of money growing gerberas (which were sold in Aalsmeer's auction) and retired early. On our first meeting, he explained, "My dad worked here his whole life, but whereas I work on the floor here with the *allochtonen*, he was a grower, which is more prestigious. I remember I used to come here as a kid, and now, look at me. I never ever ever, I mean never, thought I'd wind up here. It's ironic. I mean literally right here on this spot. But then I started working here, and then it just kind of gradually sunk in, and now I feel at home." With so much personal history there, Karl felt a strong sense of place.

"I like it here, I do," he added. "Never boring, not to me. Never a dull moment. Anything you want, any kind of person in the world, almost, you can find here. And it's not hard work, either, I think. I mean, I'm sorry, don't get me wrong, but some of these Moroccan boys, these young guys, they work here because it's an easy job. Easy money. For some people they do it so they can go to school, since it's part-time work. But not everybody. I really like it. People might not be like the highest class or whatever, but I'm more comfortable with them. I mean, I'm not high class either."

"It's interesting to see how we all turned out," he continued. "I know one guy who's now a big-wig in everything." He pursed his lips and made a snooty face, referring to someone who became a successful trader for an export company. "He started out working for my father. We worked together, actually. But now

I still work on the floor, I'm shit, and he moved up. We're still working in the same place, actually, but you know, in completely different worlds. Yes, it's like that here…" Karl went on to explain that the workforce is highly segregated, and that, even for him, with personal ties to other parts of the auction and the industry, his main contacts and his social world are on the floor where he works.

In such a masculine, and often macho environment, I wondered what it was like for Karl being gay, and out, at work. "It's not really a big deal," he said. "If someone doesn't like it, well, that's their problem. I'm not going to censor myself. But others might [censor themselves], you know, I think it's mostly to do with my personality. Everybody knows me, I'm quite popular. I mean, I'm also a slut, and I flirt with everybody. And you know, most of these tough young guys accept me, no problem. Some of the older guys, like especially ones who are religious or weren't born here, I know they don't like it, but so what."

One late morning at the end of his shift, as we walked around the auction warehouse, Karl pointed out equipment and explained how it worked, often in nationalist terms that vaguely recalled FloraHolland's marketing language. "Have you seen this system, this conveyor lift?" he asked, pointing at one end of an enormous conveyor system running along the ceiling. Day and night, Coca-Cola-red pincers clamp onto and lift flower carts – specially designed with adjustable shelves to haul buckets of flowers and heavy plants, FloraHolland owns or rents over a million of them. The system carries these carts between one side of the highway, the part of the building that houses the auctions below which Karl and I were talking, and shuttles them over an enclosed bridge to the other side, where many import and export companies have their headquarters. The conveyor system is several kilometers long and, by avoiding constant back-and-forth truck traffic, saves considerable time and resources, and reduces diesel pollution. Waving an arm across the length of one section of the conveyor, Karl said, "I don't think Dutch people could ever even conceive of such a thing, you know. This contraption was built by the Germans. Germans are like you Americans, and maybe like the Chinese, too: they think BIG. You know, us little Dutch people, we're always thinking small and local, like we're all from these *kleine dorpjes* [little towns]."

"Ah, okay," I responded. "But look at this gigantic place, the biggest in the world. It's Dutch, right? Isn't that thinking big?"

"Yeah, I guess. But people's mentality is what I mean. They think so small, so local, just about your neighbor or whatever. It's pathetic really, I think."

Karl's mentality reflects considerable international experience. He's lived in Australia, and traveled extensively in both North America and Asia. (One night I visited his apartment in Uithoorn, he showed his guests slides of his recent trip to India.) His ex-boyfriend of several years is African-American and works in a bank; Karl has also worked in the Cirque du Soleil (in the office, not as a performer). In addition to the flower business, which he knows a lot about, he spoke to me about science fiction and fantasy books and films, masculinity and flowers, hypnosis, and race.

One day, when I approached him on a work break, Karl stripped off his gloves, stuffed them in his back pocket, and sighed. He told me some days he really just hates his job, and would like to do something outside the flower business, something completely different. Like others in FloraHolland, Karl told me he would like to write a book about the place. "I think I could write maybe even a novel, something that takes place here but is a science fiction book." Gesturing to the warehouse panorama, he continued. "Like: it's after the Bomb, and now everybody's living underground. And it looks just like this." As we walked, he pointed to girders, machinery, the conveyor belt, and there were sounds of clanking metal, the hydraulic hiss of delivery truck shocks. He shouted so I could hear him over the din. "In the story, we now all live below the earth! People have little windows way up to the surface and they manage to get things down! It looks like these!" he said, pointing to a ventilator shaft and two square windows along the ceiling bright with clouds. "Of course, everyone's different, too," continued Karl as we ambled to a quieter area. "All the white people, they get even whiter. And of course the black people get blacker. But eventually the black people get the idea to go out again on to the surface of the planet. After like 350 years. And they slowly realize that now they can survive there, but not anybody else. So they move up onto earth, and the situation in our world now is sort of reversed. Now THEY'RE in charge..." His voice trailed off wistfully. "That would be something, now, wouldn't it? But the world is a crazy place. You never know what might happen." I commented to the effect that it didn't sound like a hospitable environment for flowers, except maybe for some unusually hardy orchids that can live on active volcanoes. "You're right," said Karl thoughtfully. "It would be a totally different place: no more Aalsmeer, no more tradition."

~

Although the auctions are intimately bound together with the Dutch present and its past, they have a kind of timeless quality, since auctions have had similar social and economic roles in vastly different cultures, times, and places. Though they existed in pre-capitalist societies, they became more prominent in the modern capitalist period, and may in this respect resemble money, as many pre-capitalist societies also had coins and monetary systems, but as the capitalist system took root, money and the ideology of money penetrated social life more thoroughly. Perhaps auctions are linked to primordial community attitudes toward value, and stand outside the rise and fall of particular cultures or economic systems. Besides the historical continuum of auctions, temporality is an important practical element of any auction, especially the flower auctions. In Aalsmeer, not timelessness, but time is of the essence because the passage of time affects the freshness of cut flowers, and therefor their value. With split-second sales and thousands of daily transactions, the clock is the pivotal instrument at the auctions.

Though many assume auctions tend to represent the bare machinery of the free market, economists nevertheless devise rules for particular auctions in order to perfect that machinery, and/or to benefit the sellers and organizers of the auction. In recent years, some economists (such as Paul Klemperer) pursuing this line of thinking have used game theory and advanced mathematics to devise complex models for different kinds of bidding strategies and, by tweaking the rules of operation, have investigated effects in real world auctions, such as those of U.S. government bonds and e-band width. Some of these insights have led to innovations in auction rules and design. But since the social world is inevitably more complex, dynamic, and unpredictable than models can account for, results of some of these studies have been mixed.

In 2007, research in this vein looked at Aalsmeer's cut flower and plant auctions, in a paper called *If Winning Doesn't Matter, Why Do They Keep Score? A Structural Empirical Analysis of Dutch Flower Auctions*. Calculating the micro-second reflexes of hand-eye coordination, the authors compared reaction times between winning and losing bids to measure the reserve price against the timing of the bids. They were interested in which factors led to faster bidding. But carefully entering the data of hundreds of thousands of transactions into elaborate formulae ultimately allowed them to draw rather modest and banal conclusions about the speed of the bidding, for instance "that reputation is very important at the AFA [the plant auction]," something which is self-evident to any trader, or any grower, since growers work hard to cultivate their reputation. Economic work on auctions is often like this – perhaps insightful and revealing about the logistics and technologies involved with buying and selling, but not very savvy about basic questions of value, since auctions are seen through a sort of tunnel vision, as highly complex mechanical contraptions that can be refined and manipulated through sophisticated techniques and ever more finely tuned mathematical modeling.

It's worth noting that auction designs that relied on this way of seeing have occasionally led to seller furor and frustration. In the 1990s, companies and governments turned to economists to design auctions for selling mobile phone companies, and they used game theory to predict how bidding would go. Auctions, it seems, were selected as the method of selling for noble and democratic reasons: to ensure fairness, to prevent the property and access from merely going to those companies with the most political muscle. But something curious happened when the auction designs were carried out in real life – a crucial factor had been overlooked. When British mobile phone spectrum was auctioned, an unforeseen dynamic developed: collusion between bidders. Bidders worked together to find the best price for themselves! No type of cooperation formed part of the designer's picture of the way auctions work, or might even potentially work. Participants working together surprised them because previously economists designing auctions assumed that buyers behaved strictly according to individualistic codes. The modeler's flaw was to assume that everyone would act independently; instead they cooperated. Auction designers understood this as an obstacle for more sophisticated architecture to subvert.

Although collusion involves scheming together, it is not the same as the basic cooperation one finds in any auction. When buyers collude, it is to subvert the system by bamboozling the seller. Collusion happens when two or more bidders make illegal arrangements not to bid up the auction price. But tacit collusion – where bidders signal their intentions or make 'offers' to other bidders through the bid itself which can also depress prices – is perfectly legal. Klemperer became famous for helping the British government to sell high bids on mobile phones, in the wake of the notoriously flawed Swiss auction in which telecom companies vying for rights colluded to submit low bids, and the government was forced to sell off its rights at dirt-cheap prices. In Aalsmeer, as in most auctions, buyers don't have to conspire to keep bidding low. Instead they share a tacit understanding that the system is sound and fair, and that the seller will receive the best price based on the buyer's (sincere) individual and communal assessment of value. At least two other basic features of Aalsmeer's auction make collusion irrelevant. One is that growers set a minimum price below which they will not sell. (It's the grower's institution, so they set the rules. But on the other hand, if their flowers or plants don't sell, they must pay a penalty to the institution, so it's in their interest to keep their minimum price reasonable.) The other factor making collusion improbable involves the obvious case that unlike the world of oil and telecommunications, horticulture is cheap and highly perishable.

The point here is that forms of cooperation stubbornly remain important factors in auctions and other market behavior, but designers and participants typically overlook this, since they seem to have a blind faith in a particular vision. Namely, that markets are free and fair, and the system's balance and integrity relies on the trader's inherent competitive and selfish nature. On the other hand, it's important to emphasize that pointing out principles of cooperation does not mean an absence of competition, nor imply the kind of democratic, communal values one might find in, say, an anarchist factory collective in Argentina. While there isn't as strict a pecking order in Aalsmeer as one might find in the stock market or a high price government auction, there are big players and small players. There are echelons of influence.

In the plant auction, when Gonzalo told me that the traders were really just slaves and *campesinos* of the system, he was only giving part of the picture. For most traders most of the time, that's probably a pretty fair assessment. Most at FloraHolland are small: between eighty and eighty-five percent of traders buy just fifteen to twenty percent of the products sold in Aalsmeer. But the big fish, the top five percent of traders, buy almost fifty percent. Of the thirty-five hundred registered buyers, several hundred work exclusively in the Dutch market, and are thus local figures that tend to earn a modest income. There is a hierarchy of traders, which is apparent in where they seat themselves in the auction theaters. By tradition, the bigger traders sit in the center and toward the front of the arena. This used to give the large traders some advantage in the time before the digital clocks (in the early 2000s), which show photos and display extensive market information about the product. These days, when trade is conducted via headset and laptop, it doesn't much matter where a trader sits, or even, increasingly, whether they're in the auction at all, since they may purchase online from any location. The grouping of traders in the auction doesn't really indicate a pecking order. In fact, big and small traders can switch positions – a big trader can lose and slip in his financial and market position just as a small trader can rise and gain wealth and position. Traders understand that due to the market forces beyond their control, and/or because of good or bad judgement, they could wind up in another situation – it's part of their shared reality.

While the Aalsmeer auctions are barely a century old, the institutional form of selling is at once ancient and contemporary, both pre-capitalist and stitched into the patchwork of the current world economic system. Though already an institutional element of the classical world, auctions seem somehow to embody the raw essence of capitalism, a kind of arena where the parabolas of supply and demand most clearly intersect, represents the most unbiased method of sales, and in this way constitute the core of the market. But at the same time, there's something slightly sneaky about auctions, perhaps because of the unpredictability and occasional volatility of prices. Some Dutch argot reflects this almost seedy sensibility. "In de veiling nemen" or "door de veiling sleuren" (literally, to take someone in, or drag someone through, the auction) is to trick someone, to pull their leg. I never heard anyone use these expressions in Aalsmeer; they appear to be archaic slang from a generation or two ago. In the 1930s they first appeared in print when a popular Rotterdam writer named Willem van Lependaal used them in his stories. Nevertheless, the expressions suggest a distrust of auctions. In Dutch, veilen, the verb meaning to auction, dates back as far as the fourteenth century, and even then referred to a primitive kind of public bidding.

In languages with stronger Romantic ties, many auction words derive from Latin, including, of course, 'auction' itself, which comes from *augeo*, which means to enrich, and increase or augment. Also closely related to the contemporary sense of auctioning is the Latin *augur*, as in to augur or foretell, as in an augury or omen. An augur was an official diviner in ancient Rome, someone who often used objects or signs to make predictions and whose authority was socially endowed, though assumed to come not from the community but from a supernatural source. (In those days, it was a God; today's almighty is the market.) In other ways, too, this sense of divination or auguring carries over implicitly into the auction, since the auction is also an arena that inaugurates, or formally ushers into the world, a commodity by assigning it a price. This inauguration also has occurred with people, in the cases of slaves and of wives who were sold in the earliest auctions on record. And there are other lingering traces of ancient auctions in both contemporary sensibility and language. The Romans called the auction a 'subasta,' (still the Spanish term; Italians say 'asta') which is a contraction of two Latin words, sub hasta, literally "under spear." Roman soldiers would auction off the spoils of war by driving a spear in the ground to demarcate the market, and sell the booty to the highest bidder, or 'emptor.' This led to Roman slave auctions in the forum being held under the sign of a spear, and kept the word in use. Typically, the auctioned slaves were captives of some Roman military conquest, and the profits helped to subsidize the campaign.

In pre-modern times, auctions were not as widespread as they have become with the advent of capitalism, but even in the ancient world they had functions akin to those of the modern era. As long ago as Roman (and before that, Babylonian) times, auctions served to resolve problems of establishing the value and ownership of objects – those gathered primarily from looting and pillaging; and the value, ownership, and identity of people – those unfortunate men bonded into slavery, as well as young women sold, often along with other property, into marriage. With regard to slavery, auctions seemed to have had a similar function in both the ancient and the early modern era, because when people became slaves, they acquired a new identity as well as a new owner, and this transformation in status required both social sanction and a ceremony to structure, legitimize, and record the event. In the contemporary period, auctions continue to establish the value and ownership of objects, an aspect especially pronounced in police auctions of recovered stolen goods, and in auctions of the estates of deceased people. Under such circumstances, the auction clarifies the value and the ownership of the property. But the really interesting aspect is not in the uncertain value of the things or in who they belong to, but in the communal character of the sale, for both the price and method for establishing value is legitimized by community approval and endorsement.

Horticultural Aesthetics

There are things
we live among 'and to see them
is to know ourselves'
George Oppen

The annual International Horti Fair held in Amsterdam RAI presents an important platform for cutting-edge technologies, services, and providers, and attracts visitors from around the world eager to showcase what they have to offer, to see the latest and future trends, and to meet people. One of the biggest global horticultural events, the Horti Fair evolved alongside, and partly through, the Aalsmeer auction. The original Flower Trade Show developed in Aalsmeer in 1963 from Bloemenlust and CAV (Aalsmeer's founding auctions); in the 1970s it moved to the current FloraHolland center in Aalsmeer, and focused on what was called 'food crop horticulture and technique' and 'floriculture, floricultural technique, and trade.' Combining after 1972 to make the NTV, which pushed forward Dutch horticulture's international agenda, the show quickly became the premier promotional event for Dutch horticulture and today attracts around 50,000 visitors from over 100 countries. Over the years, I've attended several of these week-long events, and 2008's was typically quirky.

Through Amsterdam RAI's vast show hall loitered thousands of people, mostly consisting of men wearing dress shirts and jeans. Booths offered demos and horticultural tackle, and tents hosted exhibits varying from conveyor belts circulating potted orchids beneath LED lights to floral arrangement competitions taking place before speakers booming House music. In these Horti Fair venues, the breadth of technical enterprise behind the production, presentation, and transportation of commercial flowers and plants is on display. Like other aspects of the industry, the event is firmly embedded in Dutch civic life. Horti Fair's 2010 chairman, Ewald van Vliet, was the former alderman of Westland, the first mayor of Lansingerland, and represents a sort of bobo or big linker, a power player and uniting figure in politics and horticulture. Individuals like this illustrate just one way horticulture connects with political, social, and commercial institutions in the Netherlands. In addition to these sorts of figures, annual events also do a lot to support the industry, ranging from the bloemencorsos, which emphasize aesthetic and folkloric facets of Dutch horticulture, to trade shows like the Horti Fair, which encompasses business, technical, and aesthetic aspects.

In 2008, the Horti Fair in Amsterdam RAI offered some curious displays of floral aesthetics, including a tent devoted to 'the art of the possible' featuring artificially colored flowers. Few people seemed interested the afternoon I visited, and stepping through the striped flap of the entrance, my eyes fell on the single rose illuminated in a glass display case. Each of the three people standing before it seemed surprised, or slightly repulsed. Two of them quickly moved on, and I was left with Hans, a fiftyish former rose grower and current breeder who bore a striking resemblance to Bruce Willis. Hans wrinkled his nose. It turned out that he knew the rose's designer, and averred that he was slightly embarrassed for the guy, an acquaintance. The rose was sprayed purple with silver glitter, a burlesque thing in a sleek black vase. If this long-stemmed bloom under a spotlight had been a performer, it might have been late Elvis – rhinestone studded, entrancing, and mawkish. Hans and I were transfixed by its gaudy glamor and the sheer shellacked surface of its flawless form. Roses dipped in tints and misted in sparkles don't arouse many consumers in the Netherlands, but are most popular in France, which was the market for this rose. Something about its artificiality, or the emotions it triggered, or the awareness of all this fanfare, capital, and marketing around flowers and plants suddenly seemed rather odd.

As I nodded and gawked at the display, it struck me, as though for the first time, that flowers really are commodities, and that as important as auctions, institutional practices, history, infrastructure, and networking are to this global business, the horticultural industry is fundamentally about the creation and evolution of these fragile objects. The realization that this commodity drives the industry seemed both obvious and strange. Clearly, the trade is organized around selling plants and cut flowers, but what seemed so remarkable was the extent of infrastructure, money, and planning that goes into it, the level of technical wizardry in growing and transportation, the pageantry of institutional events, the compelling appeal of the flowers, and the passion and sentiment of so many figures in the industry. The cumulative effect was impressive and seemed unparalleled. And yet, in many respects other agricultural trades might not be so different: the industrialization of the process certainly isn't unique, and many farmers have sentimental attachments to their crops or their animals. Also, in lots of ways, flowers resemble other commodities. As with bananas or wheat, flowers are mass produced; like copper and tomatoes, their value is set each day via auction; and they have a quality economists call fungibility, which means that like coal or sugar each identical unit has equal value – one orange gerbera should be indistinguishable from any other from the same lot. Production is carefully controlled to create a homogenous crop, to eliminate individual distinctions and imperfections. It's only a slight exaggeration to say that growers, breeders, and buyers alike aspire for each bloom to achieve a sort of archetypal form akin to a platonic ideal. Color, bud size, stem length, and much more must be reliably generated again and again. Both producers and consumers want predictable, stable qualities with little variance; blemishes, aberrations, and idiosyncrasies reduce the market value.

But if there's clearly a science to production, the products themselves are aesthetic objects, and part of their appeal is that they're enticing, delicate, and evanescent. Commercial flowers are luxury goods, and are typically distinguished from mineral or food commodities as optional and even superfluous, since one buys flowers only once one's basic needs are taken care of. But while it's true that in the twentieth century, the dramatic rise in wealth and a market for commercial goods enabled the emergence of the commercial flower industry, the same can be said of many agricultural products, livestock, industrial metals, and plenty of other commodities. These industries and commodities are what they are today because of a large, middle-class consumer market. No one doubts that we need food, but not commercial flowers, to survive. But actually, this reasoning doesn't carry too far, since it's equally true that human society could endure without bananas, beef, oranges, and many other supposedly essential commodities. Nevertheless, these various commodities are hardly interchangeable with horticultural products; they do belong in different categories. After all, on occasions of affection, mourning, celebration, and intimacy, people don't typically exchange string beans. Flowers are most distinct from other commodities not because they're less essential, but because of their sentimental attractions and meanings.

They tug at our emotions, nourish a sense of beauty, characterize traditions, and inspire wonder – an anomalous sort of commodity. Marx may as well have been referring to twenty-first-century commercial flowers when he wrote, "A commodity appears, at first sight, a very trivial thing, and easily understood. Its analysis shows that it is, in reality, a very queer thing, abounding in metaphysical subtleties and theological niceties". That shimmering rose in its Horti Fair showcase may have lacked metaphysical subtleties and theological niceties, but its appeal certainly inspired curiosity; it was indeed a queer thing, and its peculiarities lay not only in its appearance but in its effects on us. Above all, the horticultural product is bound up with emotional and aesthetic needs and impulses. For consumers of cut flowers, these objects always and inevitably communicate social and cultural meanings. Ornamental flowers have no utilitarian purpose, nor do they ensure the smooth functioning of the contemporary world economy, but how we assess their value and how we exchange them both socially and commercially do suggest some things about cultural logic, and about how and in whose interests the market works. In this sense, so-called luxury items are very revealing. Our taste – what we prefer, consume, and how we go about consuming things – communicates a ton of social and cultural information about many things, including affection and other emotions, identity, aesthetics, societal position, gender, class, nationality, and community.

Horticulture's social significance is crafted through aesthetics by many professionals along the production chain, particularly breeders and florists, as well as those in a lab or greenhouse. As in the early days of tulip cultivation, scientific, commercial, and cultural interests overlap in the creation of floral aesthetics. And even more than during those early days of Dutch horticulture, today the floral commodity is grown, marketed, and distributed in an international context. In this world system, the Dutch set aesthetic and market trends, which are partly, but not entirely, forged through technology, capital, efficient production and distribution, and other material factors. Breeders and florists influence market trends and aesthetics, but more broadly, aesthetics evolve and are sustained through relationships and practices – male networks, infrastructure, institutions, and social traditions. The first century of the Dutch flower auction system has produced or encouraged a number of activities and traditions that self-consciously invoke an imagined past – tulip-naming ceremonies and bloemencorsos most notably, but traditions like Valentine's Day and Mother's Day are also largely sustained by the flower industry. Many of these traditions are about honoring, enhancing, and enriching relationships. So the conception of horticultural aesthetics is closely involved in the emotional and cultural meanings and social function of plants and flowers, which in turn, shape the production of the commodity.

Understanding the dynamics of horticultural commodities at auction tells only part of the story of the cut flower's cultural performance. For a fuller appreciation of this performance, one might consider the commercial flower or plant in Forest Hylton's words, as "a social hieroglyph – not as a thing, but as a complex relation between networks and organizations of people, as well as between states and bureaucracies – [and if we do so,] we may glimpse some of the distinguishing features of the contemporary world". But flowers are also important in themselves, as objects. They are inscrutable without looking carefully at them as things, too, and examining how people invent, breed, design, market, and consume them. To focus exclusively on their social footprint would be like trying to understand the appeal of a film by tallying box office profits but without ever seeing it or evaluating its context, or analyzing a politician's appeal by ballot statistics alone: you would miss an essential quality.

Looking carefully at luxury goods involves a consideration of the aesthetics of their presentation. The depiction of horticultural commodities has a long historical background. How and when did flowers become commodities? What has the Netherlands contributed to the creation of flowers as a commodity? The answers are more suggestive than definitive. They involve not only contemporary traditions and social and commercial institutions, but aesthetic practices in the Dutch Golden Age including mapmaking, tulip production, and still life. Mapmaking provided one way for the Dutch to "market the world," as historian Paula Findlen has put it, to trade not only commodities but to promote a worldview with the Dutch Republic at the center of a global economy. In this period, tulips became a metonymy for the social upheaval and the transition to a market economy. And still-life painting produced in the seventeenth century drew attention to objects (particularly perishable commodities, including flowers), and this way of looking at things both reflected and helped to create the new kinds of human relationships emerging in this nascent market-capitalist culture. Still life helped to stoke popular enthusiasm and values for cut flowers. And some of the same figures involved in the tulip trade and VOC (familiar *burgemeesters* and *stadhouders* such as Frederick Ruysch) also collected still life – both circulated in male networks, a particular kind of masculine, profit-driven, aesthetic circuit and value system.

~

Although George Oppen likely referred to images of U.S. atrocities in Vietnam when he wrote: "There are things/ we live among 'and to see them/ is to know ourselves'", the reflexive sentiment in these lines applies well to our affinity with commodities. The lines assert a relationship, a sort of economy, between things (which aren't specified), people, and knowledge, regardless of whether the tone is philosophical or political. Seeing the things one lives among, really looking at them, is in fact a central tenet of the Dutch still life of the seventeenth century, and Julie Hochstrasser frames her understanding of the paintings in this way. In *Still Life and Trade in the Dutch Golden Age*, she asks what the region's "sudden and rather astonishing focus on material culture – bluntly on objects in fact – reveal to us about the history of the Netherlands, Europe, and the world in the seventeenth century".

Along with the period's colonial expansion, the Atlantic slave trade, scientific discoveries, economic innovation and prosperity, the Dutch Golden Age generated an incredible amount of art, which included not only still life, but historical scenes emphasizing allegories and religious motifs, maps, portrait painting, and other scenes of everyday life. Because of the abundance and availability of paintings (about 70,000 per year during the century), ordinary people often displayed art in their homes. Historian Michael North also records that "works of art, ranging from simple prints and copies to original paintings, hung in almost all Dutch houses… [although] probably less than one percent of seventeenth-century pictures have survived. (The legacy of such output led J.H. Huizinga to open his long essay *Dutch Civilization in the Seventeenth Century* with the statement: "Were we to test the average Dutchman's knowledge of life in the Netherlands during the seventeenth century, we should probably find that it is largely confined to odd stray notions gleaned from paintings".) Still life (*stilleven* in Dutch) constituted an enduring segment of this visual media. It featured both familiar and exciting new objects in a medium that highlighted – and helped to arouse in viewers – their mysterious, seductive, and otherwise appealing qualities.

Still-life paintings featured local products like gouda cheese and herring, Southern European imports like grapes and lemons,

New World treats like tobacco, as well as tea and other spices from the East. Painters captured the astonishing range and variety of these objects of global trade that flowed through Dutch daily life. Baltic grains went in to the bread featured in so many still lifes; oranges, hazelnuts, and olives that came from the Mediterranean; wines transported from France and Spain; pepper, cloves, Chinese porcelain and much more imported by the VOC; and salt, tobacco, and sugar that arrived from the New World on Dutch West India Company, (West Indische Compagnie) ships. As painterly subjects, these objects also tended to fit in sub-genres, which in turn had typical themes, such as 'breakfast paintings,' which displayed upper-class delicacies along with a religious reminder to avoid gluttony. Flowers became another popular subject. In the most seductive still lifes, the familiar became strange and the strange familiar: goods that had been ordinary began to seem special in the aura of painting and imagination, and new goods came to seem both thrilling and necessary. The still life helped not only to commodify flowers, but to create the first consumer driven commodity culture around the multiple goods flowing into Dutch ports during the time when Amsterdam sat at the helm of the world system. Among the common messages of these pictures, this visual language of the commodity communicated "the pride of primacy", in Hochstrasser's words.

And if during this era, economic and scientific dynamism spurred each other on, a passionate aesthetics helped to make sense of the dramatic changes occurring, since "visual culture was central to the life of the society" as historian Svetlana Alpers has argued. Still life captured some of the attraction and possibility of the new goods flowing in, the devices for observation and study, and recorded some of the novel ways of seeing. Aesthetics was inherent in all this, and manifested most apparently in collecting, gardening, and visual art. As both secular consumption and scientific interests were rising, production of floral still life surged. Some scholars of still life see explicit relationships between interest in the natural world – in plants, insects, and animals – and the origins of floral painting. To illustrate the close connections between art, science, and commerce, consider the Ruysch family. Frederik Ruysch was a well-known botanist, anatomist, and collector, famous for his anatomical dioramas, and immortalized in Jan van Neck's 1683 portrait, *The Anatomy Lesson of Dr. Frederick Ruysch*. Ruysch apprenticed his daughter Rachel, aged fifteen, to the prominent still-life painter, Willem van Aelst, and she went on to become well-known herself, one of the few women in the painter's guild, and a highly regarded artist specializing in floral still life. Another daughter, Pieternel, married Jan Munnicks, who drew flowers for Amsterdam's Hortus Botanicus.

One reason that Dutch still life continues to fascinate viewers is that the subjects seem so strikingly immediate and relevant, despite clear differences between the contemporary global economy and the seventeenth-century Amsterdam-centered system, as well as between viewer perspectives now and then. Nevertheless, "[t]he allure of those rich commodities served up on silver platters without any troubling details regarding their acquisition reverberates shockingly in the glitz of today's advertising images that can gloss so seductively over just such disturbing realities of production," observes Hochstrasser. Curiously, this still-life moral economy involving goods, people, and ethics is precisely the perspective Fair Trade advocates now emphasize. Whether focusing on bananas, chocolate, or increasingly, flowers, consumers are urged to consider the circumstances in which these commodities are produced and sold. Seventeenth-century viewers weren't necessarily urged to have moral problems with the slave trade or the plantation system, but by featuring a lump of refined sugar along with a parrot or an African figure (as in several of Jan Davidsz de Heem's paintings) these issues are implied. Whether one's reaction was approving, fascinated, proud, or disgusted, viewers were invited to consider the circumstances of global trade through which these commodities circulated. And if, now, still life offers a window for us to glimpse the past, it sometimes also seems as though those in the past were peering through the same window toward the future, to us. Many of the historical circumstances of the Dutch Republic, when reduced to the general or the elemental, don't seem far removed from the contemporary environment: wars fueled by religious fanaticism, the burgeoning and collapse of empires, a global awareness among citizenry, a new media that reflects and refracts the world, a fascination with consumption as well as the thrill and thrall of worldly goods and our relationship with them.

Svetlana Alpers characterizes seventeenth-century Dutch visual representation as "an art of describing," in contrast to a narrative art such as that produced in Italian Renaissance painting. "Dutch pictures are rich and various in their observation of the world, dazzling in their display of craft, domestic and domesticating in their concerns. The portraits, still lifes, landscapes and the presentation of daily life represent pleasures taken in a world full of pleasures: the pleasures of familial bonds, pleasures in possessions, pleasure in the towns, the churches, the land". And with careful work, Hochstrasser contends, we may approximate "the 'feeling value' of these objects within the Dutch mentalité of the time, and speculate as to how that can inform our understanding of these pictures". With kindred precaution, Huizinga notes that "[p]art of the meaning of this art will always escape us," though we may understand some things, and know that "[t]here is meaning behind every flower in a floral painting…"

Dutch still life is often characterized as the art of thinking through things. These paintings continue to appeal to viewers because they present an unexpectedly penetrating social gaze, rich in ideas and sympathies. Though embedded in their seventeenth-century context, by exploring one's relationships with objects, intimacy, and the world, they gesture at modern notions we still struggle with and are intrigued by. As Mark Doty so elegantly put it in his meditation on Jan Davidsz de Heem's *Still Life with Oysters and Lemon*, this Dutch still life conveys:

> "That this is the matrix in which we are held, the generous light binding together the fragrant and flavorful productions of vineyards, marsh, and orchard – where has that lemon come from, the Levant?

That the pleasures of what can be tasted and smelled are to be represented, framed, set apart; that pleasure is to be honored.

That the world is a dialogue between degrees of transparency – globes of the grapes, the wine in the glass equally penetrated by light but ever so slightly less clear than the vessel itself, degrees of reflectivity.

That the world of reflection implicates us, as well – there, isn't that the faintest image of the painter in the base of the glass, tilted, distorted, lost in the contemplation of his little realm? Looking through things, as well, through what he's made of them, toward us?

That there can never be too much of reality; that the attempt to draw nearer to it – which will fail – will not fail entirely, as it will give us not the fact of lemons and oysters but this, which is its own fact, its own brave assay toward what is.

That description is an inexact, loving art, and a reflexive one; when we describe the world we come closer to saying what we are."

When Doty says that when we describe the world we come closer to saying what we are he has hit on a recurrent theme in theoretical discussions of commodities, from Marx to Barthes, and that is the overlap of people and things. Each takes on characteristics of the other, and both are transformed in this economy, restricted by the market's potent gravity. Still lifes are meditations on these processes. Looking at *pronk* still lifes (sometimes called the art of the ostentatious, from *pronken*, to flaunt or prance about), Hal Foster sees a culture of fetishism. With their typically shiny and luxuriant surfaces, Foster says they have the effect of "lubricating" the viewer's gaze, creating a commercial preoccupation that is provocatively ambivalent. On the one hand, during the era of the Republic, the Dutch Protestant social order tended to frown on the idea that a material object could have a spiritual value. They sneered at different African culture's ardor for talismans or amulets, which the Dutch, borrowing from the Portuguese, called *fetissos* (literally, fetishes). But "as religious fetishism was suppressed, a commercial fetishism, a fetishism of the commodity was released; the Dutch denounced one overvaluation of objects, only to produce another of their own".

Roland Barthes similarly noted a pious sense in still life and other Dutch painting of the era. Though by the seventeenth century specifically religious iconography ceased to dominate, a kind of religious aura nevertheless glowed from the secular scenes presented. He wrote that the proliferation of objects in such images had, in effect, "washed away religion only to replace it with man and his empire of things"). That memorable phrase 'empire of things' captures both the Netherlands' colonial expansion across the globe and the burgeoning consumer culture at home. He goes on to comment on the portraits of regents, "[w]hat is it then which distinguishes these men at the pinnacle of their empire? It is the numen... that simple gesture by which divinity signified its decisions" via those Dutch burghers and merchants, "this class at once social and zoological," these traders in goods and in still-life paintings. What is so significant is the numen (the spirit or divine power) of their gaze, because actually, the participants are not concerned with the money and the objects surrounding them, despite all the abundance that characterizes Dutch painting of the period. Ultimately, argues Barthes, the gaze focuses on you, which is to say, on us, the viewers. "You become a matter of capital, you are an element of humanity doomed to participate in a numen issuing finally from man and not from God".

~

This formative period for both consumer culture and Dutch horticulture has more to reveal through a key relationship between aesthetics and economics. These paintings expose the complexities, ironies, and suggestive absences of what has been called a Dutch "cultural iconography". More than the religious and symbolic approaches traditionally used in art history, this inclusive conception incorporates visual and material culture alike to explore not merely visual representation but the wider historical context and cultural milieu. The tulip craze fit in with larger social structures and emotional phenomena of the time, expressed through masculine networks and commercial institutions, and generally related to curiosity, wonder, excitement, and the connections between art and nature. In order to gain entrance to upwardly mobile or elite circles, one needed cultural capital, which in seventeenth-century urban Dutch society included knowing about both art and flowers, and often people from the very same gentlemen class were involved in both, since collecting art often went hand in hand with collecting tulips. This world of collecting connected directly to social status, the public demonstration of taste, and this close society of collectors revolved around exchange relationships and gifts. And in the world of still-life painting, tulips, and other collectibles, aesthetic values resonated against and reinforced one another. At the beginning of this transitional era, personal and intellectual relationships were often pursued and cemented through gifts – something that shifted quickly and dramatically with the encroachment of market forces, the popularity of painting, and the flourishing of aesthetic practices. Along with other objects of still life, commodification of the tulip came quite naturally, and this is part of how the tulip came to epitomize crisis.

We know that the financial aspect of the crisis is largely myth. Amounts paid for tulip bulbs at the peak of their boom in the winter of 1636-1637 were not as high as is commonly thought today. The famous tulip bulb sold for the price of a canal house was an apocryphal tale, coming from a moralistic pamphlet and not from records of sales. Goldgar has shown that the actual ledgers reflect a significant rise in tulip bulb prices, but not wildly out of proportion from the price fluctuations of other commodities, and although bankruptcy records for the period are sketchy, not a single one can be conclusively linked with the burst bubble of tulipmania. Far from the country in tatters and ruin commonly portrayed in popular media then and remembered today, growth continued through the postcrash years, industry and investment rose, overseas expansion marched on, and general standards of living improved in the Republic. In fact, it was in about the 1650s or 1660s that the Dutch empire reached its true dimensions. Though not an economic calamity, Goldgar emphasizes that nevertheless tulipmania was a serious moral and social crisis.

In a short span of time, Dutch society changed drastically. People were confronted with the rapid growth of urban societies, immigration, a fast and highly visible increase in wealth, an economic system that pioneered new forms of buying, selling, and planning, and also, something both troubling and exciting, the entrance and circulation of heretofore unimagined, exotic goods from places and people scarcely conceived of. Suddenly their local towns, markets, and harbors were seen to fit in a world that was much larger and stranger than previously suspected. Historians like Steven Greenblatt have highlighted wonder as one of the popular responses to the radically different people, beliefs, and goods entering European markets from the New World and other locations. But Simon Schama demonstrated that "riches seemed to provoke their own discomfort, and affluence cohabited with anxiety". And Hochstrasser and Goldgar emphasize that apprehension was a common response not only to the new wealth, but to the striking changes taking place. A familiar way of life was ending, social practices and rules of exchange were abolished or transformed, and with the scale of poldering and other development projects, even the landscape beneath their feet took on a different order.

The rupture in Dutch society, the real tulipmania, reflected anxieties about the dramatic transformations going on around them, including a strong shift toward what today we call market values. The fascination with tulips epitomized both the delight and fears over the society in radical transition. Given the long-standing culture of face-to-face exchange, intimate social and economic networks, respect for trade, and the popularity of collecting, the abrupt collapse of tulip prices sent out shock waves. The suddenly worthless tulip bulbs inevitably raised questions and provoked uncertainty about knowledge, value, and taste. As story and rumor spread about the prices people were paying for these curious commodities valued for their beauty, tulips and the tulip trade came to stand for all that was wrong and dangerous about the social and economic changes underway. Tulips and the trade became scapegoats, helping to spur popular myths about the folly of speculative capitalism and the social decline it inexorably causes.

Marcel Mauss argued that metaphysical and mythological aspects of the exchange process infuse many objects, their owners or possessors, and often as well, ideas about the object's origins. But why might a horticultural commodity become the focal point of the crisis – and not telescopes, ship building, painting, or any number of things or contemporary processes that might conceivably have been construed as emblematic? And why tulips instead of more familiar and traditional flowers like roses, lilies, or carnations? Goldgar suggests that, in addition to the tulip's links to social status and elite networks, the tulip trade depended on trust, since bulbs were sold in winter months while still in the ground, and the resultant blooms would not come out for several months after the sale took place. So tulipmania "fractured social relations by reminding burghers how fragile their connections were. If a debt of honor" became unreliable and unenforceable, it threw into peril a culture of negotiation and arbitration upon which stable society seemed to rest.

Because gift economies don't involve the exchange of money, it's easy to see them as totally unrelated to commerce. But Mauss argues that some commonalities subtly underlie gift economies and contemporary practices of trade, since contemporary economic and legal systems emerged from the sort of gift-exchange value systems that were once nearly universal. There are remnants of much older systems embedded in our current institutions. Yet in other ways, these sets of values and practices seem mirror images of one another. As David Graeber has observed: "In gift economies, [...] exchanges do not have the impersonal qualities of the capitalist marketplace. In fact, even when objects of great value change hands, what really matters is the relations between the people; exchange is about creating friendships, or working out rivalries, or obligations, and only incidentally about moving around valuable goods. As a result everything becomes personally charged, even property. In gift economies, the most famous objects of wealth – heirloom necklaces, weapons, feather cloaks – always seem to develop personalities of their own. In a market economy it's exactly the other way around. Transactions are seen simply as ways of getting one's hands on useful things; the personal qualities of buyer and seller should ideally be completely irrelevant. As a consequence everything, even people, start being treated as if they were things too". That is the shift. In a market economy, you become a matter of capital, as Barthes said.

In another context, Walter Benjamin comes to a similar conclusion. Swooning over a book he bought at auction, he wrote that "ownership is the most intimate relationship that one can have to objects. Not that they come alive in him; it is he who lives in them". Yet elsewhere, Benjamin draws a different lesson. In one of his best known essays, the mechanical reproduction of art eliminated or eclipsed its distinctiveness, what he called its "aura." As copies proliferate, art's power is muted, blunted, refashioned into something else, something "uprooted from tradition", which has a tendency to support dominant ideology and solidify class divisions. Though Benjamin's critique of mass production applied mostly to visual art, one suspects a parallel phenomena going on with the bulk, uniform production of flowers that also occurred during the same period, and catered to the same consumer markets. Over the course of the twentieth century, flowers transformed from a fragrant, perishable luxury into a sturdy, scentless affordable good for the middle class. Techniques of mass production and distribution are what enabled this transformation, this industrialization of the process. While these techniques differ in obvious ways from what occurred in the Dutch Republic, both times and places designate periods of profound popular changes in our relationships to commodities, in how they're produced, consumed, and regarded.

The focus on the invention of commodities and our relationship to them aren't the only parallels between then and now. The global context in which such goods were produced, distributed, and consumed became synonymous with the system in which they circulated. But more subtly and more significantly, this context became an important dimension of the objects themselves, part of their iconography. It was not just that they were transported from faraway lands to be sold and consumed, but that part of that distance, that cachet, became insinuated in how they were depicted and imagined. In other words, part of the meaning of commodities was worldliness. To consume them, or even to witness their passage, was to partake in modern society. For the Dutch especially, an urban, cosmopolitan sensibility infused the trade in commodities. More than any particular item, or process of production and consumption, the Dutch trafficked in worldliness. Writing in the eighteenth century, Daniel Defoe accurately conveyed the situation: "[The Dutch] really are the Middle Persons in Trade, the Factors and Brokers of Europe... they buy to sell again, take in to send out, and the greatest part of their vast Commerce consists in being supply'd from All Parts of the World, that they may supply All the World again". This view was well founded, not merely impressionistic. As Wallerstein has argued, managing bureaucracy and information was key to becoming the steward of the world system, and the Dutch handled this quite effectively. So, for example, Western Europe came to rely on Amsterdam's weekly commodity price list that by 1634 included 359 different items, and by 1686 grew to 550, according to Julie Hochstrasser. Not only had the Republic become the conduit for commodities, it set international value and standards for them – a role not unlike that of the Netherlands today with global horticulture.

Though industrial speed and efficiency have dramatically increased, and today there's a high degree of interconnectivity, already in the seventeenth and eighteenth centuries, commodity chains encompassed different nations and continents, and tended to reach from the centers of the world system to the limits of its peripheries. And especially in the Dutch Republic, the production and distribution process took place through social and commercial networks that emerged from that humanistic society of gentlemen. As the world system developed, flowers became a significant part of the making of what has been called "the first modern economy". Jack Goody has outlined "the gradual emergence in Europe of a heightened activity in practice, in representation, and in scientific and poetic discourse, especially in the context of the incorporation of that continent in a world market which for a period it then dominated. One particular feature of this growth was the widespread use of cut flowers in urban life, strikingly so in Holland..." Though clearly not the only commodity around, along with the cornucopia of delights from America, the Orient, and the Levant, flowers occupied commercial, aesthetic, and imaginative spaces in this new social economy. But as much as any particular product or dynamic of the world system, it was the idea and attraction of worldliness itself that the Dutch pioneered. Said another way, social and aesthetic forms and practices were key aspects of the system.

Illustrations and visual art captured many of these forms and practices. Widely circulated illustrations on Dutch maps and book covers might depict a Persian rug, a turbaned man, an Inca priestess, or a silk-robed Chinese emperor. In the profusion of images coming out of the Dutch Republic, maps constituted both practical and aesthetic models of geography. These visual documents presented actual ways of seeing the world, and they proliferated. The images that accompanied typical maps featured an eclectic mix of exotica celebrating the expansion of the Dutch world, and they conflated global space. The Dutch controlled many trade routes connecting Europe to the East (Java, Japan, China, Macao); to the Americas (Brazil, the Caribbean, North America); and to the South (including the route around Cape Horn in South Africa and vast swaths of the African continent, used to propagate and profit from the Atlantic slave trade). Their commercial dominance, innovative trade practices, and guile enabled the Dutch to profit from the growing market for commodities and the sort of objects that the owners of *Wunderkammern* (cabinets of wonder or cabinets of curiosities) sought for their collections. And at the same time that they supplied many of the objects, art, and curios, they developed compelling visual representations of that domain, through cartography and painting. Benjamin Schmidt has called this phenomena "the marketing of the world" that appealed to readers, viewers, and consumers across Europe, and this image of the world was tantalizingly 'exotic'. Moreover, these images also often lent support to specific Dutch business ventures. Johan Nieuhof's careful and complete description of Brazil was sympathetic to the Dutch West India Company at the height of its power, for instance. Business ingenuity went hand in hand with aesthetics, or vice-versa.

This amounts to more than historical background of how flowers became commodities; these images and ideas constitute part of flowers' "cultural biography," and in various ways, this formative period carries over in contemporary values, practices, and ideas. Though some aspects of commodities may be mysterious ('metaphysical and theological'), many of the abstruse qualities of things become concrete and more comprehensible when looked at vis-à-vis their cultural biography. The anthropologist that first articulated why a life story offers such a useful metaphor for things explained it like this. "In doing the biography of a thing," wrote Igor Kopytoff, "one would ask questions similar to those one asks about people: what, sociologically, are the biographical possibilities inherent in its 'status' and in the period and culture, and how are these possibilities realized? Where does the thing come from and who made it? What has been its career so far and what do people consider to be an ideal for such things? What are the recognized 'ages' or periods of the thing's 'life,' and what are the cultural markers for them?" Finally, "...what is significant about the adoption of alien objects" such as tulips is "the way they are culturally redefined and put to use".

The analysis of still life and tulips explores this last aspect of flower's cultural biography. Understand them through their 'life story,' call them cultural icons or social hieroglyphs: looking not only at how these things were represented but at how they fit in the world system reveals the desires and uncertainties of Dutch society during its modern formative period, and suggests some of the ways that a cultural link between aesthetics and economics was forged. No single aspect of this environment should be understood in isolation. Prosperity, collecting, gardening, science, visual art, and a cosmopolitan sensibility all contributed to the society, and suffused the meanings of new commodities, including flowers. With a twenty-first-century gaze, it's hard to imagine how extraordinary a lemon or a clove or a tulip might have seemed. But for seventeenth-century habitués of these global channels, the marvel of exotic goods was very real. The seduction came not only from their taste, look, novelty, or the lure of their mysterious origins, but from the complex narrative implied by their arrival via the commodity chain. The worldliness of goods – encompassing the desires and ambivalences of this new economic and cultural system – increased their appeal. The objects stood in for a range of values and processes, which made their beauty that much more pleasurable, and which fueled that much more fantasy and covetousness.

~

Jade turtles, opal scarabs, blue-green butterflies encased in glass ornaments, orchids growing from the eye sockets of a stone animal skull: these and other marvels of art and the natural world have appeared in Florian Seyd and Ueli Signer's Wunderkammer, an annual show that's part gallery, part flower shop. Housed in a historic Amsterdam warehouse, the two florists partnered with Bloemenbureau Holland and KNOP (the Dutch

Orchid Growers Association, Kring Nederlandse Orchideeen Producenten) to create a sort of flower salon, which they have done each May since 2005 with themes like "Tropical Dreams" and "Is This the End or a New Beginning?" The Wunderkammer references European Renaissance and Dutch Golden Age history to attract viewers, setting up a sort of theater of the world where nature and art overlap. In their heyday, a collection might have included a narwhal tusk, a diorama of human fetal bones, geodes, and a two-headed sheep preserved in a jar. Cabinets of curiosities were ornate collections of exotic and curious objects from around the world – some came from nature, some were modified from nature or were valuable man-made things. But these cabinets consisted of more than just elaborate tchotchkes of the fabulously wealthy and extravagant. They truly reflected one spirit of the age in Europe: wonder. Through a combination of science, art, and theater, viewers were often spellbound, and the owner's status greatly enhanced. Describing one of the best known and best preserved Dutch cabinets, that of Frederick Ruysch, Stephen Jay Gould captured the general purpose of such collections: to dazzle or "to stun, more than to order or to systematize, became the watchwords of this enterprise". Other wealthy Amsterdammers also possessed wonder cabinets, and like Ruysch, were implicated in local networks of power and influence. One of the VOC's founder-members, Gerrit Reynst, had two sons, Gerard and Jan, both of whom contributed to the economic and aesthetic life of the Republic as collectors, and Gerard alone as head of Amsterdam's Wisselbank. (A precursor to contemporary central banks, the Wisselbank sat literally at the center of the city's power). The Reynst brothers' Wunderkammer consisted of naturalia (animals, fossils, minerals) and artificialia (paintings, vases, coins), and their collection became most famous in 1660, when several dozen paintings and sculptures were given to King Charles II in hopes of repairing Anglo-Dutch relations. In contrast to this prodigious history, Signer and Seyd's Wunderkammer is mostly gimmick (the goal seems less to provoke and impress viewers than to entice customers). But they do invoke a past, and invite participation in an experience of the exotic, wondrous, and opulent, along with a bit of theater and history. Part of the lure for ordinary viewers today is to imagine entering that environment of lavish wealth and worldly curiosities of seventeenth-century regents and the very affluent. The marketing of a playfully imagined Dutch past is a recurring theme in Dutch horticultural aesthetics, one promoted and nourished by organizations, breeders, and florists alike.

The contemporary fashioning of horticultural aesthetics comes largely from florists, and in other ways, from breeders. But the production chain overlaps quite a bit, so no single sector really operates in isolation. Just as auctions set prices but aren't the only factor determining value, florists and breeders drive aesthetic innovations without being totally autonomous creators. The trend in the production chain is toward more and more integration; breeders, growers, distributors, exporters, and organizations all work together, all intersect considerably in both formal and informal ways. As FloraHolland's Bernard Oosterom put it, "Growers visit retailers and retailers visit growers," by which he meant not merely that these professionals drop by on each other once in a while, but that they regularly collaborate and recognize shared interests. Retail florists matter to growers and others along the production chain because they have direct contact, and often maintain enduring relationships, with consumers. Face to face contact means a lot in the sale of such emotional commodities. These commodities are first created by breeders, and later fashioned by florists.

Breeders and florists share commonalities, but differ in significant ways, too. Florists are artisans and cultural producers. Their craft shapes many aspects of the horticultural industry, by coming up with designs that influence the consumer market, by setting trends, supporting causes and organizations, and in the Netherlands especially, by their relationships with people in other parts of the value chain. Also, political and cultural icons like Lady Di or First Lady Michelle Obama employ florists to provide a signature aesthetic, and their choices and designs may reverberate back through the production chain. Breeders, too, devise horticultural aesthetics: their creations are shaped by artistic, ornamental, and market considerations, and their choices influence the chain in terms of price, volume, transportation, and many other factors. Breeding involves fashioning all sorts of characteristics – color, longevity, scent, stem length and strength, resistance to fungi or pests – and is dedicated to generating aesthetics. But breeders are somewhat insulated from the unpredictable swings of the market, like when snowstorms that keep consumers from buying inflict damages on florists, importers, exporters, and others along the chain. Sales do affect the breeder's profits, but breeders are less vulnerable to market vagaries. They also earn royalties from the intellectual property rights and patents on their creations, which hooks their interests in policy debates to the world of high-tech multinationals, a power block far removed from florists.

But in the Netherlands both breeders and florists are organized, like other sectors of Dutch horticulture. They talk to each other and work together; they have formed collective institutions that protect shared interests through promotion, and legal and economic advocacy. So in addition to what they generally share – creating horticultural beauty – they cooperate, have mutual concerns, and engage in common practices. The Dutch florist's organization is called the VBW (Vereniging Bloemist-Winkeliers); Dutch breeders have Dutch Creations, which is the association of leading horticultural breeders in the Netherlands, and CIOPORA, the International Community of Breeders of Asexually Reproduced Ornamental and Fruit Plants. The knowledge sharing and networking between breeders and florists is increasingly fluid, as demonstrated by the appointment of Bram Rijkers as Dutch Creations' marketing manager from his former position as sales representative for the VBW.

Florists in the Netherlands are organized, and they have a recognized trade. Of the approximately 3,300 Dutch florists, the VBW enjoys a membership of nearly 2,000, which is over 60 percent of the total. Remarkably, this is seen as a low portion to be involved; VBW director Marco Maasse says it's because many *bloemisten* are independent-minded, and also because the organization lobbies for the whole sector, so even non-members enjoy some benefits from the VBW's work. The VBW continues to grow, and Maasse hopes to make the florist's sector larger, more organized, and better integrated. The sector earns one billion euro annually and employs 11,000 people (most of whom are part-time or seasonal employees of established florists). 25 percent of florists buy directly from Dutch auctions, so in terms of horticultural networks and the auction community, they're centrally positioned, and participate in the industry as both traders and florists. By promoting and crafting holidays like Mother's Day, florists also carry on tradition (and incidentally, in the Netherlands, the average Mother's Day purchase is 34 euro.) Many florists make a special effort to involve kids, bringing both boys and girls to the auction and to the shop, teaching them about the auction system, horticulture, arranging, and caring for flowers.

Due to their position straddling between the auction and the customer, beauty and the market, aesthetics and economics, florists have unique perspectives and often share thoughtful reflections on both practical concerns in Dutch horticulture and broader, abstract issues. In an interview with the *Grote Handelsblad*, for instance, Maase draws connections between price, value, worth, and beauty: "De bloemist is het beste kanaal dat waarde kan toevoegen. Het enige kanaal dat van een 'steel met een bolletje erop' een boodschap met emotie kan maken". (The florist is the best way to add value. It's the only way that buying 'a stem with a little bloom attached' becomes an emotional purchase/transaction.) Maasse is equally clear about his pragmatic goals for the VBW. He wants the florist's sector to be larger, more organized, and better integrated. A VBW campaign called 'omarm de bloemist' (embrace the florist) aims to make the role of florists better understood and more respected, and more essential to the horticultural business, by cooperating growers, florists, and buyers at FloraHolland. He also explains that the position of the florist in the supply chain is growing due to strong cooperation with partners and other members in the chain. As well, individual florists and respect for their profession has expanded through promotional events like Florist of the Year and numerous awards sponsored by FloraHolland, the Keukenhof, local bloemencorsos, and many other venues. But above all, success as a florist in the Netherlands depends on "personal contacts," according to Maasse, speaking at the Floriade conference in early 2011. In direct and indirect ways, personal contacts lead to greater exposure, enhanced reputation, and more and better opportunities. But publicity is also crucial. The Flower Council of Holland recently celebrated that one of its campaigns reached 100 million people, mostly in Europe, via saturation in new social media, areas the horticultural sector has moved into actively.

Although Dutch florists have embraced the latest technology, and only began to organize themselves in the late 1990s, clearly their profession is not new. Flower arranging has a long history in the Netherlands, as floral still lifes illustrate. During the seventeenth century as well, a number of unique vases and other objects and techniques of display came into being. In the late seventeenth and early eighteenth centuries, Delft ceramicists produced lavish flower pagodas, which were stacks of dishes mounting to towers that allowed for tall, ostentatious floral displays. In the connected worlds of design, art, fashion, and horticulture, these objects, too, have lately been recreated to reference a 'classic' past of the Dutch Golden Age. Most recently, these flower pagodas commemorated the renovation of the Rijksmuseum in Amsterdam. (And the reproductions were made by artisans from the Royal Tichelaar Makkum – an enterprise itself with Golden Age roots, as one of the Netherlands' oldest companies). Also on the contemporary agenda, the World Horticultural Expo held in Venlo in 2012 referenced the Golden Age, if only obliquely, with its forecast "theater of green emotion" that hopes to create "een wereld van vervreemding en verwondering" (a world of estrangement and wonder).

The designer of this theme, Anouk van Dijk, is the daughter of successful florist Marcel van Dijk, who also participated in the show. According to Marcel, arrangers work closely with growers, so that "we de sector zo goed mogelijk neer te kunnen zetten" (to help to present the [horticultural] sector as best we can). This point bears emphasis because it expresses a common attitude throughout the industry: working together for the benefit of a broad collective. It's hard to envision a florist in the U.S., for instance, showing this communal spirit for the whole sector, but in the Dutch horticultural industry, such sentiment is normal, even tacitly expected. Recently at the European Conference of Florists (Florint), VBW's former manager, Toine Zwitserlood, made a presentation on the value of the trade associations in the horticultural industry, in which he underscored and expanded on the sense of community fostered by Dutch professional networks. He argued that a compelling explanation for people joining trade organizations is not merely that they help protect their interests, but – as with our attraction to flowers – for emotional reasons. Membership serves many needs, which he listed: a feeling of solidarity; standing stronger together; a feeling of ownership and involvement; it's ours, for us and by us; a feeling of security; protection from outside threats; a feeling of profit, a lot of added value in it for me. The ultimate goal of collectives like Dutch Creations, the VBW, and FloraHolland, said Zwitserlood, is to "create a real florist society". As both means and end, collectives impart meaning and belonging, encourage the sharing of ideas, and instill a strong feeling of democracy.

In myriad ways, then, not only are growers and traders essential to the industry, and to FloraHolland, but breeders and florists are also integral to Dutch horticultural institutions, traditions, and promotional events. The annual Horti Fairs in Amsterdam highlight flower-arranging presentations, and these are often co-sponsored by both florists and breeders. At 2010's Horti Fair, the most photographed and celebrated arrangement came from one of the Netherlands' biggest breeders, Schreurs. It was a sphere of crimson roses whose long stems were attached in a spoke structure that visitors could watch florists Joop and Ria van Leeuwen assemble. With its strength and near-perfect symmetry, the architecture of this ball of large-headed Red Naomi roses seemed to defy physical laws. It resembled a dandelion going to seed, or a chandelier lit by the bright red bulbs just opening. Other florists working for Shreurs and Dutch Creations (the umbrella breeder's organization) have recently made more striking exhibits, such as Stef Adriaenssen's "Flight of the gerberas," which uses 3,500 red gerberas and mimics aeronautics in a sort of Rube Goldberg machine. The Flight's movement comes from a rotating ramp of welded steel that emerges from its container and floats to the door, in order to portray "that the Gerberas are getting away from the greenhouse of the grower to the consumer!" Both the description and the enthusiasm of that exclamation point are notable. Adriaenssen conceived of this wacky contraption, in other words, as a kind of meta-commentary on – or imaginative model of – the production of horticultural commodities.

Breeding companies employ florists, so through both artistry and science, they mold horticultural aesthetics. Their organizations are also major industry power players. Their decisions and their lobbying of policymakers have global consequences. To see how this is so, consider that eighty percent of roses sold worldwide today come from just eight breeding companies. (And, as of 2010, there were only thirty-five rose breeding companies in the world.) As has been the trend with auctions, Dutch breeding companies have merged to become exponentially larger, more powerful, and more effective in influencing segments of the production chain. Armada provides one example. Forged in 2006 from five leading companies in breeding, propagation, marketing, and the sales of ornamentals, one of Armada's advantages is to be able to finesse different parts of the production at once. Among other activities, their breeding division pushes the interests of breeder's rights, licenses, and the sales of cuttings and young plants outside Europe (notably India). Many breeders who are part of Dutch Creations also belong to CIOPORA, the main international flower and plant breeder's organization, 60 percent of whose membership is in the EU. Devoted to protecting property rights, today CIOPORA counts more than 130 members from five continents. Though female florists are common in the Netherlands, the industry cannot count many active female breeders. One exception was the creator of the Ayaan tulip, the dark maroon-brown bloom named for Ayaan Hirsi Ali, by Lydia Boots of Lybo Hybridizing, who hybridized 'Gavota' and 'Gander's Rhapsody' (two other well-regarded flowers). Due to its dark mystique and the ongoing attempts to make a 'black' tulip, the Ayaan earned Boots some market and industry recognition. Though respected, not everyone thinks breeders deserve their often exalted positions, arguing they do little more than levy a tax on grower's hard work.

By contrast, across the industry, florists' contributions seem widely appreciated. People see them as artists or craftspeople, figures who make beauty with beauty. Floral arrangement is thought of as "puur handwerk," a pure craft or skill, as a sort of affectionate manual labor, so that "de bloemen groeien uit je vingers" (flowers grow out of your fingers), as is sometimes said. With craftwork, knowledge, skills, and values are passed on through social interaction, something which occurs between individuals, but individuals operating within institutions (either narrowly or broadly defined). To acquire these skills, one participates in tradition. Whether as carpenters, lab technicians, or conductors, craftspeople dedicate themselves not to pursuing profit, but primarily to their work, since that provides a sense of intrinsic value. People who insist that ornamental flowers are superfluous because they serve no survival purpose may also object to the notion that florists are craftsmen, since unlike carpenters or weavers, they don't produce something pragmatic for daily tasks. But even if one accepts that their work isn't 'practical', is such criticism really relevant, since an aesthetic sense and a connection to tradition are clearly important to many of these artisans?

Besides, taking the assumptions of this point of view to their conclusion, doesn't the vision of a society in which everything has only a functional use belong to dystopic science fiction? Florists I have spoken to see flowers as an essential aspect of daily experience, and not only because their livelihood depends on flowers. While it is a business, and many Dutch florists have a family background in the horticultural industry, most of them see their choice of profession as one option among many. They're florists not for the money or for lack of other opportunities, but because they enjoy the work. "My life is surrounded by beauty," several have told me. And it is not just the abundance of blooms and plants that brings satisfaction. Making a personal emotional connection with people around their love or grief can also feel tremendously fulfilling. The craft has its own rewards, as well: it's gratifying to create arrangements just to be beautiful, to please the senses, to appeal to aesthetic and emotional needs, or hopes, or expectations. Craftwork is seated more in community than in the market. Peter Otto, the manager of 'cooperative affairs' at FloraHolland, drew an important contrast between the commercial flowers and craftwork: "big chains like Albert Heijn sell products; florists sell emotion."

That's the defining characteristic of floral commodities, their aesthetic and emotional appeal. Some of FloraHolland's promotional materials state this straightforwardly: "Emotion is reserved only for the versatile and colorful commodity that forms the core of this powerful trade empire." FloraHolland Aalsmeer is not just a commercial center for sales and distribution, but an important node in the network of florists and the production of horticultural aesthetics. It is a critical resource for florists, and a big player in floral design. FloraHolland regularly hosts florists and each week displays new arrangements at the entrances to its auctions, but at the site itself also, florists come together, and interact with other sectors of the chain as both florists and traders buying through the clock.

Other florists that don't buy through the clock, do purchase garden supplies, cut flowers, and plants through FloraHolland's wholesale center, Cultra, with its "cash and carry" on-site facility. Located in one section of the auction building, it is a world unto itself, with forty-five thousand square meters of space. It includes two wholesalers of cut and dried flowers (Weerman and Dobbeflowers), a wholesaler of indoor and garden plants (Waterdrinker), two wholesalers of hardware and floral supplies (Duif and Basic&Trends), one wholesaler of packaging (Zwapak) and one wholesaler of hydroponic plants (Nieuwkoop Europe). In Cultra, one encounters florists not only from the Netherlands and neighboring Germany and Belgium, but occasionally too from other places around the world. One April morning, I happened upon a group of Slovenian floral teachers hosted by someone from the Dutch Flower Academy. They were watching a floral design demonstration, set up on some tables outside Waterdrinker, and one of them told me he was less impressed with the arrangements than with the quality of gladiolas and other flowers used. Purchased that morning at auction, they were fresher than many of the flowers with which he was accustomed to working.

As an institution, FloraHolland popularizes floral aesthetics, not only through these numerous connections with florists, but by sponsoring regular aesthetic competitions, and through cooperation with organizations and institutions. The Boerma Instituut (Holland's International Floral Design School), for instance, sits just 1500 meters from FloraHolland Aalsmeer and is housed in a former greenhouse. Another instance of how horticultural institutions are embedded in local communities, Aalsmeer residents often host international students attending the Boerma Instituut. Floral training gives instruction and experience on the gamut of issues that florists face, from basic knowledge of horticulture and the use of chemicals and pesticides to color and composition in the art of arranging. They also learn the techniques for dyes and glitter which adorned that compelling purple rose at the 2008 Horti Fair.

~

Florists and breeders take active part in two prominent horticultural traditions in the Netherlands, bloemencorsos and the Keukenhof gardens, both of which are well known for their extravagant aesthetics. Taking place between March and September, these seasonal events have very different styles and appeal, but are complimentary. Bloemencorsos attract locals, the Keukenhof draws tourists, and the industry markets and celebrates them both.

In early August, if you pass through Westland's verdant countryside, you might find fleets of colorful floats gliding through the waterways. In 2008, over the course of three days, along the 70-kilometer stretch of canals between Delft, Vlaardingen, and Maassluis, over 250,000 people assembled to watch hundreds of performers on dozens of barges sliding by. One such 20-meter barge called Chinese Wall featured a dragon-headed prow and a spike-tailed stern of tightly packed green carnations that snaked through the water. On board, situated among an abundance of flowers and crenellated cardboard parapets, were four men and two women with white painted faces, all of whom were dressed in ebony and cherry silk robes, and sported multicolored hats or black 'Asian' wigs. With his arms folded and hands hidden in his sleeves, the man posing as a Chinese emperor stood above a banner which read "Carpe Diem," and from time to time, he bowed. A few meters away, another float, called "Origin of the World," hosted five ethereal figures wearing loose-fitting gowns that riffled in the wind, each person donning a hat with broad curling horns, or butterfly wings, or antennae with matching aquamarine dishes bouncing at the ends. Each boat was loaded with thousands of flowers – gladiolas, gardenias, gerberas, dahlias, and more, in all manner of chartreuse, electric pink, indigo, orange... And thousands of people crowded along the banks of the canals, watching, cheering, lounging in lawn chairs, and sipping beer in the sun.

This frame of the floating parade represents a snapshot from just one of the Netherlands' bloemencorsos. An even better attended procession, Westland's, drew over 300,000 spectators in 2011, an impressive number given that the Westland municipality of south Holland has a population of only 100,000. (For over sixty years, until 2007, Aalsmeer had its own corso, but decided to end it and join forces with that of Westland.) Each year, the bloemencorsos feature a different theme using flowers, plants, fruits, and vegetables produced in the region's greenhouses, in pageants that include music, performances, contests, elaborate costumes, spectacular designs and other arresting decorations. The flower parade's origins date from the early twentieth century (about the same time as Aalsmeer's flower auctions) and their growth over the past hundred years mirrors the rise of the horticultural industry, which sponsors and encourages them. Though the flower parades began partly as a way to foment popular support for the industry, and marketing remains an important element in the events, many see the bloemencorsos as part of a timeless tradition, something really Dutch. Like tulip-naming ceremonies, they are a recent invention. But unlike tulip-naming ceremonies, which are publicity stunts for unveiling new tulips and are attended by industry executives, breeders, politicians, and royalty, bloemencorsos are widely beloved, involving dozens of local civic groups (baton-twirling troops, theater and musical organizations, neighborhood clubs) as participants, and many more people as spectators and supporters. Participants and onlookers revel in the imaginative spectacle, and florists relish the chance to come up with something that might stand out in such outstanding company. One of the florists I met, Geertje Stienstra, talked about the excitement and challenge of designing something for a float. "Whatever you make, it has to be able to withstand several days in sun, wind, rain, whatever summer weather the Netherlands brings. But it should also be elaborate, colorful, playful, creative, and unexpected – and new."

Stienstra is a member of the VBW, is featured on the Dutch Creations website, and often buys flowers and plants at FloraHolland Aalsmeer's Cultra, which was where I met her one December afternoon. She studied flower arranging for four years, and has been working professionally for almost twenty years, specializing in weddings, funerals, shop decorations, and demonstrations. In 2002, she designed several floats in Eelde's bloemencorso, and has performed demonstrations at Horti Fairs, and placed well in many competitive arranging contests, including 2001's "100 Bridal Bouquets for Maxima." Asked what is the most important quality of a good florist, she pursed her lips and frowned for a moment, then said "I guess more than the knowledge, colors, composition and all that stuff, which matters a lot, the most important thing is to have the right feeling. The right feeling for the event, the people involved, sensing the right flowers to communicate that." Aesthetics should always work to evoke the appropriate emotions, she maintains, whether in a bloemencorso, at a funeral, or among the gardens of the Keukenhof.

Bloemencorsos are about honoring the hard work of those in horticulture and celebrating the commodities they produce; bloemencorsos are also about excess, abundance, craft, and beauty. Occurring on long, leisurely summer days, they are flamboyant and easy-going galas. By contrast, the Keukenhof presents a far less convivial atmosphere, but one equally steeped in Dutch horticultural tradition. Constructed on the grounds of a fifteenth-century countess's estate, the Keukenhof is touted as the largest garden in the world. (The land was used for hunting and to grow herbs for the castle kitchen [*keuken* in Dutch], hence Keukenhof). In the seventeenth century, VOC captain Adriaen Maertensz Block built a second castle on the estate for a summer home. Today, the Keukenhof's carefully managed aesthetics are striking, controlled, and have an air of refinement, a whiff of the elite. These are some of the Keukenhof's sights: 50-meter parallel stripes of red and white daffodils edged with ferns; a multicolored tulip mosaic that recreates one of Rembrandt's best known self portraits; a row of seventeenth-century tulip hybrids spaced along a walkway like votive candles. Located not far from Haarlem and Leiden in the Dune and Bulb region (Duin-en-Bollenstreek), the Keukenhof is devoted to the Dutch bulb-growing sector, with tulips being the main attraction, and only tulips of Dutch origin. In 1949, with the hearty endorsement of Lisse's mayor, a group of growers and buyers began a sort of garden attraction on 32 hectares of land then owned by Duke Van

Linden. Each grower had his own stand to promote his flowers, and today the format hasn't changed much – at least, it's still a major showcase for Dutch growers and Dutch flowers more generally. The Keukenhof's ambience is one of wealth, but also of amazement with what nature and the cultivation of nature can produce. In addition to emphasizing tradition and selected aspects of Dutch history, the Keukenhof maintains this 'well-bred' impression by enlisting the support of high-profile figures such as models and actors, but especially through Dutch royalty and the endorsements and participation of ambassadors.

The Keukenhof is an important institution for Dutch horticultural aesthetics, but its audience is largely international, unlike the bloemencorso's, which are mostly attended by locals. More tourists visit the Keukenhof than any other site in the Netherlands (nearly a million, which is extraordinary since it's only open for two months per year). The Keukenhof not only promotes flowers and bulbs, but markets a sort of elevated and elegant 'Dutchness' imbued with a stately and prosperous past, a sense of distinction via flowers that as a tourist you're invited to savor. But of course, the price per ticket for this experience is 14.50 euro and the savoring, it is hoped, will whet the appetite for horticultural purchases. The Keukenhof's managing director Piet de Vries explained in 2010 how he hopes that the tourists' visit "has encouraged them to plant bulbs in their gardens and to buy more fresh cut flowers. Also we hope they really enjoyed the event. Then they will act like true Keukenhof ambassadors, stating that if you didn't visit the Keukenhof you didn't visit Holland". But what vision of Holland are they endorsing and nurturing?

A conservative institution in the sense that it aims to preserve flowers and floral traditions from the past, the politics of the Keukenhof also seem to tilt to the right side of the political spectrum. In addition to tulips named for first ladies and European royalty, some of their tulip-naming ceremonies pay homage to nationalist figures in the Netherlands. In 2003, for instance, exactly one year after his murder, the Keukenhof unveiled the

Pim Fortuyn Tulip in a solemn ceremony. Tulips with these sorts of designations have special marks of distinction: they're assigned identities, and their clean, sleek, 'classic' aesthetics become associated with a politics, and a world view grounded in a 'timeless' image of Dutchness that collapses a sort of Golden Age kitsch and yearning with a contemporary xenophobic outlook. But while the tulip names and ceremonies communicate values, their actual influence and the depth of their resonance seem dubious, since few consumers identify their tulips by name. It does not matter to florists, traders, exporters, and of course consumers that the flower is called Ayaan or Fortuyn, or that it was blessed by Queen Beatrix or Queen Paulowna. Nevertheless, these ceremonies and aesthetics adorn powerful, conservative institutions and figures. The Keukenhof emphasizes one face of Dutch horticultural aesthetics; bloemencorsos bring out another.

Regardless of the venue, flowers in the Netherlands are integral to views of the continuity of the past and the future – tradition, ritual, and aesthetic and economic legacies all contribute to the flowers' power of distinction. The Keukenhof and bloemencorsos represent contrasting images of the industry, the nation, and ways of seeing floral commodities. Flowers possess a combination of low and high, humble and royal; they're homespun and earthy yet noble and eminent. They have the aura of salt-of-the-earth cultivars and the elegance of royal families, the Pope, and heads of state. Flowers have the rustic roots of an ordinary grower and are blessed by Queens and honored by presidents and prime ministers. In this way, they're presented as something both exquisite and ordinary, exalted and run of the mill, while in both senses, above all, they're traditional. But the notion of aesthetics in the Netherlands extends beyond horticulture, painting, writing, design and the plastic arts to include the very land itself. The Dutch word kunstwerk means artwork, or a singular work of art, a masterpiece, but the term has a wider use in the Netherlands than its literal English translation. In addition to painting or pottery, kunstwerk also refers more generally to projects of engineering and human ingenuity, like bridges or dikes. The most conspicuous example would probably be the Delta Works, a vast water-management project with hundreds of miles of dikes and over three hundred structures, including dams, sluices, locks, and storm surge barriers. Noting the grand scale of this human achievement, many have likened this feat of engineering to the Statue of Zeus at Olympia, the Temple of Artemis at Ephesus, and the other five Wonders of the World. But kunstwerk also applies to more ordinary infrastructural projects like polders and canals. That the same word may be used to describe sculpture, poetry, and human-made modifications to the environment suggests quite a dynamic and flexible understanding of what is meant by a work of art. In this way, there's an artistic dimension to broader and seemingly unrelated aspects of Dutch horticulture such as the steering policies to manage space and infrastructure (as with Greenports). Even the Dutch word for fertilizer, kunstmest, uses the word for art (kunst) in an abbreviation for kunstmatig, or artificial.

In a country where the terrain itself is seen as a sort of artwork – something forged and modified through cooperative planning and aesthetic vision – the flowers produced from that land have particular distinction, whether they bloom out of the soil or come to perfection in a greenhouse. Dutch flowers stand in the foreground of the contemporary cultural landscape, a place earned through the stoking of Golden Age nostalgia, the popularity of invented traditions like bloemencorsos, and the powerful, high-profile celebrants of tulip ceremonies. But in whatever context, floral value and flowers themselves are so deeply insinuated, so intimately tangled with the varieties of sentiment, daily life, and economic practices that they may best be grasped (or may only be described?) through figurative language. Are flowers ever just flowers? As Michael Pollan observed, "This stands for that: flowers by their very nature seem to track in metaphor...", whether in popular traditions, the terminology of botanists, or the imagination of writers and artists. Metaphor pleases with its unexpected connections that nevertheless seem true; it often strikes us as beautiful the way metaphor makes the strange familiar and the familiar strange. In a sense, this is what Dutch still life did: in those paintings, things are so utterly themselves that they seem to glow from within with the world's many aspects. They refer to much beyond themselves.

In mid-seventeenth-century Holland, tulips and tulip bulbs became symbols of economic disaster caused by speculative greed. They stood for a range of market values that ultimately triumphed but were also popularly scorned. Today tulips have different meanings, but are no less figuratively rich. They're practically synonymous with the Netherlands, associated with Dutch character, and even the popular narrative of tulipmania is a story people love to tell. As a tall-tale, it approaches the status of a creation story, a narrative of the origins of modern Dutch society. It sheds light on the zany folly of Dutch excess, a calamity that's safely distant and light, but also relevant enough to gain traction and reliably evoke smiles. Yet it's not smiles, but similes that best characterize discussions of flowers. They seem to demand comparison: they're always like something else, even in discussing their social and historical place in the Netherlands. They're "social hieroglyphs," or we must properly understand them as "cultural iconography," and appreciate how this Golden Age history contributed to their "social biography".

Although specific meanings to people vary over centuries and geographies, almost everywhere flowers hold rich associative and allegorical significance, and are often central to rituals of union and death, conceptions of beauty, cosmological order and the afterlife, and emotional expression. Among "prehistorical and historic peoples of the Southwest and Mesomerica," for instance, anthropologist Jane Hill concluded that "a complex system of spirituality centered on metaphors of flowers formed an integral part of [their] cultural repertoire" after studying Uto-Aztecan speech communities. For these people, the transcendent spiritual realm was a sort of utopia partly in and partly outside of ordinary life, which Hill called the Flower World. Their languages and cosmology are rich in horticultural metaphors. Though the Uto-Aztecan Flower World may seem far removed, some of the scope of this should feel familiar to those fluent in our dominant culture's repertoire, where floral metaphors are deeply embedded in custom and language. We know that our reality is partly shaped by conceptual and linguistic practices and habits, by what has famously been called the metaphors we live by.

A person can be a potted plant, or a vegetable. Romance often buds or blossoms, but the fruit of love may well wither on the vine. Seeds of hatred or friendship or other emotions may be planted and later ripen and are sown. When someone is angry, upset, or disapproving, they may shoot a withering glance. Powerful phenomena are said to be deeply rooted; to affect a violent change is to extirpate (to uproot). Social movements flourish, though history may judge the effects baneful or beautiful. Mao, launching the Hundred Flowers Campaign in 1957, declared: "Letting a hundred flowers blossom and a hundred schools of thought contend is the policy for promoting progress in the arts and the sciences and a flourishing socialist culture in our land." The list of examples could go on, but the basic point wouldn't change: metaphors for flowers and plants are ensconced in English and many other languages. As uncontroversial as this seems, why it is the case remains a mystery. As Georges Bataille wrote in his well-known essay "The Language of Flowers": "It is surely impossible to use an abstract formula to account for the elements that can give the flower this quality".

The 'language of flowers' was also a potent trope in nineteenth-century Britain, where among certain classes different flowers and floral colors conveyed many messages, including respect and affection, fidelity and chastity, passion and romantic love. Though the specific meanings may have been new, the emotional communication of flowers was not. In his study of flower cultures through the ages Jack Goody notes, "Sexuality lies at the core of the flower's existence and played a prominent part when it was taken up in human life". Victorians were notoriously titillated by orchids; they found them prurient and blatantly sexual, and were part of the British empire's domestic culture. In fact, botanist Joseph Banks's lecherous exploits in Tahiti in the nineteenth century helped to cement a relationship that Patricia Fara has called "the Three Ss – Sex, Science and the State". An overtly sexually repressed public was quite enchanted with horticulture's graphic anatomies, alluring terminology, and explicit descriptions of fertilization.

Charles Darwin himself found orchids particularly thrilling and wrote about them enthusiastically. Though composed at the same time as *On the Origin of Species*, he decided his treatise on orchids did not fit with this volume. But he was convinced that "An examination of their many beautiful contrivances will exalt the whole vegetable kingdom in most persons' estimation". Sexual reproduction was of particular interest. Is it unrealistic to hear a little more than strait-laced, unmetaphoric diction in the 'naked, sticky surfaces' of his scientific writing, where for nine dramatic and minutely observed seconds he described the insertion of probosci to an orchid's labellum? He effused: "Let a moth insert its proboscis (and we shall presently see how frequently the flowers are visited by Lepidoptera) between the guiding ridges of the labellum, or insert a fine bristle, and it is surely conducted to the minute orifice of the nectary, and can hardly fail to depress the lip of the rostellum; this being effected, the bristle comes into contact with the now naked and sticky under surface of the suspended saddle-formed disc..." Readers who might find this description slightly pornographic are not alone. Similar to the tulip's sweeping popularity in the Netherlands, English Victorians pursued orchids with vigor and vim. They sought orchids from the Orinoco in Colombia to Papua New Guinea, and prized them at home through clubs, gardens, literature, and talk in elite circles. So-called 'orchid fever' or 'orchid delirium' took place in the context of Darwin's work, a wealthy expanding empire, and the accelerating science of botany. This British phenomenon was connected to the nineteenth-century global hunt for plants and flowers, what has been called "colonial botany". Orchids mesmerized Victorian society (Michael Pollan described them as "the inflatable love dolls" of the plant kingdom): clearly, metaphoric richness in horticulture is not at all unique to the Netherlands.

Nor is a supposed social mania based on flowers. Orchids and tulips aren't the only flowers in history to be associated with social frenzies, fads, or crazes. Ancient Egyptians, Greeks, and Romans seriously valued flowers, sometimes to the point of covetousness, as in the Alexandrine fashion of Garlandomania, a popular ritual of crowning one's lover's head with roses. Nor was the passion for orchids anything new. Eric Hansen finds other examples of orchid fever as long ago as ancient China, and cites, among other evidence, Confucius' (551-449 B.C.) declaration of the orchid as "the king of fragrant plants". And both Hansen and Susan Orlean have shown us that a widespread passion for orchids is alive and well in the early twenty-first century. But in earlier eras, people were gripped not just by flowers and representations of flowers but by the words used to describe them. The language was provocative, ticklish, and reinforced gender norms. Flowers were tempting and luscious but also coy and dainty, waiting passively for the active pollination of birds and bees.

Even in the contemporary lexicon of botanists, biologists, and naturalists, the anatomy, actions, and chemistry of flowers are virtually synonymous with gender and sexuality. Botanists sometimes refer to both tulip bulbs and the bifurcated tubers of some orchid seeds as "testiculates". The nomenclature of early botanists and naturalists described stamens as floral penises and separate structures containing seeds as wombs, and still today, bees are "flying penises". At the center of the rose lies its 'gynocium,' from the Greek meaning women's dwelling, and 'male' stamens encircle it. The gynocium of the rose is composed of 'carpels,' commonly known as ovaries, inside of which sit thousands of egg-shaped bodies, called ovules. Ovules fertilized with the 'sperm' of pollen grain will mature to seed filled 'fruits.' Every flower represents a self-contained reproductive compartment, a tiny reproductive factory. The closed carpel is what distinguishes a flower from a cone or seed pod, making angiosperms (literally, 'seed' sperm, inside a 'vessel,' angiosperm). All flowering plants are angiosperms, as opposed to pine or juniper or palm, which are gymnosperms. Flowers like roses that contain both stamens and carpels are 'bisexual' and 'perfect,' while flowers like marijuana are 'unisex' and 'imperfect.' These terms emerged from eighteenth-century European botanists (a group not known for their progressive outlook on gender issues), a gentlemen class, men of wealth and/or privilege, who understood 'man's' role as subduing, controlling, and dominating nature. "Perfect bisexuality" likely reflected their view of nature's order, that an ideal flower was one where, as they described it, the male stamen "married" the female carpel by conveniently delivering its pollen within the same bloom. It wasn't until the nineteenth century that it was shown how few 'perfect' flowers actually 'marry themselves'. Also, many flowering plants, like asparagus, have both perfect and imperfect blossoms – botanists call such an arrangement 'polygamous.'

Other professionals devoted to flowers use terminology similarly thick with metaphor. On graduations, christenings, and other occasions when lilies are bought, sometimes florists 'castrate' them by snipping off their anthers in order to prevent any of the flower's bright, greasy pollen from staining linens, gowns, and jackets. (Mischievously raising an eyebrow, an American florist once described the practice to me as "avoiding a Monica Lewinsky," after her infamous semen-stained dress.) And the sexual innuendo is more than a way of speaking. Flower images have also evoked passion: they're no less frankly corporeal, and often seem flagrantly erotic. Once Carl Linnaeus had helped to make botany erotic in the public imagination through his new scientific system of identifying and defining plants by their sexual characteristics, the erotic voltage of the language as well as the accompanying images seduced many Europeans. It was not unusual for botanical textbooks to be considered pornographic. If it's challenging to imagine how not only horticultural terminology but the pictures of flowers and plants could seem so risqué and sensual, just browse through some of the paintings of Georgia O'Keeffe. Today of course, one cannot talk about flowers, roses in particular, without also, sooner or later, talking about sex and love.

But the carnal aspects of flowers don't always refer to the erotic, especially when it comes to art. One case in point is visual artist Juan Manuel Echevarría. In work produced in the 1990s, he replaced the intimate inner parts of flowers with human bones to explore the violence and trauma of his native Colombia, as anthropologist Michael Taussig has movingly described and examined. In some, with stems arched like ribs, and stamen, phalanges, and sacrum combining to form a skeletal structure, Echevarría's images "are so obviously not flowers". The rips and tears of their bodies are poignantly imagined, very human, and in addition to contemporary torture and colonial violence, reference Enlightenment science. The titles Echevarría gives his catalogue of mutilated and suffering flowers also plays off the Latin names of these flowers. But with designations like Dracula Nosferatu, the tone is often tongue-in-cheek and irreverent, with a dose of wicked irony. When I look at these pictures that combine aspects of the natural world with human elements in a kind of faux-Enlightenment setting, I don't think so much of the Inquisition or contemporary regimes that torture. Instead, I'm reminded of the dioramas of early Dutch anatomists – namely, those of Frederick Ruysch.

A figure connected not only to wonder cabinets and still-life painting, Ruysch was one of the best known and most talented medical scientists of his day. His Wunderkammer, later purchased by Peter the Great, typifies the genre's combination of science and art. Using human bones and organs, for instance, he created dioramas with moral messages, such as the leg bones of a fetus kicking the skull of a prostitute. He skillfully embalmed human organs and fetuses using secret recipes of his own device that included wax, resin, talc, and cinnabar pigment. Like his contemporary still-life artists who painted flower vanitas that were often meditations on mortality, Ruysch created tableaux that instructed, entertained, and showed off his stunning dexterity, powers of observation, and techniques of preservation. He used the anatomies of dead people to create aesthetic objects and scenes that would endure – in a sense, defying death. His collection of oddities included a jar of baby Siamese twins, severed hands and heads set on beds of lace sewn by his daughter Rachel, and a box of fly eggs removed from the anus of "a distinguished gentlemen who sat too long on the privy," as his own description reads. These and 2,000 other such presentations filled five rooms in his house on Amsterdam's Bloemgracht, or Flower Canal. Contemporary viewers of what remains of his wonder cabinet are liable to find the displays ghoulishly outrageous, absurd, or deranged, particularly those involving fetuses and infants, but Ruysch regarded his work with tenderness and scientific rigor, as did many viewers of the time. Understanding his work in this way may be difficult, but is also kind of marvelous and even moving. With a drawn bow of desiccated artery, one fetal skeleton appears to play a tune on a miniature violin to accompany the lyrics "Ah fate, ah bitter fate." Another skeletal figure grasps a string of pearls beside the caption "Why should I long for the things of this world?" This question is worth pausing over.

In unprecedented ways, longing for the things of this world was very much on people's minds at that time, with the influx of so many new and exotic goods from around the globe and the emergence of a modern consumer culture in the United Provinces. For the Dutch of Ruysch's period, it was a time of curiosity, anxiety, and wonder, dramatic economic growth and expansion of trade and broader knowledge of the planet, massive infrastructural projects at home, and the production of new art (including Dutch still life) at a staggering scale. From this vortex of activity and industry came the invention of commodities, and the origins of modern Dutch horticulture. Flowers were an essential part of early consumer culture that evolved in the Netherlands in the seventeenth century; as social objects and as luxury items, they were a part of ordinary life, they figured in the conception of the world system with Amsterdam at the center. Today some version of that history is recycled as a marketing tool, or a way of celebrating past glory, and in some ways, flowers function as props that lend reality to an imagined Dutch community set among theatrical parades adrift in countryside canals. But, although the bloemencorsos are local events and shape the creation of aesthetics, the ongoing evolution of floral commodities, in terms of aesthetics, production, and consumption takes place in a global arena with the Netherlands at the center. Not only growers and traders, but florists and breeders, are very conscious of this. And the work that goes into the marketing of a flower like the Horti Fair's sparkly mauve rose comes from the lab or the greenhouse, but also emerges from social interactions and networks found in trade shows, clubs, meetings, and other aspects of Dutch horticulture's close-knit social infrastructure.

Planet of Flowers

I am letting two old roses stand for everything I believe in.
I am restricting the size of the world, keeping it inside that plastic pot.

Gerald Stern

It was once said that the sun never set on the British Empire; today one might make a similar claim about the Dutch flower industry. From East Africa to East Asia, from Israel and Palestine to Ecuador and Brazil, Aalsmeer's auctions span the globe, selling flowers grown in 60 countries and exporting to about 140. Over the past several decades, the dynamics of horticultural production, transportation, and consumption have been shifting to more complex patterns and arrangements, and while the Netherlands remains at the center, the very idea of what it means to be at the center is changing. Industry planners, exporters, and growers alike have expressed anxiety that the Netherlands might eventually lose its grip on the business due to the increasing strength of competing growing regions and consumer markets. Though sales and distribution continue to flow through the Netherlands and FloraHolland, Dutch networks and horticultural institutions seem to be evolving toward the roles of middlemen – indispensable brokers, facilitators, and suppliers of knowledge and services. Some planners predict Dutch horticulture will continue to maintain its conceptual, financial, aesthetic and trend-setting position, but not necessarily occupy a fixed geographical hub in the same way the auctions do today.

Although such developments don't take place overnight, the process may already be well underway. While Dutch growers still cultivate more tulips and tulip bulbs than any other country, that's already not the case with other top-selling flowers. In the 1990s, Colombia became the number one producer of carnations, and in just a few decades, Kenya and Ethiopia have come to produce more roses than the Netherlands – significant not only because roses are the top-selling flower worldwide, but because the founding flower of Aalsmeer's auctions is the rose. There are many reasons for these sorts of transitions, including the obvious factors one might suspect: land, labor, water, and sun are far more plentiful and cheaper in the equatorial regions of South America and East Africa than in the Netherlands. But this is far from the whole story. And these areas haven't so much displaced or usurped the Netherlands as added to and adjusted the workings of the value chain in both obvious and subtle ways. Most commercial horticulture continues to be produced in the Netherlands (still today, roughly half of what passes through its auctions), though each year the percentage of total volume decreases as other regions continue to increase production.

While global horticulture does not merely mirror global political and economic trends, it does not stand outside such forces, either. A basic principal of both capitalism and the flower industry is that they must continually expand. Expansion of the Dutch horticultural industry has occurred in very deliberate and controlled ways – through state and quasi-state funding, support from the Dutch institutions and auctions as well as the auction community, all of which takes shape through networks, flavored by Dutch cultural practices and business style. The shift toward online sales and the increased participation of international growers in Dutch auctions have introduced some big modifications to the system, yet even with these innovations, both the Netherlands' position and Aalsmeer's auction maintain pivotal roles. How does this work? As international growing increases, how does the Netherlands maintain itself at the center of an increasingly global industry? And since Aalsmeer's auctions were founded by growers to protect grower's interests, what happens to them as the cooperative institution expands internationally, incorporating more and more grower-members from abroad? To get a handle on these issues, I spoke with growers from many places and took a careful look at both the roles of the Aalsmeer auction in international expansion and at the global value chain. To see how the operation works, I highlight several countries around the world, but focus most on East Africa, since it's most relevant to the Dutch flower business, and I know it best after spending time in Ethiopia.

Growing far from the Dutch auctions means greater complexity, vulnerability, and unpredictability in transportation, an aspect of commodity production that's crucial but often overlooked in popular analyses. Currently, flowers and other perishables account for approximately 15 percent of worldwide air cargo, and costs of airfreight can represent up to 80 percent of the total product price, so transportation involves a crucial calculus, one that has often burned many growers. Fuel prices can be exorbitant; strikes and bad weather can ground flights; the politics and policies of airlines, governments, and airports can kink up production flow. Flowers begin to lose value from the moment they are cut. Not surprisingly, many people in the industry continually seek ways to minimize risks and maximize profits. The methods vary but airlines notoriously rip off patrons. In 2006, the U.S. Department of Justice and the European Commission, along with authorities in Canada and Australia, concluded a long-term investigation which found price rigging and cartels among several airlines. Between 1999 and 2006, many airlines coordinated pricing policy to maintain artificially high surcharges on fuel and security. In the U.S., seventeen airlines were fined 1.6 billion dollars, including the Dutch Frank de Jong of Martinair, who was sentenced to eight months in jail and personally fined 20,000 dollars. In November 2010, the European Commission levied fines on eleven airlines totaling 799 million euros, and singled out Air France-KLM (which also operates Martinair) for egregious behavior, fining them alone 340 million euros. The airlines also face numerous civil lawsuits, about 300 of which (or 5-10 percent of total complainants) come from the flower industry, and they seek 21-42 million euros in retribution.

Some South American growers have minimized these risks by sending their flowers to Rotterdam by ship. Because a cut flower's value is tied closely to its freshness, this might seem an improbable method of transport, but shipping offers several advantages. It's far cheaper, actually; it reduces the flower's carbon footprint (which is more and more important to both growers and to European consumers); and in spite of the 12 days by boat versus 12 hours or so by plane, the flowers remain just as fresh, due to refrigerated container technology. Once a flower is cut, cool temperatures keep it from wilting rapidly, but its life is seriously shortened by going in and out of refrigeration, as happens when flying – moving from storage on the farm to a truck, from that truck to the plane, and from the plane to the truck that carries it to the auction. Even though it takes place in a mere 24 hours or so, the trauma of flying really reduces a flower's longevity. But by sea, the flowers are sealed in their heavy container at the farm and not reopened until they enter cold storage at the auction. In that way, many varieties of cut flowers can remain as fresh as or fresher than those flown in. Also, the sea route is less hindered by hazards like blizzards and volcanic ash clouds. But there are some downsides, too: not all cut flowers do well by this method, timing and security pose difficulties both at the place of loading and during transport, and customs officials and international trade policies, ostensibly combating drug traffic and terrorism, are loathe to allow more sealed containers into the European Union. For decades, South America has established sea transport for bananas and other fruit; adding or substituting flowers as cargo was a relatively easy logistical accomplishment. There's a history, practice, and infrastructure already in place. Nothing comparable exists yet in East Africa.

Now as a producer, you face a host of difficulties, from aesthetic and genetic challenges to political negotiations. For foreign growers especially, stem length, thickness, and composition are crucial because they change the flower's weight, and thus increase fuel costs – for instance, a flight containing 44 tons of flowers from South Africa to the Netherlands consumes 60 tons of jet fuel. Every aspect of the flower must be attended to and accounted for. Calibrating such considerations as thorns and stem woodiness with the structural ability to hold up the bloom can become a tricky and costly operation, involving breeders and propagators as well as growers. Furthermore, if you're in East Africa, it's not just your flowers that travel by plane. Various samples and equipment go back and forth between the Netherlands and East Africa; chemicals and fertilizers are produced in the Netherlands; labs in the Netherlands regularly perform soil testing collected from East African farms. These sorts of requisites complicate matters for foreign-based growers, whether they're Dutch or not. In many ways, day-to-day activities don't differ much whether you're cultivating flowers in the Netherlands or East Africa, but outside the Netherlands, you're often working by remote control, since so many of the products and services you need (to say nothing of the auction and the consumer market) are thousands of kilometers away, on another continent.

Far more than a mere relay system, global production and distribution structures depend on complex coordination and negotiation subject to political and economic jockeying and power games (and in other industries, to piracy, hijacking, labor unrest, and more). Zimbabwe offers one example of the challenges of producing far from the auction. One of the earliest African countries to cultivate flowers for export and, as its neighbors subsequently did, Zimbabwe used its national airline to deliver flowers to Europe. While the goal was to generate revenue, the national airline was less efficient and reliable than KLM, and so back in 1989, growers began to favor KLM over Affretair. Affretair could not compete with the Dutch airline's services and number of flights. So to tip the scales in support of local industry, Zimbabwe then raised landing-rights costs for KLM. KLM and the Dutch government responded, in turn, by refusing Affretair landing rights at Schiphol, causing millions of dollars in loss for Zimbabwean growers who had contracts with Affretair. Their only option was to land in Germany, and deliver to the auctions by truck, losing precious time, as their products' quality and price diminished. Though this occurred 25 years ago, airfreight battles are not a thing of the past. In 2006, *Addis Fortune* reported that "A price war was sparked between Ethio Horti

Share Company and Sher Ethiopia Plc after an email message was sent by Sher to 77 growers announcing new cargo services to Europe. The email said that the company would begin leasing an airplane to transport flowers and vegetables to Luik, Belgium..." The Netherlands-based Lauden Airways underbid Ethiopian airlines, offering growers two advantages: lower costs and a fixed rate. Sher, the Dutch rose grower with the largest flower farm in Ethiopia, had brokered the deal. Immediately, Ethiopian airlines and the Ethiopian government began to coordinate a response. Eventually, through a combination of government negotiations, compromises, and incentives, the deal with Lauden was scrapped and most floricultural exporters now use Ethiopian Airlines. I asked for a reaction from two Dutch growers, Peter Linssen of Linssen Roses and Wim Ammerlaan of AQ Roses, who together have almost 400 hectares of land and export daily to FloraHolland's auctions. Both downplayed the tug-of-war aspect of airline and political competition as an ordinary part of doing business anywhere. In what may have been an effort not to air dirty laundry, they told me for the most part they were happy with Ethiopian Airlines' service. But regardless of how frank or reluctant they were expressing these views, both affirmed the obvious: that reliable, efficient, and affordable air transport is essential to their cut flower business. Air transport for East African growers typically eats up 40 percent of profits.

Cultivating flowers along equatorial regions in South America and East Africa offers big advantages. Land is available and very cheap; water is free, or very cheap; costs for heat and sunlight are zilch; there's plenty of labor and wages are low (for instance, the Ethiopian minimum wage, which is normally what workers on flower farms typically earn, hovers at twelve birr, below the United Nations' one dollar twenty-five cent per day poverty threshold). The EU charges little or no duty on South American and African agricultural products. What's more, you can get monetary and logistical assistance from Dutch horticultural organizations and financial institutions, and if you 'partner with a local entrepreneur' may even receive development funds.

The widening geographical spread of Dutch flower growers has enabled them to more deftly manage the market, allowed for the industry as a whole to expand, and for profits at Dutch auctions to swell. Nowadays, varieties that thrive in warmth and sun are grown in regions that naturally provide those elements, while flowers that favor cooler climates or conditions that demand more advanced technique and control are produced in the Netherlands. Low-priced but high-volume flowers like carnations and many kinds of roses became too expensive to cultivate at home by the late 1980s, and moving production south has encouraged many domestic Dutch growers to focus on niche markets, and allowed them to excel in higher value and specialized products. In this way, the core cluster in the Netherlands has moved up the value chain. Producing in an array of international locations has also permitted Dutch growers to more easily cultivate and sell certain varieties flowers over longer periods of the year and at higher quality, taking advantage of seasons in both northern and southern hemispheres to bring a consistent variety of fresh flowers to the auctions all year round.

~

Auction planners and executives initially sold the idea of expansion to the membership by appealing to their interests. Growers want a stable and reliable price for their product, and while for decades the auction had removed many of the problems involved with sales, nevertheless, the fluctuation of prices from season to season caused problems. Production would slow and become more expensive for growers in the winter months, and by the early 1990s the auction had trouble meeting demand for Valentine's Day and other big sales periods during the cold season. Foreign-grown flowers, it was argued, would help stabilize supply levels, and thus help ensure more consistent prices at the auction year round, and even potentially reduce the growers' costs on certain varieties. For instance, tea roses, those lighter-colored hybrid varieties, require warm temperatures and a lot of light.

Equatorial regions in Africa and South America provide ideal temperatures, and have nearly synchronous periods of day and night, which are particularly copascetic for many roses. Although technological advancements would and did increase yields and efficiency, it was clear that meaningful expansion would have to take place outside of the Netherlands. And there was an even more powerful economic reason to expand. These new up-and-coming growers might one day come to challenge the auction and could eventually threaten the Dutch dominance. A cheaper supply, a faster supply route, and an alternative center of distribution would take time to develop, but could conceivably happen, and that was what concerned auction planners and those in the horticultural industry that kept their eye on trends and potentials. Better to include these outsiders, they reasoned, and tie them into our system, than allow them to emerge as competitors and develop alternative centers of sales and distribution.

As long ago as the 1960s, Dutch horticultural planners began to envision large-scale growth of flowers in southerly regions, but at that point the state of technology and logistics made large-scale expansion or transfer unfeasible. The oil crises in the 1970s, and the ensuing instability in transportation, energy supply, and market prices further discouraged planners from seriously exploring expansion beyond the region. Nevertheless, there were some foreign growers (in Spain and Israel particularly) who supplied Dutch auctions. They weren't full members, meaning they paid an annual fee to sell via the auction, but couldn't vote on policy, and lacked certain other privileges of full members as well. By and large, until the 1980s, supply of Dutch auctions came from the Netherlands. At that point the arguments about transportation, competition, and growth began to compel planners.

Not everyone thought that international expansion was a good idea, however. Some did not initially support the admission of foreign-grown flowers to the auction, and likewise in 2006, a minority voted not to admit foreign-based growers as full members of the cooperative. Though criticized for exhibiting parochial attitudes or for looking-to-the-past-not-to-the-future, these growers may have had perfectly sound, self-interested reasons for their wariness. They saw the move as relatively risk-free for the institution, but very dangerous for them, as they might be signing off a lifetime's work, and generations of investment, in rose cultivation. Aalsmeer grower Hans de Vries doesn't mince words: "The auction executives didn't and don't give a shit about small-time growers. They sold out the Dutch rose growers," he told me. (And De Vries himself does not cultivate roses!) Not all growers are so blunt or outspoken, but you can't argue with the way things have turned out just a few decades after the process began. Both the fears of those reluctant 'backward-looking' growers and the hopes of ambitious auction planners have in some sense borne out. Rose production has partially transferred abroad, and some growers in Aalsmeer or other parts of the Netherlands have gone out of business, have begun to cultivate other kinds of flowers, or have themselves gone abroad to grow – but even so, the Dutch rose industry has not vanished: far from it. At the same time, the auction has consistently grown, and maintained itself at the center of the horticultural trade, which in various direct and indirect ways confers numerous benefits on Dutch growers. The foreign-cultivated roses, carnations, and other flowers pass through the Dutch auction clock, and strengthen the auctions' profits, power, and influence over the global market by ensuring its ongoing centrality.

A few figures might make these trends seem more concrete. For the first time ever, in 2008, imported tea-hybrids were greater than Dutch supplies at Dutch auctions – 1.2 billion stems. For an auction cooperative founded on the sale of roses, and one that for nearly a century dominated production, this was a remarkable moment. Rose imports to Europe have steadily climbed over the past ten years, coming from Dutch and non-Dutch farms mostly in East Africa; in 2007 Kenya became number one with 2.5 billion, next in line was the Netherlands at 2 billion, and third was Ethiopia at 458 million. One extraordinary aspect of this is the percentage rise in supply – while Kenya and the Netherlands increased three and four percent respectively, Ethiopian production soared by 104 percent, a trend that it has maintained for the short time the industry has existed. In one way, such growth was only possible because it was part of the Dutch horticultural cluster. But the cluster only absorbed this region in the first place because of its rivaling potential. Bert Ottens, FloraHolland's Ethiopia representative, offered this cost-benefit argument to me one afternoon in Addis. "If you want to continue to be the hub of the flower industry, you need to accept growers from everywhere. You cannot turn your back on them, because they are already there, and if they're not with you, they're competition."

Brazil

Holambra, in Brazil, was founded in the late 1940s by a group of Catholic farmers from the Netherlands' Brabant who were led by a graduate of Wageningen University named J.G. Heymeijer. Heymeijer possessed the right combination of drive, knowledge, and charisma to organize and inspire a Dutch settlement in far-flung Brazil. His undergraduate thesis had focused on the emigration of Dutch farmers to France, and, showing further enthusiasm for and identification with Dutch agriculture, he had edited a volume called *Wij Boeren* (We Farmers). His small group of *boeren* settled in an undeveloped area not far from São Paulo, and named their village Holambra, for Holland-America-Brazil. (Curiously, it is not far from another relocated community, this one established a century earlier by pro-slavery secessionists fleeing the pre-civil war U.S. South to fashion a town called América, which to this day holds square-dancing contests.) But for a variety of reasons including climate, cattle farming in Holambra did not work out, and soon the group of transplanted Dutch were cultivating citrus groves and other agricultural produce.

By the late 1970s, Holambra was also producing a respectable amount of gladiolas, much of which was exported to the Netherlands. Between 1963 and 1980, Holambra went from eight hectares devoted to flowers (mostly glads) to 1,180 hectares (an astonishing growth rate that Ethiopia would surpass decades later). Central to this spectacular success, according to the growers, was the group's *samenwerking* (cooperation), and the fact that they had come together to form a cooperative based on what they knew in the Netherlands. Holambra even developed some prominently Dutch cultural and architectural features, such as windmills and 'canal houses' (but no canals), characteristics that subsequent Dutch horticultural outposts in Ecuador and East Africa lack. One might compare Holambra to eccentric billionaire Yang Bin's replica of a Dutch village in northeast China, replete with drawbridges and a version of Amsterdam's Central Station. But where Yang's village resembles a personalized theme park, and an abandoned one at that, Holambra was established by Dutch immigrants, and by now has over ten thousand residents and six decades of history. Furthermore, Holambra is directly tied to Dutch horticultural auctions, not only through its past, but via ongoing practices and trade. Each year, Holambra hosts Expoflora, a prominent trade show, well attended by Netherlands-based importers and exporters. Holambra even has developed its own auction with two clocks, a maneuver aiming to institute more regional authority and to capitalize on Brazil's burgeoning domestic consumer market. Many people involved with Dutch horticulture have regular business and exchange with Holambra's growers and auctions. I spoke with a retired executive from the Aalsmeer auction who visits there often, offering advice, and forging relationships, and who thinks fondly of the Brazilian branch of the horticulture business as a distant cousin on the Dutch family tree. Holambra's distinctive horticultural signal has not only emblazoned a star on the world flower business map, it has reached the radar of certain heads of state. In a 2009 speech at the University of São Paulo, prime minister Balkenende singled out Holambra from Brazil's considerable agricultural accomplishments as "a Brazilian success story, with Dutch roots," and expounded on this horticultural village with ongoing "Dutch traditions and

Dutch culture." Holambra represents a commercial and cultural relationship both countries seem eager to pursue.

Colombia

Colombia produces a staggering amount of flowers. In 2009, in its fortieth year of cultivating commercial flowers, Colombia became the top producer and exporter of carnations, one of the most purchased flowers worldwide, and became second only to the Netherlands in total volume of cut-flower exports. Most of Colombia's flowers are destined for the United States, and so the industry there relates only indirectly with the Netherlands. But due to its size and what many in the industry describe as its 'leadership position,' events there impact the international market, and influence a range of economic and horticultural factors far beyond its borders, especially regarding health and safety standards. According to Ascoflores, the Association of Colombian Flower Exporters, the industry employs upwards of 150,000 people, over 70 percent of whom are women. Ascoflores, which began in 1973, has in recent years made efforts to highlight 'good news' about the flower industry. They started a peace-building initiative in the countryside, for example, which receives partial USAID funding. They also say that in defiance of popular international images of Colombian drugs and violence, the flower industry offers a more pleasant representation of the country.

But many scoff at the idea of the flower industry presenting a positive face of Colombia to the world, or respond by claiming that if it is representative, it's for ugly practices like union busting, using toxic chemicals, and exploiting the labor force predominantly made up of young women. The Associated Press has reported how, after workers won protections against long hours and dangerous exposure to chemicals from Colombia's largest flower grower, Dole, the company elected to close thirteen of its farms, citing competition from East Africa and China. Cactus, an NGO based in Bogotá, has carried out medical research that indicates almost two thirds of flower workers suffer from maladies linked to pesticide exposure, such as miscarriages, muscle pains, nausea, rashes, and conjunctivitis. In addition to risking their health, Cactus found, workers are typically fired if they become pregnant, in spite of their legal entitlement to maternal leave and other formal rights. Due to a steady stream of criticism, the tide of awareness among U.S. consumers has risen, and many people now associate Colombian flowers with these sorts of abhorrent practices.

Slowly and reluctantly, the industry has responded. Ascoflores, which represents seventy-five percent of Colombian growers, has been pressing its members to adopt a voluntary code of conduct. Many Colombian growers adhere to this code, or claim to. Other countries, including Ecuador, Kenya, and now Ethiopia as well, have followed suit with their own voluntary codes, certificates, and other proposals for self-policing. They might sound promising, and depending on the goal – a public relations show aimed at maintaining the status quo or sincere effort to reform the industry – the efforts may or may not be admirable. But in either case, the code of conduct seeks to sidestep legal enforcement and independent oversight. Many people both in and outside the industry express little enthusiasm for these voluntary safeguards and policies. Based on reports from Colombia (and similar ones from Kenya), auto-regulation in horticulture seems about as reliable as in the oil and financial industries, or in sweatshops. The scale of violations in the horticultural industry has been great enough to be represented in exposés and documentaries, as well as in commercial films.

Maria Full of Grace follows the story of a young Colombian woman who quits her dreary job on a flower farm to smuggle cocaine to the U.S., and *The Amsterdam Kill* sets its drama among drug cartels smuggling their goods in flower containers passing through Aalsmeer. Actually, the connections between the cut flower and illegal drugs industries extend beyond the movies. To different degrees, Ecuador and Colombia both receive favorable trade advantages from the U.S. – zero or low tariffs on their flower imports in exchange for working closely with

U.S. authorities to combat the production, trafficking, and sale of drugs, an arrangement summed up by a legal regime known as ATPDEA, or the Andean Trade Promotion and Drug Eradication Act. ATPDEA mostly benefits Colombia, and only secondarily helps Ecuador. Updated and revised every several years, in many ways the ATPDEA is the father of the Colombian flower industry, since it was this regime of policies that enabled the country's cultivation and exportation of flowers to thrive and prosper. Without it, Colombian flowers would have had more competition in the U.S. market, a situation with obvious repercussions for other flower-exporting nations. Almost needless to say, safe, cheap, and reliable trade routes interest South American producers not only of flowers but also of cocaine, since both commodities are widely consumed in Europe and the U.S. Though authorities make stabs at preventing transport, and occasionally seize large shipments, no one really knows how widespread drug traffic via flower containers might be. All we know is that from time to time there are significant busts, as occurred in December 2009 with a shipment arriving in Spain from Colombia, a familiar enough phenomena for police to dub the sting operation "Flower Power."

Ecuador
Of course, cooperation with the U.S.'s War on Drugs is a highly charged political matter, both inside the U.S. and internationally, and many regard the ATPDEA with a healthy dose of skepticism. Gonzalo Lazuriaga, the Chairman of the Board of Expoflores, the Association of Flower Producers and Exporters of Ecuador, understands ATPDEA as one of Uncle Sam's 'big stick' tools to combat 'socialist' policies in what has been understood by U.S. planners since the Monroe Doctrine as its backyard. Lazuriaga told *Floraculture International* that "[t]he new ATPDEA will last for one or two years, after which it will be replaced by a new act. The idea behind it is not a fair one because in the end it's in the country consuming the drugs that action should be taken. New socialism will prevail anyway."

In my experience, these sorts of spirited geopolitical critiques are not unusual in the flower industry. Lazuriaga's comments demonstrate another perspective within the industry, a voice that's neither the unapologetic exploiter and despoiler of natural resources, nor that of the 'apolitical' entrepreneur. His criticism of the geopolitical status quo reveals a social conscience. Granted, some of this might also have to do with his country, and with political effervescence in South America these days. Ecuador's left-leaning president Raphael Correa has not only challenged Washington's neoliberal orthodoxy and insisted on a timetable for withdrawal of troops from the U.S military base installed for decades in the South American country (and granted asylum to U.S. bête noir Julian Assange). Correa has also instituted social and economic reforms as part of the 'soft' left known as the pink tide. "New Socialism in Ecuador means salaries are on the rise," notes *FloraCulture International*. "Since the beginning of 2008 salaries have risen by up to 18 percent. The average worker on a rose farm in Ecuador takes home around 480 dollars a month, including benefits, making flowers the best industry to work in."

The horticultural Aaasa corporation built a school for forty kids outside of Quito in Tabacundo, and also provides adult education for their parents and others in the community. The general manager of this flower farm, Ricardo Canelos, states passionately that education and welfare of the workers go hand in hand with producing environmentally friendly horticulture. "In my opinion a sustainable rose is produced at a farm which meets the international social standards, avoiding pollution of the environment." Admirable sentiment, and while not especially rare, certainly unusual – across Ecuador, and industry-wide, fair trade practices have yet to be adopted on a large scale. Ecuador's industry started later than Colombia's, but instead of playing catch-up or little brother, it has attempted to distinguish itself from its 'superpower' neighbor. Though Ecuador and Colombia share some important issues, they also have serious distinctions concerning cut-flower and plant production, as well as sales and transport. They're both signatories to the ATPDEA, but

Ecuador doesn't face the same drug or violence issues, has a more progressive president, uses the U.S. dollar as national currency, and has actively pursued trade with the Netherlands and with international buyers via internet. In addition to expanding fair trade, this seems a smarter strategy for developing their industry. It's still a young industry, too.

China

As with many areas of economic dynamism, those who look at global trends have speculated on the future role of China in the international flower industry. The most significant kinds of flowers cultivated in China include carnations, gladioli, gerbera, orchids, and roses. The rose trade is not primarily for export to the West, and so China is not (yet) a competitor for the Netherlands. But Dutch horticultural entrepreneurs watch carefully for developments in China, and many have been actively involved in joint ventures, building infrastructure, seeking markets for Netherlands-grown bulbs, or new territory to cultivate seedlings. Chinese horticultural exports (mostly in potted plants and seedlings, not cut flowers) have steadily increased, headed mainly to Japan, Singapore, Thailand, Saudi Arabia, and the Netherlands; Chinese imports have also been growing, coming from South Korea, Japan, Holland, Costa Rica, and Taiwan. Dutch planners have actively involved themselves in the Chinese flower business in numerous ways, as in the Greenport-Shanghai initiative, the planned futuristic ecocity already described. In addition, back in 1997 China began its first horticultural auction in Yunnan province with input from Dutch consultants and modeled on the Netherlands system. Since then Yunnan has emerged as a major flower producer, growing over 50 percent of China's flowers. Such growth was possible not only due to available land and favorable climate, but because of the synergy of a Dutch-style horticultural cluster – you find supportive government policies, several top-notch agricultural institutions, a lot of flower producers, and now as well, an auction system to handle marketing, sales, and distribution. Lately, FloraHolland Naaldwijk has been working closely with Kunming International Flower Auction (KIFA) to establish an Aalsmeer-style auction system drawing on growers from Yunnan and targeting a wide distribution.

Kenya

Kenya was the first place in the region where export-oriented commercial horticulture really took off, and the Dutch were crucial, though not alone, in establishing the system that today generates billions of euros in revenue per year. Kenya's horticultural sector has overtaken both tea and tourism to become its leading foreign-exchange earner. 69 percent of Kenya's flower exports (three-quarters of which are roses) go first to auctions in the Netherlands. Some of the first people to establish farms and to build networks were colorful Dutch figures like Hans Zwager, whose 2005, four-hundred page autobiography is called *The Flowering Dutchman*.

Born in Holland in 1926, Zwager studied classical and jazz music, and became an accomplished pianist. During Germany's occupation of Holland in the Second World War, he escaped to Belgium and later joined the Nederlandse Bank's branch in Nairobi, Kenya. In Kenya, Zwager and his wife began a flower farm and built a home in Oserian (the Djinn Palace), on the shores of Lake Naivasha (which was the setting of the film *Out of Africa*). Today not only is the Zwager's Oserian farm one of the largest rose producers in the world, they are also well-known conservationists and have been recognized both locally and internationally for their positive contributions to the region and to the industry. They created a wildlife sanctuary on over 8,000 hectares of land that protects several endangered white rhinos, which live alongside hundreds of zebras, gazelles, ostriches, leopards, and cheetahs. Zwager's greenhouses run on electricity generated by geothermal energy from natural steam holes on his property. His farm has become a showcase for the positive potential of this model of export-led horticulture. On a state visit to Kenya, then Chairman of China's Communist Party Jiang Zermin saw the Oserian Flower Farm and was reportedly "deeply impressed." In 1998, Kenyan President Daniel Arap Moi awarded Hans Zwager Kenya's Medal of Honour, the Moran of the Burning Spear, and his son Peter Zwager has been inducted as an honorable Masai tribal elder. Begun over thirty years ago, the farm in Oserian was one of the first East African farms to sell at Dutch auctions in Aalsmeer and elsewhere. Once it was established and there was more potential for expanding horticultural networks, other Dutch growers and investors began to see the advantages of cultivating flowers around Lake Naivasha. The Kenyan state allowed foreigners to buy land inexpensively, and investments poured in.

Unfortunately, Oserian's glowing image does not represent the whole industry. Civil society groups, independent researchers, non-profits, and journalists present a starkly different portrait of commercial horticulture in Kenya, about as opposite as you can imagine from the environment-friendly and culturally sensitive presence of the Zwagers. *The Guardian*, for instance, has reported on the possible fraud and tax evasion in the flower business, and the Kenyan Revenue Authority is investigating the flower sector, including the Zwager's Oserian farm, Karuturi, and Flamingo/ Homegrown, all based around Lake Naivasha. Christian Aid has calculated that Kenya may be losing as much as $500 million dollars a year on its flower exports. But investigations of some companies and organizations are tricky for several reasons. One is that about 60 percent of what is counted as international trade actually consists of internal transfers within multinational companies, according to the Organization for Economic Cooperation and Development, so it is difficult to trace exactly where such institutions might hold particular earnings. The other is that many of Kenya's elites have financial stakes in the flower industry, and do not want corruption or tax evasion exposed. Likewise, powerful international players neither wish to lose profits nor to see their names tarnished.

A damning documentary by a Dutch filmmaker called *A Blooming Business* opens with the testimony of a young Kenyan woman who looks into the camera and says "this is what flowers mean to me" and presents her arms, which have been mutilated from handling chemicals unprotected; when the camera settles on her face, we see how her upper lip and cheek are similarly shriveled and mottled. The film has inspired strong reactions from the public and the industry alike, mainly in the Netherlands, where it was screened at Amsterdam's International Documentary Film Festival, and in England, which has the biggest market for Kenyan flowers. Another woman in the film describes how she has put up with sexual harassment and even rape from her supervisor, fearful she would lose her job and be unable to provide what little she can for her children. The film hauntingly captures how local, international, and moral economies connect.

Flower farms crowd the lake's shores, so that only one narrow passage remains open to the public – for the Masai, who come with their cattle to drink, for local women to wash clothes, for fishermen to launch their boats. We see how the industry has devastated the local economy and ecology, since both have depended on Lake Naivasha for fishing, agriculture, drinking water, and more. Flower farms surround the lake, siphoning off millions of liters of water per day and leaching back chemicals and fertilizers. The farms contribute to overcrowding by drawing thousands of people to the area for work, and prevent local communities from accessing fresh water. After several decades, the results were predictable: a shrunken lake, sunken water table, pollution, contaminated water, greatly reduced fish populations and habitat under threat, and all those conditions magnify and proliferate as they impact the communities that depend on water, land, fish, and trade. Given this environmental destruction, it almost seems beside the point to debate whether or not the abusive labor practices are widespread, representative, or, as the industry people have responded, just constitute a few bad apples.

Numerous reports from environmental and civil society groups around the world echo the messages of Van Zandvoort's documentary. Yet the perception within the industry remains rather different. Representatives of the business side of the flower industry dispute this version of reality, but because they do not publish environmental studies of their own and impede financial transparency, their counter narratives tend to focus on a few 'success stories,' voluntary policies (but not regulation or law) regarding labor and environmental standards, and statistics on generating profits, but without any demonstration of how or where those profits went or how they have been invested. Kenya continues to be celebrated as a major success story, even if, from time to time, someone acknowledges 'mistakes'. But the damage is getting harder to excuse or ignore. Already back in 2007 there was a proposal before the Dutch parliament to ban the importation of Kenyan flowers after a spate of news reports decrying "slave-like" conditions for workers. While the proposal was rejected, debate in the Netherlands has continued about the ethical practices of flower growing.

But curiously, and especially in England, both sides of the debate appeal to moral arguments about African labor, the environment, and the global value chain. Some people suggest that buying Kenyan-grown flowers is a kind of moral duty, to help these struggling Africans. "This is about social justice and making it easier, not harder, for African people to make a decent living," argued the UK's International Development Secretary Hilary Benn a few years ago. He asserted that emissions produced by growing flowers in Kenya and flying them to the UK can be less than a fifth of those grown in heated and lighted greenhouses in Holland. "People want to buy ethically and do their bit for climate change, but often don't realize that they can support developing countries and reduce carbon emissions," he told the BBC. Appealing to British consumers, he urged the public to buy Kenyan flowers in order to reduce poverty and lessen environmental impacts, while being romantic with your loved ones. The British minister's plea inspired ridicule. Siding with social justice, fair development, and environmental groups, the European Federation of Professional Florist Associations found Mr. Benn's argument "very strange," given the cases of child labor, unregulated use of pesticides and other toxins, and the questionable assertions about the flower industry's history of success in promoting local wealth and sustainable horticulture.

Ethiopia

Before 2000 the nation's flower industry did not exist, but now Ethiopia is the world's third largest rose producer, thanks to bountiful resources and labor combined with Dutch capital and expertise, as well as favorable state policies from both Ethiopia and the Netherlands. All of this, in turn, has spawned growth and investment in Ethiopia, and the horticultural industry has been a high priority for the Ethiopian government. At the end of September, 2010, the Ethiopian Agriculture and Rural Development State Minister, Dr. Aberra Deressa, announced that in the first three quarters of 2010, his country had earned over 250 million dollars from flower exports and employed over 100,000 people. "The government believes it is just the beginning," he said. "The government is fully committed to the sustainable expansion of the production of cut flowers, fruits, vegetables and fresh herbs for export," and to show that commitment, flower growers get a five-year tax holiday. According to the Ethiopian Horticultural Exporter's Association's (EHPEA) most recent figures, in 2011/2012 floriculture contributed 80 percent of the total foreign revenue earning and created over 180 thousand jobs, 85 percent of which are held by women. In addition to roses (at approximately 80 percent of exports, by far the dominant flower) Ethiopian growers also produce hypericum, lily, carnation, and gypsophila; the five main production areas are topographically diverse – Ziway, Koka, Suluta, Sebeta, and Holeta – each with slightly different temperature, elevation, and quality of light that in turn help determine the best conditions for particular varieties. For Dutch rose producers, particularly tea hybrid growers, the writing has long been on the wall. Philippe Veys of Olij Rosen, an international rose breeder headquartered in the Netherlands, says: "the tendency for increased supplies of imported tea hybrids will continue; in fact their market share will become bigger since the hectarage in the Netherlands continues to decrease. The expansion in Africa, on the other hand, continues to increase." But success is mixed for both Ethiopia and the Netherlands.

For Holland, rose growers may suffer, unable to compete, since plentiful, inexpensive foreign roses drive down price, and that in turn, pressures them. And in the last decade, the production area of roses in the Netherlands has shrunk considerably: of the 765 rose nurseries covering 932 hectares in 2000, roughly 300 hectares remained by 2013. But the picture is more complex than these numbers suggest. Ethiopian farms are not exactly putting Dutch growers out of business, for one thing, and rose sales at Dutch auctions continue to increase, and the grower-owned cooperative institution of FloraHolland stands in good stead. While it's true that through this shifting ballast of trade volume, some Dutch growers have lost out, in general, the Dutch rose sector is still thriving. It's just that 'success' looks different than it used to. Dutch growers are not producing more roses, or more varieties, than they once did. But some growers have switched location to East Africa and have seen profits soar; some have chosen to specialize in varieties that do better in northern latitudes and under Dutch growing conditions than East African environments. Others in the sector have gained business in producing fertilizers, chemicals, and greenhouse technology; and with their protected intellectual property rights, Dutch breeders have enjoyed a bonanza through this international growing. Yet it's true that many Dutch rose growers are frustrated. It's estimated that to generate revenue, Dutch growers need a yield of 100 euro per square meter, whereas their African counterparts only need 30-40 euro per square meter to eek out a profit, and most costs are dramatically higher in the Netherlands.

East African rose producers have further, special relevance to the Aalsmeer auctions which is both material and sentimental. As the founding flower of the auctions and appearing today on FloraHolland's logo, the rose an important symbol of the trade and a reminder of humble origins. Of the approximately fifteen thousand varieties of flowers and plants sold each year in Aalsmeer, nearly a third are roses. While the rise of the rose industry in other countries has meant a dramatically increased number of stems sold at the auction and the handsome profits that go along with higher trade volumes, it has also signaled the death knell for some local flower farms. While rose production in the Netherlands will probably never disappear altogether (as many once feared), Netherlands-based growers remain competitive only by aggressively pursuing niche markets, and avoiding direct competition with their now much larger and more powerful cousins in East Africa. The shift in production location has gone hand in hand with a shift in power within the institution of FloraHolland, away from the local growers who make up the cooperative's membership and into the laps of auction executives who set the policy agenda.

The great transfer in (and growth of) production over the past several decades from the Netherlands to East Africa and other regions is not quite as straightforward as one might suppose. Unlike many industries that have killed local business by outsourcing labor and production to distant parts of the globe, Dutch horticulture operates by expanding local networks to a global scale. This means that while some production occurs on foreign land, it remains part of 'Dutch success' in several important ways: many of the farms are Dutch owned, and profits remain largely in circulation of the Dutch network (via breeders, propagators, and other players, not only through the auction but also through necessary services such as soil testing and the sale of fertilizers and pesticides). Furthermore, the Netherlands and the institution of FloraHolland both benefit because as some of these foreign-grown flowers and plants pass through the auction clock before moving on to wholesalers and retailers, and thus 'count' as Dutch products and, if they cross the border, as Dutch exports. And Dutch roses have been re-marketed or rebranded as classic, while East Africa's are considered almost ersatz – good, but of a slightly lesser quality and not as fresh since they have to fly from another continent, and they sell at cheaper prices.

Within the Netherlands or around the globe, one might say that the 'invisible hand' guiding Dutch horticultural business success is not 'the market,' as many contend. Rather, financial institutions – whether private, state funded, or quasi public – have made crucial differences in Dutch flower growers' expansion abroad. And these institutions and programs are not really invisible or secret – many in the industry could tell you personally about how they have been helped – but they do contradict popular ideas about the machinations of 'the market,' 'international development,' and much of what is called private industry. The state provides direct financial assistance to horticultural enterprises, and creates favorable policies through subsidies, incentives, and tax breaks, as well as through other tailored programs and organizations. By now, these institutions are several decades old.

The discourse and mentality that supports and justifies them, however, dates back even further. As early as the 1920s, the Dutch were touting international investment as a kinder, gentler way of relating to Indonesia, Africa, and the colonial world more generally. A 1924 report from the New York-based Netherlands Chamber of Commerce illustrates the thinking. Uncovered by political scientist Frances Gouda, the report describes how the Dutch experience in the East Indies reveals, in its own words, "the truth of the philosophical dictum about the harmony of contrasts: a small mother country and a wealthy colonial empire... the inhabitants of the mercantile 'Low Countries' as masters of agriculture on the mountainside". Whether it was profits from the trade in nutmeg and clove during the seventeenth century, sugar production in the nineteenth, or flowers in the twentieth, the Dutch were indeed masters of agriculture, with all the resonance that phrase implies. But by the 1920s there was a difference – an admission, or at least an implied recognition – of the brutality and exploitation of colonial practices, whose ruthlessness was exacerbated by the acknowledgement that the malfeasance was based on economic self-interest, and not on some kind of altruism. In this way, Gouda concludes "the language of atonement for past transgressions gave way to a jubilant plea: the time was ripe for Holland to reach 'the summit of *freiwirtschaftliche* (free trade) policy' and to enact its pioneering role in the internationalization of economic life", a course that in fact they had set out on centuries earlier. The process accelerated in earnest during the 1950s and 1960s.

Institutions such as the Netherlands Overseas Financing Association (NOF) were founded in the post-colonial period as a way for the Netherlands to maintain some international footing in Indonesia and other regions that may have resisted the practices of plantations and other familiar policies of an overt Dutch presence. In 1959, as many Dutch businesses were forced to leave Indonesia, the Dutch government, together with twenty businesses and banks, set up this NOF fund, which private industry and public policy advocates alike recognized had lucrative and relatively safe business possibilities. It was a direct response to the policies of decolonization. Recognizing in the 1960s "that investing was a better tool," by 1970, the NOF broadened and deepened its mandate to become a special kind of institution called the Netherlands Development Finance Company (FMO), which would use both public and private funds to advance commercial interests in the so-called developing world. Today, Dutch international development organizations like the FMO exercise considerable political and economic 'soft power' in advocating for Dutch financial benefit. This is no secret, though the self-interest is now portrayed as fostering 'sound corporate governance,' 'reliable institutions,' or 'transparent business practices.' As the organization puts it, the "FMO often plays a pivotal role in embedding sound corporate governance in our partners' and clients' own organizations". In the 1980s and 1990s especially, the FMO funded major horticultural expansion, particularly in Kenya. The FMO receives taxpayer subsidies but is 49 percent owned by the private sector, primarily by multinationals such as Unilever and Philips, which ostensibly have nothing to do with flowers and plants, another indication of the broad embeddedness of Dutch horticulture. Today, the FMO enjoys an active presence in over 80 so-called developing countries and countries in transition, many of them in Africa, and boasts an investment portfolio of around five billion euro.

The FMO is not the only organization of this kind. There is also the Center for the Promotion of Imports from Developing Countries (CBI) in the Netherlands, which Dutch Agricultural Attaché Geert Westenbrink has lauded as an important element in establishing the Dutch horticultural cluster in Ethiopia. Created in 1971 as part of the Dutch Ministry of Foreign Affairs, the CBI aims to support the expansion of exports from poor countries with plentiful natural resources in order to support development. Some Ethiopian growers who 'partner' with Dutch entrepreneurs receive CBI support: such funds have provided necessary start-ups for a number of flower farms. These days, as well as the FMO and CBI, the Land-en-Tuinbouworganisatie (LTO) Nederland has also provided valuable assistance to international Dutch horticultural business ventures. Presided over by Albert Jan Maat, who from 1999-2007 headed the European Parliament in Brussels, LTO Nederland is the Dutch Federation of Agriculture and Horticulture, an entrepreneurial and employers' organization representing almost 50,000 agricultural entrepreneurs. With the involvement of such high-profile 'big linkers' as Maat and its broad membership, obviously, it is an organization of real stature and weight. It also suggests the elevated place of horticulture within a larger framework of agricultural policy and planning. The partly state-financed LTO sponsors study trips abroad, and provides funding, logistical support, and information to Dutch horticultural and agricultural businesses, both domestically – notably with a glasshouse program – and abroad. Two Dutch flower growers I spoke with in Ethiopia had originally come there on trips inspired and funded by LTO Nederland. That is what greased the wheels for their transition from the Netherlands to Ethiopia.

In addition to LTO Nederland, smaller scale 'micro-investment' schemes also aid Dutch horticultural expansion. Another reliable benefactor is PSOM/PSI, a Dutch government funded grant scheme for developing countries whereby a new enterprise set up by a Dutch company with an Ethiopian one may be awarded 50 percent of costs, with a maximum investment of 1.5 million euro. For the past several years, Ethiopia and China have been the number one and two focuses of PSOM/PSI projects. In a program earmarked for development aid, PSI gives financial assistance to "Ethiopian-Dutch partnerships," which have been used as start-up funds for flower farms. Along with financial institutions, aid organizations, and the Dutch embassy, FloraHolland itself instigated and invested in international expansion, and was a major muscle behind the birth of international commercial horticulture in Ethiopia, encouraging individual growers to take the initiative in Ethiopia. And the Agricultural Growth Team at the Netherlands' Addis embassy has provided training and advice for local growers, and has contributed 1.5 million US dollars along with 300 million from the World Bank to a growth program trust fund, aiming at sustainable production and targeting women and youth for training. Nevertheless, while horticultural development has been important to Dutch policy, and some of the first foreigners to take advantage of the Ethiopian government's new programs for investment were Dutch flower growers, in fact, policy priority is not on horticulture at all.

The enormous appetite of Ethiopia's commercial horticulture inspired agricultural production for export (maize, soy, and palm, as well as seed oils) and to a land grab by competing global players, India, China, and Saudi Arabia among them. Ultimately, the largest and most enduring legacies of Dutch spawning of Ethiopian horticulture may be on agriculture more broadly, via the production of seeds and seed oils. "The seed initiative will help much more than just the horticultural sector," Geert Westenbrink told me. "We are the biggest importer of edible oil in Europe. That's why we embarked on the seed venture." According to a UN-sponsored investigation, between 2004 and early 2009 alone, foreign investors purchased two and a half million hectares of land in Ethiopia, Ghana, Madagascar, Mali, and Sudan for agricultural development. But the first group to take advantage of land-grab opportunities in Ethiopia were flower growers, many of them Dutch. Some of these Dutch flower growers came from the Netherlands, where land is scarcer and costs are higher, and some horticultural businesses have jumped ship from Kenya to Ethiopia. Karuturi has expanded into Ethiopia while maintaining, but not increasing, its land in Kenya. Several other big players in Kenya such as Sher have moved to Ethiopia along with smaller Dutch growers.

Though they may not own land in Ethiopia, many foreign companies with deep pockets and plenty of capital hold long-term leases on vast territories. (The Dutch flower growers I interviewed mentioned ten, fifteen, and twenty-five year leases, paying twenty-five dollars per year per hectare. By contrast, Kenya sold much of its land outright; even with these open-ended flimsy leases, the Ethiopian government maintains the possibility of restraining foreign companies.) The biggest of these, Karuturi Global, has acquired several hundred thousand hectares of land around Ethiopia; its Kenya holdings are similarly astronomical. Due to the sheer size of these foreign-run lands and the flight of economic earnings, these operations are sometimes described as countries within countries. To offer a sense of the global context, according to Indian rose grower and agricultural powerhouse Karuturi, land of similar quality in Malaysia and Indonesia would cost about $350 per hectare per year, and tracts of that size aren't available in India. A poor, densely populated nation of 80 million offered plenty of people ready and willing to work for almost nothing – ideal conditions for large-scale farms and international companies. Flower farms owned and operated by Ethiopians are comparatively rare.

The attitude of Ethiopian growers toward the auction is a lot like many of their Dutch counterparts, a mixture of elation, confusion, and anxiety. On the one hand, it's a relief to not have to particularly worry about sales and marketing – the auction system and buyers mostly take care of that. But on the other, the flowers you've poured so much investment into are sent off to a giant warehouse on another continent, and their fate rests in the hands of strangers. After months of planning, negotiation, and growing, the sale is over in nanoseconds: the process may seem unnerving and suspicious. I asked Santosh Kulikarni, a farm production manager in Holeta, Ethiopia, about his relationship with the Dutch auctions. Kulikarni hails from Mumbai, but came to Ethiopia after working for several years on a flower farm in Kenya. A friendly, cosmopolitan man in his mid-forties, Kulikarni wore a red baseball cap as we strolled through several greenhouses, and he pointed things out to me – now, the latest organic agents developed at Wageningen University for dealing with spider mites (a bane for rose growers), now calling to a kerchiefed woman among a new breed of peach-and-lemon-colored blooms.

"You speak Oromo," I commented. "That's impressive."

"I speak enough to communicate with them, and I need to," he explained. "But to answer your question about the Netherlands…" he said, trailing off into a thoughtful pause. He stopped walking, shook his head, and shrugged. "We are totally dependent on the auction. And yes, I've been to see them sold, not in Aalsmeer, but I went once to an auction in Japan. Long time ago. Oh my God! No! I could not handle it. Not for me. I just thought, if I have to sit here and watch this, I'll die. Really."

"Too much stress?"

"So too much stress!!! Leave that business to them. I will grow the flowers."

Not all foreign growers feel this way, but most do have a relationship with the auction, and like Kulikarni, many have shared their strong sentiment. Kulikarni's boss is the head of the Ethiopian Horticultural Exporter's Association (EHPEA), Tsegaye Abebe, and the roses from his 20-hectare farm are sold in Aalsmeer. When I asked Abebe about his relationship to the auction, he just smiled calmly and said: "Oh yes, a very nice place. I've been there many times. Many times. It's my home away from home, really."

"That's interesting," I responded. "A lot of growers in the Netherlands and here have told me that the auctions make them nervous."

"Ok, yeah, it can be a little confusing," he emended himself. "But overall, the system works well for us."

Abebe seemed eager to convince me that Everything Is Just Great in Ethiopian commercial horticulture, and was full of these sorts of generically positive comments. We met twice, and at our first encounter, he shook my hand and gave me his card. "We [EHPEA] have been making a lot of improvements. We are the new face of Ethiopia," he told me without a trace of irony, and drew his index finger across the card, which had printed an attractive young Ethiopian woman picking some greenery and the phrase in quotation marks "The New Face of Ethiopia." Later, he gave me a copy of the first issue of EHPEA's magazine, published in the fall of 2009. Its cover featured a picture of Abebe standing beside the Ethiopian prime minister at the spring 2009 Hortiflora trade show in Addis sponsored by FloraHolland. "The prime minister has been very supportive of flowers," he told me. If Abebe's comments seemed bland and non-committal, that's not particularly surprising, given the country's political context, where all the press is government-controlled, elections are orchestrated to offer a veneer of democracy, and horticulture has been declared a major priority. But even if Abebe was merely repeating propaganda, his comments did make clear one important thing. Ethiopian flower growers need a business-like cultural fluency with Dutch auctions, and more broadly, with Dutch horticulture.

If this is where you will sell your flowers or plants, in order to make your best choices (what to grow, selecting and negotiating transportation, packaging, etc.), you need a good grasp of how they work. Strategic knowledge of what is happening at the auctions, and often as well, enjoying friendly relationships with people on the ground in the Netherlands, can make the crucial difference in profits or even the survival of your business. Because it is the point of sale, the auction is especially critical, but it isn't the only aspect of trade that a foreign grower selling in the Netherlands must manage. The horticultural industry, particularly the trade in cut flowers, is both capital and knowledge intensive. Also, capital and knowledge relate closely in several ways. The latest greenhouse technology, irrigation systems, and refrigeration are fundamental to a profitable commercial flower farm. In East Africa, tax holidays and other incentives have been granted not to local farmers but to foreign growers in order to attract larger-scale investment; and access to subsidies, development funds, zero or low-interest loans requires more than fluency in English or Dutch, but being savvy to what's available and possible in terms of funding, capital, business contacts, and technology. But even when all is working well, and especially on small and medium-sized farms, profits may be low or non-existent. "We're not talking about falling profit this year, just survival," Ethiopian farm manager Emebet Tesfaye recently told the *Christian Science Monitor*. "The buyers in Amsterdam [sic] control the market, and they are setting prices very low – there is no minimum price for our stems. Every loss is on the growers' side: transport, water, electricity, wages, and even fees to the rose breeders."

~

But the rose business has been rather more lucrative for other growers, particularly (though not automatically) among those with a keen understanding of the auction system and who can smoothly negotiate logistics with businesses based in the Netherlands. The Linssen farm not far from Addis has managed not only to profit but to expand since opening about a decade ago. Of course, in addition to capital and expertise, it's essential to have effective and efficient people working in the greenhouses. Peter Linssen, who generously opened his farm to me and shared his experiences, spoke with sympathy about the workforce on his farms in both Kenya and Ethiopia. Linssen, whose commercial flower farm is one of the oldest in Ethiopia, explained to me that his move occurred after his farm manager in Kenya was robbed and killed on the road for the money he had withdrawn to pay employees, and a shocked and grieving Linssen felt it was too dangerous to continue there. "It was the final signal that the price of doing business there was just too high," he said.

On the surface, the macro policies of Kenya and Ethiopia are quite similar: both have opened their natural resources to foreign growers at little or no cost, both offer cheap labor, little or no environmental regulation, and a tax-friendly environment. But for all their similarities, Kenyan and Ethiopian horticulture for export are hardly identical. As a former British colony, the trajectory of development for Kenya's flower industry has resembled the destructive consequences of monoculture and boom and bust dynamics of tea, the previous generation's main export commodity (and Kenya remains a big tea producer). Tea has generated a lot of profits, but ordinary Kenyans saw few benefits from the commodity. By contrast, Ethiopia doesn't share this long legacy of colonialism, which has resulted in a stronger, more independent central government. Partly because for decades this government was a vaguely socialist-oriented dictatorship, and was less involved with Western governments and companies until Meles Zenawi's new policies at the turn of the century, Ethiopia has been relatively cut off from foreigners, particularly the powerful commercial interests of states and corporations. But now that Ethiopia has opened up, it doesn't work exactly like Kenya once did, where development was somewhat reckless and much of the planning was left to the entrepreneurs. What this means in terms of Ethiopian horticulture today is that foreign businesses must consult a strong central government, which is not afraid to keep those companies in check occasionally, as it did in 2011 by putting the brakes on Karutiri's voracious land acquisitions. Foreign companies must also coordinate with the Ethiopian banking system. Geert Westenbrink at the Dutch embassy described the differences this way: "Kenya doesn't have a policy. Ethiopia has a policy."

In some ways, this leads to more coordination, less confusion and haphazard development, and at least in theory, could be a structure that provides some regulation. But for both Dutch growers and the Ethiopian public, this policy has its downsides, too. From the perspective of Dutch networks, a strong Ethiopian state often means roadblocks to doing business. Westenbrink told me "there's a misfit between Ethiopia and the globalized world. It's not Brazil or Kenya, those countries are easier to operate in – Ethiopia's much more difficult." Some of the challenges he identified were the "three holy cows of lingering communist government policies: no foreign banks, and the government owns all the land and all telecommunications." The banking issue seemed particularly irksome to Westenbrink, and in this he is not alone – everyone I spoke to in the horticultural sector expressed frustration with Ethiopian banks, from Dutch and Ethiopian growers to members of the EHPEA and FloraHolland representatives. Westenbrink put it like this: "The IMF, the World Bank, the Netherlands – EVERYBODY has pressured Ethiopia to open its banking system. This is fundamental to what it means to be in the modern world, really. Recently the prime minister responded to all this by saying that 'we did not suffer an economic crisis because we were not involved with foreign banks.' Well, of course that's not a very good argument, but there you have it. We discuss this again and again with the prime minister, that opening up would be best, and he listens, but this is his position. It's fully understandable, but we think it should be more open." One does not have to see eye to eye with the Dutch Agricultural Counselor nor support IMF policies in East Africa in order to understand their point. The Ethiopian banking system is slow and inefficient; very little is digitized or computerized; most transactions are still done on paper, and with cash; sales and agreements typically get held up while waiting for an official signature or stamp. (A small illustration of what doing business is like for foreigners: almost nothing may be purchased on credit, and in 2010, the country had just two ATMs, each located in elite Addis hotels.) But given the investigations of abuses and suspected losses in Kenya due to tax loopholes and other financial shenanigans, a healthy suspicion and heavy regulation of foreign banks would seem wise. Still, it's also useful to maintain skepticism over why certain policies are pursued – namely, Zenawi was no populist. It seems likely that his agenda was aimed not to benefit the majority of Ethiopians and protect the country's natural resources, but rather to strengthen the position of the central government, both in the international arena and in relation to its own population. Friendly relationships with multinational agricultural businesses fit snugly with these priorities. For investors and growers alike, these sorts of policies, first in Kenya then in Ethiopia, have created a welcoming climate for business. But the Dutch presence in Ethiopia predates the transition from Kenyan farms and this latest policy shift of Prime Minister Zenawi. The ties actually trace straight back to colonial and post-colonial Dutch Indonesia policies.

~

Many Dutch growers conceive of their project in Ethiopia as not merely to earn a profit for themselves, but also to foster prosperity in the poor, rural communities that provide the setting for their farms, and also to instruct locals on the values of hard work. When I asked Wim Ammerlaan, Jr. what he was most proud of about his flower farm, he said it was helping local people, offering employment, and teaching them valuable skills. "When we started," he said, "we had trouble making them understand that they needed to show up for work every day. Some did, but most didn't understand, they had no work ethic. But now they do. People come here and they work hard." As Frances Gouda has pointed out of similar views of Dutch colonials in Indonesia, "even if these narratives are modulated by a self-imposed ethical duty to 'civilize' and 'uplift,' they nonetheless devise a tale that is a far cry from the renowned Dutch habit of compromise – of honestly negotiating over contested space or resolving moral ambiguities". But the parallels go deeper than a common approach to business and development. In addition to the ideological and cultural links between twentieth-century colonial Indonesia and the contemporary Dutch flower business in Ethiopia, there are direct business ties.

The first Dutch enterprise in Ethiopia was a sugar production and refining facility, a company called HVA, which left Indonesia in the early 1950s to open in Wonji/Shoa, about 200 kilometers south of Addis. It is considered the forerunner of the contemporary horticultural business both because of its Dutch origins and its export model of production. HVA was one of the companies kicked out of Indonesia shortly after independence, and quickly moved its sugar production to Ethiopia, which had no prior domestic production, no sugar market, and little or no sugar imports. In 2009, *FloraCulture International* interviewed Bert van Blokland, a retired agricultural engineer who had overseen work and research for a number of years at HVA from his offices "right in the middle of the plantation," which he described as "a fantastic job." Van Blokland had studied tropical plants and plant breeding at Wageningen University, which worked closely with HVA and helped him to launch a career through HVA's business as they transferred their sugar operation from Indonesia to Ethiopia. (A PR campaign quickly whet the appetite for domestic sugar consumption, and local Ethiopians, for the first time began drinking their coffee with sugar.) Given these elements, both the timing and the planning involved in the transfer of sugar operations have a familiar feel. They suggest a similar model of international expansion via clusters – close cooperation between business, university, and government policy, finessed by cultural familiarity and personal connections. As Geert Westenbrink said in 2007 when he was newly installed in Ethiopia: "Zonder consensus gebeurt er niks," nothing happens without consensus. Westenbrink also specifically identified "an important impulse toward cooperation" between Wageningen University and Ethiopian farms, and between Dutch capital, knowledge, and development funds, and Ethiopian land, labor, and agricultural policies that welcome foreign investment. The goals and strategies of policy remain remarkably similar for sugar and cut flowers. When interviewed in 2009, Van Blokland had recently returned from a "sentimental journey to Ethiopia," and *FloraCulture International* celebrated him as a pioneer of the Dutch flower business in Ethiopia, which has taken off so dramatically.

But not everyone has such fond memories of HVA's sugar business. A former resident of the region now living in the U.S. has accused the company of causing extensive and long-term problems to local health and ongoing environmental hazards. Almaz Mequanint is not alone in articulating her criticisms, pain, and outrage, and in 2003, she published an article in the *New Internationalist* under the title "Dirty Business." After ignoring her letters, HVA International NV did respond to her complaints, and while the company refused to accept legal liability, in its response, it did not deny the substance of her accusations. According to Mequanint, "many people I know were sick from diseases caused by pollution [from the sugar factory]. Some of my father's friends were bedridden because of skeletal fluorosis." She claims to have been debilitated herself for decades with joint problems as well as tooth decay, and that her children, too, suffer a variety of ailments from spending the early years of their childhoods in the village beside HVA's plant. Mequanint recalls that in the late 1960s and early 1970s, "the exhaust fumes were so thick they formed a sort of fog around the community where I used to live. Dust, gases, and smoke had affected many people's lungs and circulation. Drinking water was heavily polluted with hazardous wastes," though to her knowledge little of the damage had been studied or in any way officially substantiated. She ended her open letter by saying of HVA International NV, "I hold them accountable for the mess they have created."

Clemens J.M. Rolink, the General Manager of HVA International NV in the Netherlands, prefaced his response by saying that while his company had no legal responsibility or culpability for the conditions, he felt "a moral obligation" to address her, since "we probably are the only party that might give some answers to [her] questions." He acknowledged that "after some years it became apparent that these wells contained a high fluoride percentage," after HVA's official study conducted in the 1970s concluded "that drinking from the wells over a long period could have a negative impact on teeth and bones, especially those of children," but that "the effects of fluoride were not known at that time," and anyway, of this and other environmental complaints, "the air pollution from sugar factories is very limited if compared to other industries like steel, chemicals, etc." Also, crucially, Rolink recounted that "during the time of nationalization... [when the military junta of the Derg took power in 1974] the Ethiopian Government claimed a large amount as compensation for the fluoride problem and at the same time accepted responsibility for all future claims." Unfortunately, the Ethiopian government has been no more accountable than HVA.

While foreigners lease land from the government, even Ethiopian property owners do not ultimately control the deeds to their land, since the Ethiopian government can take land as it deems necessary (a carryover from 'communist' Derg policies where private property ownership was prohibited). And even where the government may negotiate over deeds held by some owner, they see no need to negotiate with poor communities who may well have lived on or farmed plots of land for decades, but hold no title and so have no legal status. Some of those who have resisted these land seizures faced violence and were forced to comply by Ethiopia's formidable military. Once the land has been cleared of people, it's turned over to foreign lessees. Local journalist Agabos Debdebo says, "as a rule, the regime offers a small fraction of the property value as compensation [to those driven off], and hardly ever any adequate relocation assistance to tens of thousands of citizens affected by evictions." To my knowledge, and in contrast to other agricultural projects, no flower farms have been built on such confiscated land, though in Holeta, near Addis, local cattle once grazed where the Linssen and Abebe farms now stand. Even the biggest flower farm, around Lake Ziway, was not confiscated but transformed from a state-owned vegetable farm, yet other industries that have entered the country under Zenawi's open policies have plundered the land. Debdebos again: "In Dejen, atop the Abay River, the otherwise pristine and clean mountain air is now polluted by a cement factory spewing toxic dust... This cement plant is a Pakistani investment scheme, built on confiscated land. The cement plant, imported in disassembled parts from Pakistan, is entirely run by Pakistani workers, except for a few local day laborers."

As the landscape transforms, many ordinary people are talking about the flower industry and a lot of what they have to say is negative. Because for years Ethiopia has been isolated, and foreigners, particularly Western foreigners, are curiosities, during my time there I was approached constantly by folks wanting to talk – by people who wanted to practice their English, or just to know what I was doing, for instance, on a flea-bitten bus between two small towns. I spoke to over a hundred people in this way. Some knew nothing of the Ethiopian flower industry, but many did, and of those who were familiar with it, most felt it was exploitative. These were all random conversations with (mostly male) strangers, and I have made no attempt to quantify their responses or verify their specific assertions. But I was struck by the vehemence of their criticisms. At a bus stop in Ziway, I met one such guy, who was handsome, confident, and voluble. He told me he was a twenty-two year old university student studying environmental science, and though he stumbled a bit in English, he spoke with clarity and passion. "I am Demelash Sisa. One year I work for flower farm Holeta. These farms appear fast, like that – " he snapped his fingers. "These foreign people come and take land for free. And what do we do? We work for them." Implicated himself as a former farmhand in what he recognized as an international phenomenon, he found the situation both outrageous and gloomy. These sorts of conversations don't prove violations or wrongdoing, but they do demonstrate that, justified or not, there's widespread distrust of the industry, and strong beliefs that it is polluting the environment, and exploiting and poisoning its workforce.

The Dutch flower growers I spoke with in Ethiopia responded calmly to these sorts of allegations; clearly, my questions were not the first they had heard of such claims. They offered several explanations for local's perceptions: superstition, misinformation, rumor, and a natural tendency to distrust foreigners, particularly white ones. They welcomed me to their farms, and in their defense, they let me walk around freely, and I saw nothing like the horrors spoken of or secretly filmed on some Kenyan farms. But given their frankness and willingness to show their farms, this isn't too surprising, nor does it mean that uglier practices do not occur elsewhere. Without a systematic inspection of all the farms across the country, there's no way to know for sure how representative these Dutch farms are. On the other hand, what more proof does one need? No one disputes that in a country struggling to feed itself, these flowers are not for Ethiopian consumption but for export to Europe, nor that wages for six days work per week on many of these farms keep people in poverty. It seems fair to say at a minimum that the benefits of the Ethiopian horticultural boom are not broadly shared by its population.

Ethiopia's biggest flower farm, Sher, is Dutch owned; it's second largest, Shadi, at 410 hectares, is a joint Dutch-Indian venture. I visited Sher, about 160 km south of Addis, which extends along the shore of Lake Ziway in a stunning landscape. Sher owns the farm (but not the land) and leases parcels to different growers. The source of water is the lake, which hosts plentiful wildlife, including fish which are a staple of the local diet, flocks of flamingoes, and bloats of hippos that lurk in the shallows. Several islands dot the lake, each hosting a monastery, one of which dates back many centuries and once allegedly housed the Arc of the Covenant (the small vessel that carried the Ten Commandment tablets of Moses). The week I visited Ziway, each afternoon there was a lightning storm, and the dome of the sky flickered with as many colors as you would see at a glitter rock concert's light show. Even among these surroundings, the Sher farm strikes a grand presence with its 500 hectares of bright roofs, a sort of greenhouse city upon a hill. To put the size in perspective, consider that the average flower farm in the Netherlands is between one and two hectares (a hectare is 10,000 square meters, or 2.471 acres), and that Sher's territory covers five square kilometers.

But the size of these flower farms pales in comparison to other foreign-owned agricultural businesses in Ethiopia. Karuturi alone operates around 300,000 hectares of agricultural land in Ethiopia, an area larger than Luxembourg, and that doesn't include holdings in Kenya or other nations. Karuturi in Ethiopia produces sorghum, sugar, rice, maize, sunflower, soybeans, and palm and seed oils. Geert Westenbrink brought my attention to these facts when I asked about labor and environmental concerns on the flower farms. That doesn't take horticultural producers off the hook, but does place them in a larger context that makes what they do seem rather paltry by comparison. As foreign-owned industries impacting labor, the environment, and the economy, big agriculture seems a much more significant player. But the conditions on these farms have scarcely raised an eyebrow in the international press, and since they're even newer than the flower farms, haven't received the same levels of attention from locals, either. For both horticulture and agriculture, the economic model is the same; from the perspective of planners, policymakers, and the owners of these farms, all these ventures boost development and deserve praise. But as with their commercial ventures in Indonesia, Dutch self-interest is cloaked by a perfumed cape of enlightened generosity.

Considering the scale of the land grab occurring in Ethiopia, why do flower farms bear the brunt of outrage, while other agricultural behavior and practices seem to slip under the radar? Three reasons seem likely. First, the flower farms were the earliest to set up, so foreign presence in the landscape is largely associated with flower farms. Second, flower farming is labor intensive, and although the hectarage is far smaller than that of commercial agriculture, they may well employ greater numbers of people, who then spread the word about conditions. Finally, all along the production chain, flowers have an emotional appeal and tie in with a visceral sense of moral economy in ways that sorghum and seed oils just don't. In this way, and contrary to Westenbrink's comment about Ethiopia's backwards banking practices, Ethiopia seems very much part of the contemporary dynamics in this 'globalized' world. Though mentioned off-handedly, his comment ("there's a misfit between Ethiopia and the globalized world") seems quite rich and provocative. For one thing, it draws attention to the dynamics of international commerce, development, and to ideas about how these can and actually do work in relation to the Netherlands and Ethiopia. And the notion of a unified world system lingers in the background of such a comment, as well. Westenbrink's version of 'globalization' may well epitomize that of the overall industry, and accurately summarize Dutch policies in horticulture, agriculture, and international development. But he doesn't speak for everyone in the trade. Clearly, with figures like Aalsmeer grower Hans de Vries and Gonzalo Lazuriaga in Ecuador, other voices within the industry criticize the ways FloraHolland and the business generally have evolved abroad and at home.

~

Go anyplace on earth with a thriving commercial horticulture and you're likely to find Dutch involvement. But this is far from the whole story. Most Dutch horticultural exports don't traverse the globe, but stay in Europe, with over half sold to Germany alone. Also, a mere five percent of cut flowers from the Netherlands enter the enormous U.S. market. And East Asia constitutes a small slice of consumers of Dutch cut flowers (though less perishable bulbs do far better.) And from the supply side, half the flowers sold at Dutch auctions are cultivated in the Netherlands. This is the best way to understand how, of all the commercial flowers sold on the planet, roughly 60 percent pass through Dutch auctions. From China to Ethiopia, Ecuador, and Brazil, Dutch horticulture has extended significant networks or established big commercial links and investments. Some of this, as in the case of Ethiopia, has been encouraged and enabled by the strategic use of development funds from the Dutch government. Both the policies and the ways participants describe them are consistent with the historical trajectory of commercial endeavors ranging from the early days of the Republic to the twentieth-century Netherlands in Indonesia. Agricultural Attaché Geert Westenbrink's comment about Ethiopia and the globalized world provides a useful frame for thinking about horticultural development in terms of the internationalization of Dutch horticulture, how foreign-based industries understand and fit into a system organized around the Dutch auctions. It also gets to the heart of what 'globalization' means to those shaping Dutch horticultural policy.

While Mr. Westenbrink made this statement in the context of banking practices and did not necessarily intend it as a general observation about the country, it's worth emphasizing because it resonates powerfully in a number of other ways. Not being globalized sounds like a code for familiar ways of discussing African countries. To describe a place as not globalized is to assert that it's not part of the modern, contemporary world, that it's not merely isolated, but, one suspects, 'backwards' and 'primitive' as well. The problem, of course, is not with complaining about a banking system or pointing out a lack of infrastructure. It's with the values and ideas that often inform such observations, that these Africans live like this because they're lazy, or because of cultural characteristics, or because they lack a work ethic. Many growers also see their work as not just growing flowers but helping communities and bringing development, so it's not only on the levels of figures like Westenbrink, development funds, and the Netherlands' economic interests. Talking with Wim Ammerlaan in Ethiopia, for instance, he extolled the flower farms, directly comparing the benefits of the horticultural industry to international aid agencies. "Look what we've built here," he told me. "Five years ago there was nothing in this town [Ziway], practically nothing at all, and how long were they giving aid here? Now you have a lot of roads, development, banks, restaurants, hotels even. It has changed a lot, seriously, and not because some maybe well-meaning aid agency was giving poor people money. It's because of this industry. We're actually building things, and hopefully, it really lasts." He makes some valuable points, but it's important to recognize the parameters of this world view – since he was not alone in this opinion, and the outlook grows out of some familiar values. In this understanding, 'globalization' can only proceed along two possible routes, either through a particular model of commerce or through charity, both of which are inspired by and depend on the benevolence of knowledgeable Westerners (as distinct from those plainly self-interested Chinese and Indians engaged in a vulgar land-grab and using toxic pesticides and genetically modified techniques with impunity). In both perspectives, foreign involvement and horticulture are essential parts of the moral economy.

Because of the discourse about promoting development, creating jobs and opportunities while fostering a work ethic and teaching practical skills, critics of the export-led model of development are sometimes cast as spoil sports, or accused of failing to appreciate the good intentions and positive aspects of orthodox policies. Today, these policies allegedly aim to bring, expand, or include not 'civilization' but 'globalization.' The terminology has changed, but the sentiment and the policies of today's horticulture share noticeable similarities with earlier ventures. As Frances Gouda has argued, "a litany of tales about the time-honored traditions of Dutch tolerance and the 'ethical' governance of the Dutch East Indies molds historical memories and shapes Dutch visions of empire," and in this way, "it becomes easy to believe in a Dutch cultural record in colonial Indonesia that was characterized primarily by wisdom, thoroughness, and respect for native customs and traditions". Replace 'colonial Indonesia' with 'East African commercial horticulture' and the statement equally applies. Practices on the flower farms don't need to be as brutal as plantations of colonial Indonesia for this to be true. Conditions on today's flower farms may lend new meaning to Blake's famous line: O rose, thou art sick!

The story of the expansion of the flower industry in Ethiopia touches on a range of issues including managing our land, air and water, as well as the need for more democratic social planning, concerns vital to us all, not only those in places like East Africa.

I agree with financial blogger Yves Smith who wrote recently: "As critical resources like water come more and more under pressure, expect debates over food security and landholding, which once were the province of development economists, to become a subject of mainstream debate and concern." A few years ago Ethiopia designated 1.6 million hectares of land for companies from Gulf and East Asian nations willing to develop commercial farms, much of it in Gambella. Omod Obang Olom, president of Ethiopia's Gambella region, a close ally of Prime Minister Meles Zenawi's ruling party and friendly collaborator with Karuturi Global, spoke with Bloomberg News about the land deals. "The project will give the government revenue from corporate income taxes and from future leases, as well as from job creation," he said. "This strategy will build up capitalism. The message I want to convey is that there is room for any investor. We have very fertile land, there is good labor here, we can support them." It is remarkable that Olom unabashedly envisioned this project as 'building up capitalism' at a time when much of the world, including many people in other African nations and even in 'core' countries of Europe and the U.S., have not only declared the neoliberal development model a failure, but have pointedly questioned the wisdom of capitalism. For many looking at the global production and distribution of resources, the current system is not something that needs fortification or expansion, but instead a radical reconstruction. The problems are structural, systemic: the model of development must be changed.

Regardless of who runs the farm in Ziway, for instance, the system does not lead to thriving, autonomous local communities. Before the land and water were used to cultivate flowers, they went to produce tomatoes and vegetables for regional consumption on what was a state farm. It was not an export model generating foreign currency, nor did it provide the same level of employment as the flower farms. According to Ethiopians I spoke with who were familiar with environmental issues, this farm was a disaster. The state farm was possibly worse for the local ecosystem since more toxic and heavier amounts of fertilizers and pesticides were used. This too is important to keep in mind when evaluating the moral economy of the flower industry in Ethiopia and discussions of new models. Furthermore, per hectarage, flower farms pale in comparison to the scale of industrial farming for export of seeds oils, sorghum, soy, and more. And unlike those farms, in Ziway, they have built a hospital and a soccer stadium, and have an affectionate, if paternalistic, attitude toward the local population. The newer commercial farms run by Saudi, Chinese, and Indian companies occupy approximately 100 times the land space, but none seem to have this kind of relationship with the locals. Without denigrating the other sorts of farms, FloraHolland is eager to celebrate this friendly image.

FloraHolland Aalsmeer's centennial festivities in Addis in 2011 were attended by the Dutch Ambassador, the head of the Ministry of Agriculture, FloraHolland's CEO Timo Hughes, as well as the Ethiopian Horticultural Producers and Exporters Association. They awarded the EHPEA a plaque commemorating the successful cooperation between FloraHolland and the EHPEA, and they screened a film, *100 years FloraHolland.* Afterwards, Chairman of the Cooperative Board Bernard Oosterom spoke to the crowd in familiar, institutional language. "Today it is good to realize that you as an Ethiopian grower are connected to a strong system. It is strong because we as growers are strong. It is also strong because a major part of world demands goes to FloraHolland to buy its flowers and plants. You are connected to the Netherlands, the world's leading flower nation."

Afterword

The flowers just purchased, we'd like to leave them, along with the money, in those hands. The coins, as necessity's most minimal relief; the flowers, as insufficient tribute to the dignity of their lives, to the grace of their bodies, the eloquence of their faces. Because beauty nourishes, and as with bread, a man can also perish from its absence.

Luis Cernuda (translated by Steven Kessler)

In spring 2014, I met Tecla Aerts, a trim, blue-eyed human-resources advisor in her mid-fifties at FloraHolland Aalsmeer. An acquaintance of ours who works at the auction had given her an early draft of this book, which she read. "Suddenly I began to notice how Calvinistic this industry really is," she told me. "I mean I've worked here ten years, I guess I knew it, but I didn't really see it before. It's not only white and male and all that: there are a lot of religious people, too. There's a *bedrijfsgebed*, a company prayer, along with daily news items, that appears in people's inboxes." One of the few women of authority at the institution, a friend of Ms. Aerts', told her she had recently gone to one of the company's monthly prayer meetings, which usually thirty or forty people attend. This woman, a lesbian, apparently felt comfortable enough there to describe it as a great networking opportunity.

Though I knew of a space set aside for Salat for Muslim workers on the floor, this was the first I'd heard of Christian prayer meetings at FloraHolland, something that might conjure more severe images of intolerance for a contemporary American. But otherwise I wasn't shocked by the religiosity she described. Many flower growers in the Netherlands come from the Dutch Bible Belt, a swath of the country that's significant but rather small (and not influential compared to the U.S.). The Bible Belt tends to vote for the Christian Democratic Alliance, a center-right party, and generally subscribes to Calvinistic values: work hard, pray, take care of your neighbors, don't show off, do it not for yourself but for your community. Of course, this outlook is not confined to the Bible Belt: the sensibility is part of Dutch culture as well as its flower industry.

In reflecting on my experiences in the industry, and writing about them while living in the Netherlands, I sometimes would read "Flower Vendors", a prose poem published in the early 1950s by Cernuda, a Spanish poet and friend of García Lorca. It addresses Northern European protestants that supposedly only understand work and profit, and evokes sympathy with those (catholic) peasants in the south who have little but their own dignity and the appreciation of beauty, selling flowers to passersby. But I also believe the poem captures a widespread, if under-acknowledged or even disparaged, view, one that underpins the moral economy of flowers, of gifts, of art and poetry, of so many ineffable things we hold dear, including life itself. Similar words were spoken a few years ago by a Gazan farmer raising carnations, when he said he wanted the world to associate Gaza with flowers, that "peace and love start from Gaza". And a lifelong Dutch flower farmer who lived under Nazi occupation conveyed the same sentiment when he told me that even in times of war, "especially in times like that – people have to have something Good. They must have something Good, something Beautiful. Beauty is very valuable, very important."

There's nothing especially protestant, Calvinistic, or necessarily religious about these beliefs, but they do jibe with the ethos I picked up from many growers and florists, though few traders. Ms. Aerts' news about pious activities and tone at FloraHolland didn't particularly shock me. Some other parts of our conversation, however, did startle me – in a good way – and resonated with other experiences I recounted in the book. She enjoyed the characterization of *ouwe jongens krentenbrood* and told me she and some colleagues has decided they needed more diversity at work, that the old boy's network was too narrow and restrictive, so they began a women's network, probably a first for FloraHolland. "This could really benefit the company, too," she added. "We need more women, and we need to do things in a more 'feminine' way – which means listening to people, actually listening. Not just looking at the bottom line, setting a goal, and waiting for results."

Others at FloraHolland, including several men, had voiced similar views, and they may be gaining traction. For the first time in many years, workers went on strike at FloraHolland in 2014. Their decision was partly about frustration with proposed changes to benefits in the social plan, and partly about job security, since 250 full-time employees had been laid off, and many others were given irregular schedules and/or forced to commute to different FloraHolland locations. For communication and trust to break down to the point where people walked off the job during one of the busiest weeks of the year (just prior to Valentine's Day) represented a significant low point, and forced managers and planners, along with the membership, to reflect not only on the whys and hows of the strike but to consider what the cooperative is, and what it might or should be. Of course, as one would expect from any company, there have been a range of ideas, opinions, and lessons drawn. But few think of the flower business, and FloraHolland in particular, as just another extractive enterprise.

Some blamed the strike on a combination of the ongoing economic crisis (growth of the company slowed to just 1.5 percent in 2013) and a rigid management style carried over from the previous director, Timo Hughes. He liked to emphasize the "Four Ds" management philosophy, *Duidelijk, Duurzaam, Dienstverlening, en Durf* (Clear, Sustainable, Services, and Courage), which was often mocked as *"Doe Dit, Doe Dat"* (Do This, Do That). "There's a lot of *haantjesgedrag* around here, you know? It's a culture of *haantjes*," said Tecla. *Haantjes* are roosters, she explained, and this strutting around behavior is really common. "But this might be changing. I think the lesson of the strike is that management needs to listen more. The new manager, Lucas Vos, is a power player for sure," a so-called bobo or Big Linker with a background in one of the world's biggest logistics companies (as Chief Commercial Officer for Maersk Line) and with political aspirations in the Netherlands. "But he's not a *haantje*, and he listens more," said Tecla.

We walked to a vending machine and returned to the sparse little room at FloraHolland. "I was interested to read your book partly because I work here," she told me, and blew the steam from the surface of her tea, "but also because I wrote my thesis in university on Dutch history. Ah, but this was way back in the 1980s".

"Oh! What was your thesis about?"

"Actually, it was about sodomy on board VOC ships," she stated matter-of-factly, then slurped her drink and crossed her legs so the tip of her blue suede high-heeled boot ticked against the table leg.

I smiled and raised my eyebrows. "Great topic! Tell me about that."

"Well, sodomy became a controversy in the 1730s," a century after tulipmania. "There were public trials of a captain and it was even written about in the newspapers. There's a huge amount of court material, too, since of course the Dutch always kept meticulous records."

"Right".

"And really there was no such thing as homosexuality then, at least not in the sense that people had a name for it and it meant certain things. Men had sex with men, but it was just something that happened, mostly in private. But there was no privacy on board the ships. And so all of a sudden you had all these young men going off on these voyages for a month or more. For a long time, there had been jokes, you know, about the desperate guys having sex with – I don't know – chickens." She cupped her hands as though holding a hen. I wondered why she picked chickens, if she was somehow going to expand on the culture of *haantjes*, but she didn't.

"For sure, this is an aspect of the theme of masculinity and Dutch trade that I hadn't considered," I said.

"Somehow around the 1730s, it suddenly became controversial. There was a lot of public condemnation. No one really knew what to do, so they actually put one of the captains on trial. Like, supposedly it was his job on board the ship to sort of police these guys. The ships would go around the horn of Africa, the Cape of Good Hope, and they would dock there for a while, resupplying and things." South Africa, of course, formed a part of the Dutch world at the time, and provided both a useful stopover point on long voyages as well as a valuable source for new plant species in the avaricious pursuit of colonial botany. Those voyages were part of that network involving global expansion, plants, gardening, wonder cabinets, and commodity culture.

Tecla looked at her watch. "So... down there in a court in Cape Town, that's where they held the sodomy trials."

She stood up, and we walked out of the office and down the corridor. "It was just amazing to read those court records. Written in that fine cursive script. Amazing. All that history just right there, right here –."

Notes

1. At that time, Gasunie became the largest public-private commercial enterprise in the world, comprised of Royal Dutch Shell (25 percent), ExxonMobil (25 percent) and the state of the Netherlands (50 percent). In 2005 the company split into GasTerra, a gas-trading company, which maintains the same public-private ownership division, and GasUnie, which became exclusively a gas transportation company and is entirely state-owned. (Curiously, the discovery of gas also led to a dubious economic condition known as "the Dutch disease", whereby the exploitation of a natural resource supposedly leads to a decline in manufacturing for the national economy.)

2. Before declaring bankruptcy in 2011, for 40 years Blumex was one of the Netherlands' leading flower import/export companies, and one of the first to locate its office in the Aalsmeer auction.

3. "Tulpenboeren ontkennen alles" *NRC Handelsblad*, March 15, 2008.

4. Another distinction between bulb cultivars and flower growers is that the bulb community is even smaller and more insular, where an individual might be grower, buyer, and exporter. Traditionally flower growers have stuck to the business of growing, although today this is beginning to change in the cut-flower sector with growers taking on multiple functions.

5. As the historian Anne Goldgar has shown in her fascinating book, which I refer to often here, *Tulipmania*.

6. In cut-flower and plant auctions, this is not possible, since they operate on a descending bid or 'Dutch auction' system. Chapter three explains in detail how Dutch flower and plant auctions work.

7. *NRC Handelsblad* November 3, 2008.

8. "Ik heb zelf het gewone leven weer opgepakt en werk in een bloemenexportbedrijf in Lisserbroek. Want bloemen, daar blijf ik toch het beste in." *Quote* May 18, 2009.

9. One obvious explanation is that it reflects poorly on the industry; another is that those involved were not the types often directly involved in Dutch horticulture, so the story seemed practically irrelevant; and since the players who were cheated

of their money were ultra-rich, possibly there was less sympathy in the industry for the losses than if they had been incurred by ordinary folks.

10. Burger, William C., 2006. *Flowers: How They Changed the World*. Prometheus Books, Amherst, New York.

11. "Resolving the Food Crisis: Assessing Global Policy Since 2007": 7. Available online: http:ase.tufts.edu/gdae/Pubs/rp/Resolving-FoodCrisis.pdf. The report explains how finance-driven speculation in commodities markets, in conjunction with the effects of climate change and profit-driven state and private agriculture has devastated many regions, particularly in Africa.

12. Many have been asking if this crisis marks the end of a cycle of the U.S.-centered world system. French historian Fernand Braudel argued that the world economy follows a pattern of long-term cycles, beginning in medieval Europe around the twelfth century. Certain cities, and then nation states, became centers of these cycles, and their collapse, notable for today's context, was always brought on by a crisis in credit. Venice and Genoa were the centers of the world system in the thirteenth through fifteenth centuries, followed by Antwerp in the sixteenth century, Amsterdam in the sixteenth through eighteenth centuries, and finally London in the eighteenth and nineteenth centuries. But it was only around the sixteenth century that the density of trade began to resemble a modern capitalist cycle.

13. The figure comes from their 2011 Fourth Quarter Report: http://www-static.shell.com/static/investor/downloads/financial_information/quarterly_results/2011/q4/q4_2011_qra.pdf. Though the profit figures are important, the *distribution* of profit within these very different kinds of institutions must also be emphasized.

14. In recent years, anthropologists have been asking this sort of question more generally and broadly. For instance, Oka and Fuentes write: "Why do substantial and cooperative infrastructures endure throughout history (both social and evolutionary)? In trade and commerce, where competition is key, why does cooperation emerge as a structuring mechanism? Why do groups that could gain 'more' through contest choose instead to gain 'less but sufficient' through cooperation? We argue that the key benefits of cooperation, those of sustainability and adaptive resilience, are powerful forces that cause the 'selection'

of cooperative behaviors to mitigate against external attritional pressures, namely, predation.

"We present our approach not as a one-size-fits-all solution to understanding socioeconomic behavior but as an additive-alternative to the dominant paradigm of the competing maximizing rational actor-driven evolution."

15. There isn't an exact translation to English because the profession is uniquely Dutch. A *lijnrijder* (literally, a line rider or hauler) is someone who buys flowers at auction and then sells them wholesale to regular customers on a delivery route. Renowned for his expertise and experience with a variety of flowers and plants, he is a sort of trader, entrepreneur, wholesaler, and local horticultural figure wrapped in one. The first *lijnrijders* came from Rijnsburg and the occupation really took off in the mid-1960s, as transportation and distribution allowed and demanded.

16. Human Rights Watch and Amnesty International condemned Israel for these crimes, as well as for their use of white phosphorus, a chemical weapon, against unarmed civilians. The U.N. Human Rights Council came to similar conclusions. In what is commonly known as the Goldstone Report, the UNHRC wrote: "The blockade comprises measures such as restrictions on the goods that can be imported into Gaza and the closure of border crossings for people, goods, and services, sometimes for days, including cuts on the provision of fuel and electricity", which it stated is a violation of the Fourth Geneva Convention (UNHRC REPORT: 9-10).

17. "Palestinian flowers turned into cattle feed," *FloraCulture International* November 2009.

18. "Narratives Under Siege (5): Hassan Sheikh Hijazi Flower Farm," Palestinian Center for Human Rights. Security risks was the official reason Israel gave for blocking Gazan exports.

19. Ibid.

20. Mr. Van Akker is not his real name.